BRAIN, CULTURE, & *the* HUMAN SPIRIT

Essays From an Emergent Evolutionary Perspective

Edited by
James B. Ashbrook

with Paul D. MacLean, Eugene G. D'Aquili,
Victor Turner, Roger W. Sperry, Colwyn Trevarthen

UNIVERSITY
PRESS OF
AMERICA

Lanham • New York • London

Copyright © 1993 by
University Press of America®, Inc.
4720 Boston Way
Lanham, Maryland 20706

3 Henrietta Street
London WC2E 8LU England

Library of Congress Cataloging-in-Publication Data

Brain, culture, and the human spirit : essays from an emergent
evolutionary perspective / edited by James B. Ashbrook.
p.   cm.
Includes bibliographical references.
1. Psychology, Religious.   2. Neuropsychology.   3. Genetic
psychology.   4. Human evolution—Religious aspects.   I. Ashbrook,
James B., 1925–   .
   BL53.B654   1992   128'.2—dc20   92–24726 CIP

ISBN 0–8191–8853–0 (cloth : alk. paper)
ISBN 0–8191–8854–9 (pbk. : alk. paper)

Dedicated to

RALPH WENDELL BURHOE

keen mind . . .

venturesome heart . . .

generous spirit . . .

ACKNOWLEDGMENTS

Two institutions have been crucial in the development of this work. The Chicago Center for Religion and Science and its seminars over the last decade have provided the arena in which these ideas have been nurtured, debated, and nuanced. The Center also is sharing sponsorship of the publication. Carol Rausch Albright provided editorial consultation.

Garrett-Evangelical Theological Seminary has provided encouragement and resources. The idea of the volume was conceived while I was on leave the fall of 1986; it grew during a leave in the fall of 1989; it came to birth during a reduced teaching load the spring of 1992. For these I am grateful to President Neal Fisher, Vice President for Academic Affairs Richard Tholin, and to the Methodist Educational Funds for special grants. Joan Svenningsen, administrative assistant to the Department of Pastoral Psychology and Counseling, has managed the monumental task of converting text to camera-ready copy with the cheerful competence that inspires my efforts. The Institute for Research in Pastoral Psychology and my colleagues Lallene Rector and John E. Hinkle, Jr., have undergirded the work with sponsorship and enthusiasm.

Appreciation goes to the authors for their willingness and generosity in allowing their essays to be included under the following conditions:

Paul D. MacLean for "On the Evolution of Three Mentalities," which appeared in *Man-Environment Systems*, 5 (1975): 213-24 and was reprinted in *New Dimensions in Psychiatry: A World View*, vol. 2, edited by Silvano Arieti and Gerald Chrzanowski, pp. 305-28 (New York: John Wiley & Sons, 1977). Since Dr. MacLean is an official of the United States Government, this material is in the public domain.

Eugene G. d'Aquili for "The Myth-Ritual Complex: A Biogenetic Structural Analysis," *Zygon: Journal of Religion and Science* 18 (September 1983): 247-69, with approval of the figures by graphic artist Anna Horvath which were added to aid understanding of the material.

Edith L. B. Turner, as executor of Victor Turner's work, for "Body, Brain, and Culture," *Zygon: Journal of Religion and Science* 18 (September 1982): 221-45.

Roger W. Sperry for "Psychology's Mentalist Paradigm and the Religion/Science Tension," *American Psychologist* 43 (August 1988): 607-13. Copyright 1988 by the American Psychological Association. Reprinted by permission.

Colwyn Trevarthen for "Brain Science and the Human Spirit," *Zygon: Journal of Religion and Science* 21 (June 1986): 161-200, with minor revisions for this publication.

James B. Ashbrook for "The Human Brain and Human Destiny: A Pattern for Old Brain Empathy with the Emergence of Mind," *Zygon: Journal of Religion and Science* 24 (September 1989): 335-56.

Karl E. Peters has encouraged this project and, as editor of *Zygon: Journal of Religion and Science* when the d'Aquili, Trevarthen, Turner, and Ashbrook articles were published, gave permission from the Joint Publication Board to reprint them.

Figure 1.1 is adapted from Figure 63, from a manuscript in the British Museum, in *An Illustrated History of Brain Function*, edited by Edwin Clarke and Kenneth Dewhurst (Berkeley: University of California Press, 1972) and used with the kind permission of Edwin Clarke and Pryce & Co., the literary executors of K. E. Dewhurst, and the British Library. It comes from the second half of the fourteenth century, probably from a treatise on ophthalmological medicine written by Magister Zacharias of Salerno and Constantinople in the twelfth century and showing the figure of the eye in the human head. Sloane MS 981, folio 68.

CONTENTS

PREFACE

These articles on brain, culture, and the human spirit are basic to understanding the relation between religion and science. They represent separate realms of inquiry. They come from physiology, anthropology, psychology, theology. Each author develops his own perspective as to the place of *homo sapiens* in the cosmos we know as earth. Together, however, they represent an emerging consensus. One reviewer of the manuscript wrote of its "quite exceptional coherence and development . . . so that it might well have been written by a single author."

This coherence is not surprising, given the network of relationships developed over the years by the authors and those with whom they have associated. Ralph Wendell Burhoe, to whom the work is dedicated, has been the focal point for what he calls "an invisible college for scientific study of values and religion" (1981, 14; see Breed 1990-1992, 1992). Burhoe is referring to the structures that he shaped: the Committee on Science and Values of the American Academy of Arts and Sciences; the Institute on Religion in an Age of Science (IRAS); the Meadville/Lombard Program in Theology and Science; *Zygon: Journal of Religion and Science*; the Center for Advanced Study in Religion and Science (CASIRAS), and, as his legacy, the Chicago Center for Religion and Science (CCRS) co-sponsored by CASIRAS and the Lutheran School of Theology at Chicago (LSTC), under the direction of theologian Philip Hefner and physicist Thomas Gilbert. These institutional forums have brought together scholars and researchers. In dialogue with one another, they are sculpting a consensus between science and religion.

Through these various organizations and by personal contact, each of the authors of these essays has been influenced by Burhoe. He has provided the vision for viewing brain, culture, and the human spirit from an emergent evolutionary perspective (Burhoe 1981). In editing the material I have retained the original formats, particularly the footnotes. These differ, suggesting the different times and circumstances in which each originated. The style, in short, is a metaphor of the differences in background of the authors. The content indicates the emerging consensus. I have chosen to use inclusive language to make the material accessible to our period of raised consciousness about sexist and patriarchal attitudes. In addition, I have altered long passages into shorter paragraphs, added section headings, italicized salient points, and eliminated some material for ease of reading. In every case I have retained the flavor of the author. In looking back, all of us would revise some of what we have said and certainly some of how we said it. Rather than update the pieces, I have retained their integrity. This highlights their contribution to our current understanding of the exciting relationship between the neurosciences and the human sciences.

REFERENCES

Breed, David R. 1990-1992. "Ralph Wendell Burhoe: His Life and Thought: I. Perceiving the Problem and Envisioning the Solution," *Zygon: Journal of Religion & Science* 2 (September 1990): 323-51; "II. Formulating the Vision and Organizing the Institute on Religion in an Age of Science (IRAS)," *Zygon* 25 (December 1990): 469-91; "III. Developing the Vision among the Unitarians," *Zygon* 26 (March 1991): 149-75; "IV. Burhoe's Theological Program," *Zygon* 26 (June 1991): 277-308; "V. The Struggle to Establish the Vision as a New Paradigm," *Zygon* 26 (September 1991): 379-428.

_____. 1992. *Yoking Science and Religion: The Life and Thought of Ralph Wendell Burhoe*. Foreward by Roger W. Sperry. Chicago: Chicago Center for Religion and Science/Zygon Books.

Burhoe, Ralph Wendell. 1981. *Toward a Scientific Theology*. Belfast: Christian Journals Limited.

Evanston, Illinois
May 1992

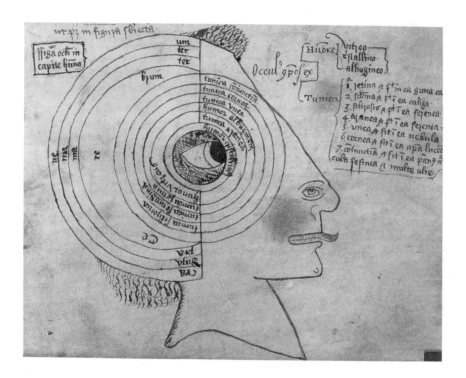

Figure 1.1 "The figure of the eye in the human head," taken probably from a treatise on ophthalmological medicine by Magister Zacharias of Salerno and Constantinople in the twelvth century.

"There is more to vision than meets the eye."

Günter Wächtershäuser (1987, 137)

1

Mind or consciousness is not something that
originates in some transcendent world outside of
nature, but is the place where nature itself become
conscious.

We need to think of human consciousness not as
separating us as a higher species from the rest of
nature, but rather as a gift which enables us to
learn how to harmonize our needs with the natural
system around us of which we are a dependent
part.

Rosemary Radford Ruether (1991, 12).

Chapter One

INTRODUCTION

by

James B. Ashbrook

The human brain is the most complex phenomenon we know. How did it come about? How does it work? What is its significance?

Answers to such questions are varied and controversial. Even so, evidence and interpretation are converging. With the cognitive sciences we have a new way of thinking about humanity, our place in nature and our relation to divinity. In the human brain, matter and mind interface directly.

Emergent evolution is a term characterizing that interfacing. It is the story of human becoming. It tells of changes from lifeless matter to breathing souls. Figure 1.1 is a curious drawing of the human eye. It probably comes from a fourteenth-century treatise on ophthalmological medicine. I suggest the large central eye represents the mind's eye and the little eye on the nose the physical eye. The mind's eye symbolizes the emergence of human consciousness. Because the sun is the source of light, humanity has regarded light and the process of seeing as a spiritual act, symbolizing understanding (Cirlot [1962] 1974, 99-100). We can see beyond the immediate; we can imagine other space and other time; we can anticipate and plan, evaluate and appraise (Lazarus 1991), reassess and reinterpret. Physical sight and psychic significance influence each other (see Neumann 1962). A dynamic relationship exists between symbolic intention and sensory perception, with the intentional processes in the prefrontal cortex being the crucial areas in consciousness (Laughlin, McManus, and d'Aquili 1990, 102-19, 93-4).

Conscious awareness and human culture have co-evolved. With other living beings we are the way we are because of our need to adapt. This is the evolutionary view (Ornstein 1991). Unlike that of other living creatures, our consciousness creates so much added information that adaptation is linked with unsuspected and unexpected possibilities. These

3

possibilities compound the nature of the context in which we must adapt. "Variation is pervasive," as cognitive psychologist Michael J. Mahoney points out, "and yet order emerges" (1991, 140). Our viewpoint influences our niche. We see with the mind's eye. This is the emergent view. Both *evolution* and *emergent* call for more explanation.

The idea of evolution burst into public consciousness with Charles Darwin's 1859 publication *On the Origin of Species by Means of Natural Selection, or The Preservation of Favoured Races in the Struggle of Life.* He believed that species evolved. They were not created separately. He ended his 1871 work *The Descent of Man* [sic] by insisting that "with all his exalted powers -- man still bears in his bodily frame the indelible stamp of his lowly origin" (Gregory 1987, 179-80). Like Darwin, other early evolutionary thinkers blurred the boundary between animals and humans, emphasizing our continuity with other species.

Darwinian ideas included: (1) classification of species according to basic sameness; (2) variation among species with suggestion why there is so much of it; and (3) natural selection with the environment shaping organisms for survival of those that best fit the evolutionary niche (Gregory 1987, 234-42).

Recent researchers have come to emphasize evolutionary discontinuities (Cartmill, Pilbeam, and Isaac 1986). They are reconstituting the boundary that distinguishes us from other creatures. Evolutionary gaps are actually evolutionary leaps, punctuated equilibria to use the technical phrase (Mahoney 1991, 127). Even so, they reflect the Darwinian position. There appears to have been no "discrete historical leap into a distinctively human evolutionary trajectory." Instead, human origin has been more a process than an event (Simons 1989). There are antecedents and parallels for many of our unique human activities. More than 99 percent of our genes match those of chimpanzees (Kolb and Whishaw 1985, 80). The features that define *Homo sapiens* appear to have come about more or less independently. These include our walking upright, ability to use tools, large complex brains, use of fire, big game hunting, gestures becoming speech, art, and symbolization.

When parts combine, emergent properties may appear. These

unexpected appearances are mysterious -- mysterious because descriptions of the parts are inadequate to explain what emerges. Development took time. Change came slowly. Only in the recent past -- the last 10,000 to 25,000 years -- did evolution of the human brain become rapid (Kolb and Whishaw 1985, 81-5).

Life began about 3,000 million years ago. It remained simple for the next 2,000 million years. Then the complexity of organization increased. Fishes, amphibians, reptiles, and birds appeared. True mammals emerged about 150 million years ago. Monkeylike mammals appeared about 25 million years ago. Humanlike animals walked upright around 3 to 4 million years ago (Lovejoy 1988). The first human symbols date back about 30,000 years. Speech may have had its origin 60,000 years ago. Rudimentary language appeared between 2.5 and 3.5 million years ago (Kolb and Whishaw 1985, 532).

Compared to the age of the universe, the culminating features of the brain appeared in a short span of time. About 2 million years ago, *Homo habilis* first used chipped-stone tools. About 1.3 million years ago, *Homo erectus* discovered fire. About 100,000 years ago, Neanderthals probably buried their dead with flowers. About 30,000 years ago, the Cro-Magnons produced elaborate cave paintings and carvings. During the last 10,000 years, the tempo of change quickened. Agriculture, the husbandry of livestock, and the representation of ideas in script (Kolb and Whishaw 1985, 83; Eccles 1989) burst forth.

Neurophysiologist Rodney Holmes (1991) links these developments to *Homo religiosus*. Religiosus refers to our ability to access "an Ultimate Reality that transcends material reality. . . . To be religious means, among other things, to interpret material and social realities in terms of Ultimate Reality." Thus, the burial sites left by Neanderthals some 70,000 years ago suggest a cranial capacity generating religious interpretation of experience. We look at the texts of nature and history in relation to Ultimate Reality.

The brain makes meaning, though that meaning differs from species to species. For frogs and birds, meaning involves distance. For mammals, it accentuates borders. Consciousness, intelligence, and religiousness are *emergent* human qualities. Nothing would have predicted their appearance.

Yet from an *evolutionary* perspective, no characteristic so clearly separates us from other species as meaning-making.

Of course, these late evolutionary developments are not all advantageous. Before the Wright brothers flew, birds could fly. Their higher rate of metabolism is associated with a more efficient respiratory function. Yet "no bird has invented an atom bomb" (Oppenheimer 1977, 7). The rate at which we are devastating our environment raises grave problems for this late emerging creature. Our ability to destroy ourselves makes us an endangered species.

What has emerged, however, is the brain's capacity to represent or model the world as a way of influencing behavior (Oakley 1985). We share this capacity for mental representation with other animals. "The mammalian brain," according to biopsychologist Jerre Levy (1977, 267), "models a reality that subsumes the past, imagines the future, and takes account of far distant spatial regions." Because of this capacity, we can speak of evidence of awareness, consciousness, and self-image in animals. Yet the capacity for language may be the most powerful representation system of all. This capacity for language shapes the content of human consciousness. The mind's eye sees more than the physical eye.

The articles in this volume deal with that emergence of consciousness, in animals and in humans. Our brain links us with other species and the rest of the created order. Culture expands the complexity of information processing to free us from some of the constraints of space and time. The human spirit opens before us varied ways of understanding and choosing to live life as we know it on this planet. Our capacity for transcendence does not free us from our environmental context. Instead, it compounds the task of living in the setting which is a gift.

More than other researchers in the last half century, neurophysiologist Paul D. MacLean has focused on the limbic system and its importance in behavior. His book *The Triune Brain in Evolution: Role in Paleocerebral Functions* (1990) brings together the fruits of his efforts. His article "On The Evolution of Three Mentalities" introduces the reader to his research. In describing our three mentalities, or the triune brain as he calls it, he characterizes evolutionary emergence. We are obliged to view our world and ourselves from the perspectives of three quite different mentalities. Two of these "appear to lack the power of speech."

In drawing inferences about the way our brain functions, MacLean summarizes his research on nonverbal communicative behavior in animals. Literature serves as a metaphor for understanding such communication. He suggests that the instinctual reptilian brain "provides the basic plots and actions." The mammalian brain "influences emotionally the developments of the plots." And the new rational brain expounds "the plots and emotions in as many ways as there are authors." MacLean contends that the old evolutionary brains are involved in fundamental ways in expressing who we are. Because of the reptilian and mammalian brains, mere logic is powerless to resolve the problems that lie closest to our hearts.

"The Myth-Ritual Complex" reflects psychiatrist Eugene G. d'Aquili's research in biogenetic structuralism. This approach relates consciousness and brain physiology (Laughlin, McManus, and d'Aquili 1974). *Brain, Symbol & Experience: Toward a Neurophenomenology of Human Consciousness* (1990), co-authored with Charles D. Laughlin, Jr., and John McManus, represents a fuller elaboration of the approach. Here he applies a biogenetic structural analysis to the myth-ritual complex.

According to d'Aquili, the structure of myth comes from the functioning of six brain "operators." He identifies these operators as: holistic, causal, abstractive, binary, formal quantitative, and value. Each represents specifically evolved neural tissue, primarily in the two cerebral hemispheres.

d'Aquili views mythmaking like other cognitive processes, as behavior arising from the evolution and integration of various parts of the brain. Human ceremonial ritual represents the culmination of a long evolutionary process. Polar opposites -- or what conceptually we regard as logical paradoxes -- are presented in myths and resolved by ritual behavior.

Motor behavior -- a trait common to all mammals -- links environmental struggle with the rhythmicity of ritual activity. In its parasympathetic and sympathetic extensions the autonomic nervous system is connected with the central nervous system. d'Aquili associates the energy-expanding or ergotropic sympathetic system with the analytic processing of the left hemisphere. In parallel, he associates the energy-conserving or trophotropic parasympathetic system with the synthetic processing of the right hemisphere. Both are simultaneously stimulated in ritual. They are also simultaneously stimulated in meditative states. The effect is a unified consciousness. Such unifying, d'Aquili believes, results in positive consequences. On the one hand, it relieves anxiety and the fear of death. On the other, it "places us in harmony with the universe."

Anthropologist Victor Turner has been pivotal in research on ritual behavior (1969; 1982). He examined the symbolic meaning of human behavior as "the result of social conditioning." In the last phase of his work his attention turned to what he regarded as "inherent resistances to conditioning." His acquaintance with work in cerebral neurology led to his fashioning what he called "a new synthesis with anthropological studies."

Turner's article "Body, Brain, and Culture" marks this shift in his thinking. Drawing upon MacLean and d'Aquili, Turner explores Ralph Wendell Burhoe's contention that "creative processes result from a coadaptation, perhaps in ritual itself, of genetic and cultural information." The division of labor between right and left hemispheres suggests insights about the place and importance of play and playful combinations of "as-if" activity. Play is intimately involved in ritual. Ritual thus appears to function "in the social construction of reality analogous to mutation and variation in organic evolution."

Significantly, Turner considers how understanding brain activity "accords with some distinctive features of the religious systems dominant in human culture." He points us toward a "free interplay and mutual support" between humanity's intuition and our genetic pool. Such a condition, he indicates, is "sometimes called love."

Roger W. Sperry shared the 1981 Nobel Prize in Medicine/Physiology for his work on split-brain research (Gregory 1987, 114-17). Years before his split-brain research, Sperry had pioneered in demonstrating neurospecificity or, as his theory is called, "chemoaffinity" (Trevarthen 1990a). He hypothesized the specificity of neuronal connections based on "chemical affinities between nerve terminals and their target cells" (quoted in Trevarthen 1990a, 5). That is, each axon or nerve fiber carries a unique chemical code that directs it to where it is to grow. Sperry regarded his shift of interest from neurospecificity to split-brain as a logical move. Others viewed it as a grand leap. In recent years, his "logic" has taken him into philosophical speculation. His essay on "Psychology's Mentalist Paradigm and the Religion/Science Tension" reflects that interest (Sperry 1982; 1991).

For years Sperry has spoken against an objective, value-free, bottom-up approach to our human world and nonhuman nature. In its stead, he has insisted upon an emergent approach. Such an approach is conscious, purposive, top-down. By this he means psychology's new cognitivism, a revised mentalist paradigm. He avoids the dualism of either a bottom-up or a top-down approach.

Rather than seeing an antagonism between science and religion, Sperry speaks of a convergence. The emergent view of nature and human nature is "less atomistic, less mechanistic, and more mentalistic, contextual, subjectivist, and humanistic." He combines a macrodeterministic perspective of the whole ecosystem with a microdeterministic understanding of "innate value preferences inherent in the human cognitive structure as a part of nature's genetic provisions for survival." Sperry calls the result a "better *quality* survival." Consciousness, as the highest and most evolved property, is to protect the biosphere. It can develop "a common natural belief system and global ethic" on which most of us can agree.

Psychobiologist Colwyn Trevarthen was a student and early collaborator with Sperry (Trevarthen 1990a; 1990b). He builds upon the work of MacLean, d'Aquili, Turner, Jerre Levy, and others. In reviewing the chemistry and anatomy of the neural core of human motivation, he extends that understanding to the newborn infant and to the transcendent reaches of the human spirit. He combines that theoretical reflection on the brain with "innate motivation for social cooperation and celebration."

Trevarthen jumps from the human brain to the "human communal mind." From there his logic moves to "the parts of the brain that form the essential crucible of the human spirit." In detailing the evidence, he describes "the human spirit in children," the result of the two-person cooperation between a newborn and its mother.

Trevarthen's survey of previous work is familiar yet fresh. He clarifies the "union of inner values and outward facts," the vitality of will that comes in self-maintenance, and the personal relationship in I-thou connections. "The human spirit," he insists, "defines itself in qualities of fellowship discovered in play and achieves fulfillment in companionship made strong with ritual."

Levy (1980) has established the contribution of biological diversity to a variety of brain organizations. These, in turn, make for a variety of social systems capable of giving us "our humanity." Evolution "was not directed toward selecting some one ideal type of brain organization and cognitive structure. . . . There is no platonic ideal," she declares, "that best characterizes the human species" (Levy 1977, 271; 1980).

Thus, the emergent view of brain oranization turns our attention from "the human social system" to "the human spirit." The last essay places the emergence of mind -- social organization and human aspirations -- back in its evolutionary origin.The chapter expresses my own neurotheological approach (Ashbrook 1984a; 1984b; 1988; 1989; 1992a) to implications in brain research. Human destiny does not mean escape from the physical universe. Rather, human destiny requires mutual interchange between the cultural realities created by the new brain and the genetic adaptation required by the old brain. Theologian Rosemary Ruether reminds us that human consciousness does not separate us from nature but "enables us to learn how to harmonize our needs with the natural system . . . of which we are a dependent part" (1991, 12). And theologian Philip Hefner insists, "survival [is] a human value," linking religion and science (1980).

Mind lifts up the *human* meaning of the evolutionary process. Mind also "give *human* meaning to the universe in which it finds itself." An understanding of destiny focuses our attention in two directions: one, downward into the organized regularities of the old brain; the other, outward toward the emergent aspects of human purposes. Such understanding of "the whole brain makes belief more credible and destiny more immediate." We sense a "mystery in the materiality of the human brain and the mentality of the physical universe."

These six essays begin with our evolutionary origins. They carry us through analogous ritual patterns and into cultural and social organization. Finally, they point us toward a transcendent dimension, the dimension of human destiny, the dimension of our human spirit. Together they set an agenda for further inquiry. They provide what British anatomist J. Z. Young speaks of as "a common code in which people can express their needs and motivations, and understand those of others" (Young 1978, 269).

I suggest there are at least three next steps. One is elaboration of the most basic variant of brain type. That variant is the diversity of organization between the female and the male brain (Dimond 1977, 491; Ashbrook 1992b). What are the implications of females being "specialized for understanding the social world" and males "for understanding the physical world" (Levy 1980, 367-71)? Another is elaboration of the diversity of multicultural patterns (Gibson and Petersen 1991; TenHouten 1985). A third deals with what neuropsychologist Stuart J. Dimond refers to as the problem of how the brain "produce[s] unity out of disunity." How does the brain "generate a dominant force to channel the discordant strands of mental action into one concerted thread of action" (Dimond 1977, 489)? How, in short, are the human spirit and biochemical processes causally connected?

The task of relating the neurosciences and religion is greater than any one individual can manage. Philosopher and clinical professor of medicine Robert Lyman Potter and Hefner each emphasize that collaborative agenda. It requires "teams of specialists" (Potter 1992; Hefner 1992). These essays represent the creation of one such "team of specialists." The mystery of mind in matter is our origin and our destiny. An understanding of our mind-ful matter looms closer. The essays that follow provide foundations upon which to build such understanding.

REFERENCES

Ashbrook, James B. 1984a. "Neurotheology: The Working Brain and the Work of Theology." *Zygon: Journal of Religion and Science* 19 (September): 331-50.

_____. 1984b. *The Human Mind and the Mind of God: Theological Promise in Brain Research.* Lanham, Md.: University Press of America.

_____. 1988. *The Brain and Belief: Faith in the Light of Brain Research.* Bristol, Ind.: Wyndham Hall Press.

_____. 1989. "The Whole Brain as the Basis for the Analogical Expression of God." *Zygon: Journal of Religion and Science* 24 (March): 65-81.

_____. 1992a. "Making Sense of Soul and Sabbath: Brain Processes and the Making of Meaning." *Zygon: Journal of Religion and Science* 27 (March): 31-49.

_____. 1992b. "From Biogenetic Structuralism to Mature Contemplation to Prophetic Consciousness." *Zygon: Journal of Religion and Science* (in press).

Cartmill, Matt, David Pilbeam, and Glynn Isaac. 1986. "One Hundred Years of Paleoanthropology." *American Scientist* 74 (July-August): 410-20.

Cirlot, J.E. [1962] 1974. *A Dictionary of Symbols.* 2d ed. Translated by Jack Sage. Foreward by Herbert Reed. New York: Philosophical Library.

Dimond, Stuart J. 1977. "Evolution and Lateralization of the Brain: Concluding Remarks." In *Evolution and Lateralization of the Brain*, edited by Stuart J. Dimond and David A. Blizard, pp. 477-501. New York: Annals of The New York Academy of Sciences, vol. 299.

Eccles, John C. 1989. *Evolution of the Brain: Creation of the Self.* London and New York: Routledge.

Gibson, Kathleen R., and Anne C. Petersen, eds. 1991. *Brain Maturation and Cognitive Development: Comparative and Cross-Cultural Perspectives.* Hawthorne, N.Y.: Aldine De Gruyer.

Gregory, Richard L., ed. 1987. *The Oxford Companion to the Mind.* New York: Oxford University Press.

Hefner, Philip. 1980. "Survival as a Human Value." *Zygon: Journal of Religion and Science* 15 (June): 203-12.

_____. 1992. Editorial, *Zygon: Journal of Religion and Science* 27 (March): 3-4.

Holmes, Rodney. 1991. "Did *Homo Religiosus* Emerge from the Evolution of the Brain?" *Insights: The Magazine of the Chicago Center for Religion and Science* 3, no. 1 (June):10-14.

Kolb, Bryan, and Ian Q. Whishaw. [1980] 1985. *Fundamentals of Human Neuropsychology.* 2d ed. New York: W. H. Freeman and Company.

Laughlin, Charles D., Jr., John McManus, and Eugene G. d'Aquili. 1974. *Biogenetic Structuralism.* New York: Columbia University Press.

_____. 1990. *Brain, Symbol & Experience: Toward a Neurophenomenology of Human Consciousness.* Boston: New Science Library/Shambhala.

Lazarus, Richard S. 1991. *Emotion and Adaptation.* New York: Oxford University Press.

Levy, Jerre. 1977. "The Mammalian Brain and the Adaptive Advantage of Cerebral Asymmetry." In *Evolution and Lateralization of the Brain.*, edited by Stuart J. Dimond and David A. Blizard, pp. 264-72. New York: Annals of the New York Academy of Sciences, vol. 299.

_____. 1980. "Varieties of Human Brain Organization and the Human Social System." *Zygon: Journal of Religion and Science* 15 (December): 351-75.

Lovejoy, C. Owen. 1988. "Evolution of Human Walking." *Scientific American*, November: 118-25.

MacLean, Paul D. 1990. *The Triune Brain in Evolution: Role in Paleocerebral Functions.* New York: Plenum Press.

Mahoney, Michael J. 1991. *Human Change Processes: The Scientific Foundation of Psychotherapy.* New York: Basic Books.

Neumann, Erich. 1962. *The Origins and History of Consciousness.* Vol. 1. Translated by R. F. C. Hull. New York: Harper, Torch Books.

Oakley, David A., ed. 1985. *Brain & Mind.* New York: Methuen.

Oppenheimer, Jane M. 1977. "Studies of Brain Asymmetry: Historical Perspective." In *Evolution and Lateralization of the Brain,* edited by Stuart J. Dimond and David A. Blizard, pp. 4-17. New York: Annals of the New York Academy of Sciences, Vol. 299.

Ornstein, Robert. 1991. *The Evolution of Consciousness.* New York: Prentice Hall

Potter, Robert Lyman. 1992. Review of *The Brain and Belief: Faith in the Light of Brain Research.* *Zygon: Journal of Religion and Science* 27 (March): 122-23.

Rosemary Radford Ruether. 1991. "Ecofeminism: Symbolic and Social Connections Between the Oppression of Women and the Domination of Nature." The Loy H. Witherspoon Lectures in Religious Studies. The University of North Carolina at Charlotte, October 31.

Simons, Elwyn L. 1989. "Human Origins." *Science* 245 (22 September): 1343-50.

Sperry, Roger W. 1982. *Science and Moral Priority: Merging Mind, Brain, and Human Values.* New York: Columbia University Press.

_____. 1991. "Search for Beliefs to Live by Consistent with Science." *Zygon: Journal of Religion and Science* 26 (June): 237-58.

TenHouten, Warren D. 1985. "Cerebral-Lateralization Theory and the Sociology of Knowledge." In *The Dual Brain: Hemispheric Specialization in Humans,* edited by D. Frank Benson and Eran Zaidel, pp. 341-58. New York: The Guilford Press.

Trevarthen, Colwyn, ed. 1990a. *Brain Circuits and Functions of the Mind: Essays in Honor of Roger W. Sperry.* New York: Cambridge University Press.

_____. 1990b. "Growth and education in the hemispheres." In *Brain Circuits*

14

Colwyn Trevarthen, pp. 334-63. New York: Cambridge University Press.

Turner, Victor. 1969. *The Ritual Process: Structure and Anti-Structure.* Chicago: Aldine Press.

_____. 1982. *From Ritual to Theatre.* New York: Performing Arts Journal Publications.

Wächtershäuser, Günter. 1987. "Light and Life: On the Nutritional Origins of Sensory Perception." In *Evolutionary Epistemology, Rationality, and the Sociology of Knowledge*, edited by Gerard Radnitzky and W. W. Bartley, III, pp. 121-38. LaSalle IL.: Open Court.

Young, J. Z. 1978. *Programs of the Brain: Based on the Gifford Lectures, 1975-76.* New York: Oxford University Press.

Chapter Two

ON THE EVOLUTION OF THREE MENTALITIES*

by

Paul D. MacLean

Herein too may be felt the powerlessness of mere Logic, the profoundest knowledge of the laws of the understanding, to resolve these problems which lie nearer to our hearts, as progressive years strip away from our life the illusions of its golden dawn.

George Boole, *An Investigation of the Laws of Thought*, 416.

INTRODUCTION

Many people point out the apparent irony that the great strides in the natural sciences seem to be speeding us toward the Hill of Megiddo and the long-advertised final conflict between the forces of good and evil. Others, still blinded by the searing light of Hiroshima, are more introspective in expressing this concern: How, they ask, can we contain and harness the devastating powers of the atom before we have learned to understand and control the potentially catastrophic forces within ourselves?

In recent years anxiety about thermonuclear war has diminished somewhat in the light of warnings that the human race and many forms of life may be on the way to extinction because of scientific developments that have made possible overpopulation, pollution of the environment, and exhaustion of critical resources.

A curve showing the growth of the world's population[13] indicates that each successive doubling of people has taken place in half the time of the previous doubling.[6] At this rate the present population would be expected to double in 30 to 40 years. U Thant, speaking as Secretary of the United Nations, made his famous pronouncement that there remained only 10 years to find solutions for the exploding population and related problems.

Warnings of this kind focus attention almost exclusively on the external environment. It is so easy to see the problems of meeting future demands for food, water, energy, and other basic requisites that planning experts seem to have overlooked the lessons of animal experimentation indicating that psychological "stresses" of crowding may bring about a collapse of social structure despite an ample provision of the necessities of life (e.g., Refs. 5 and 41). Systems analysts who have attempted to predict the limits of growth with the aid of computer technology[38] either admit to an inability to deal with psychological factors or neglect them altogether.

Michael Chance[7] has remarked that the parts of the universe that human beings first chose for study were those furthest removed from the self-- meaning, of course, the heavens and the science of astronomy. Later I mention a possible neurological explanation of why our sciences from the very beginning have focused on the external world. By contrast, and perhaps for similar reasons, there has been a retarded interest in turning the dissecting lamp of the scientific method onto the inner self and the psychological instrument by which we derive all scientific knowledge. It would almost seem that there had always been a supernatural injunction against doing so: "Of every tree of the garden thou mayest freely eat: But of the tree of the knowledge of good and evil, thou shalt not eat of it; for in the day that thou eatest thereof thou shalt surely die." [Genesis 3:2-3]

Until rather recent times religion and philosophy provided the principal spokespeople and interpreters in regard to psychological matters. Although having their modern origins in the 18th century, psychology and psychiatry could hardly be regarded as sciences until the latter half of the 19th century. The same would be true for neurophysiology and experimental psychology which encompass investigations on psychological functions of the brain.

According to Kathleen Grange,[16] the term "psychology" was used in titles as early as 1703, while "psychiatry" first appeared on a title page in 1813. Psychiatry began to receive recognition as one of the medical sciences in 1854, when Griesinger at the University of Munich united for the first time the teaching of neurology and psychiatry. Meynert, Gudden, Forel, and others followed this practice and established it as a tradition in Europe.

Since the middle of the present century, neurology has tended to follow an independent course, delving into psychological functions only insofar as particular disturbances in cerebration make it possible to diagnose the nature and location of brain disease. Psychoanalysis, which gave new conceptual and methodological dimensions to psychiatry, began to arouse public interest in 1900 with the publication of Freud's *The Interpretation of Dreams*.[14]

The late development of the psychological sciences is of itself of epistemological interest. This leads to the consideration that none of the psychological sciences devotes itself specifically to epistemological questions concerning the origin, nature, limits, and validity of knowledge. Except for sensation and perception, it is curious how little attention has been given by philosophers and others to the role of the brain in matters of epistemology.

Epistemology exists because of human societies, and human societies depend on the existence of individuals. I state these truisms to emphasize the incontrovertible centricity of the individual person with respect to public knowledge. In constitutional language, public knowledge, just as society itself, derives authority from individuals. In this sense, an individual is both supreme and indispensable.

Central to every individual is a subjective self--a self that Descartes[9] once referred to as "this me." A conceptual dissection of the subjective self requires that it be laid open not only in terms of its inner workings, but also in relationship to the societal and nonsocietal elements of the external environment. There are two sides to each of these relationships: the side that is intuitively and unsystematically experienced, and the side that becomes known through the analytic and synthetic approaches of the various sciences. The animate relationships become systematically known through the social and life sciences, while formal knowledge of the inanimate derives from the natural sciences.

"Epistemics." There is, however, no branch of science that deals specifically with an explanation of the subjective self and its relation to the internal and external environment. While such a study would draw on every field of knowledge reflecting on the human condition, it would build fundamentally on the psychological and brain-related sciences. In order to have a matching expression for epistemology, as well as an equivalent term

for science, one might borrow a word directly from the Greek, and instead of speaking of a "science of the self," refer to an "episteme (*epis teme*) of the self." Then the body of knowledge or the collective disciplines dealing with this subject could be known as *epistemics*.

Let it be emphasized that the domains of epistemics and epistemology are the same. The difference is in the point of view. Epistemics represents the subjective view and epistemic approach from the inside-out, whereas epistemology represents the public view and scientific approach from the outside-in. The two are inseparable insofar as epistemics is nuclear to epistemology, and epistemology embraces epistemics. What is entailed is an obligatory relationship between a private, personal brain and a public, collective, societal brain.

Developments in the knowledge of the brain promise to have a profound influence on epistemology. In scientific and philosophic writings, it has been customary to regard the human brain as a global organ dominated by the cerebral cortex which serves as a *tabula rasa* for an everchanging translation of sensory and perceptive experience into symbolic language, and which has special capacities for learning, memory, problem solving, and transmission of culture from one generation to another. Such a view is blind to the consideration that in its evolution the human brain has expanded along the lines of three basic patterns which may be characterized as reptilian, paleomammalian, and neomammalian (see figure 2.1).[25]

Radically different in structure and chemistry and in an evolutionary sense countless generations apart, the three formations constitute, so-to-speak, three-brains-in-one, a *triune* brain.[28,33] What this situation immediately implies is that we are obliged to look at ourselves and the world through the eyes of three quite different mentalities. To complicate things further, two of the mentalities appear to lack the power of speech.

"Objectivity." Achievements of the so-called hard or exact sciences have helped to promote the attitude that solutions to most problems can be found by learning to manipulate the external environment. It has been traditional to regard the exact sciences as completely objective. The self-conscious cultivation of the "objective" approach is illustrated in a statement by Einstein quoted by C.P. Snow.[46] "A perception of this world by thought, leaving out everything subjective became . . . my supreme aim." Monod,

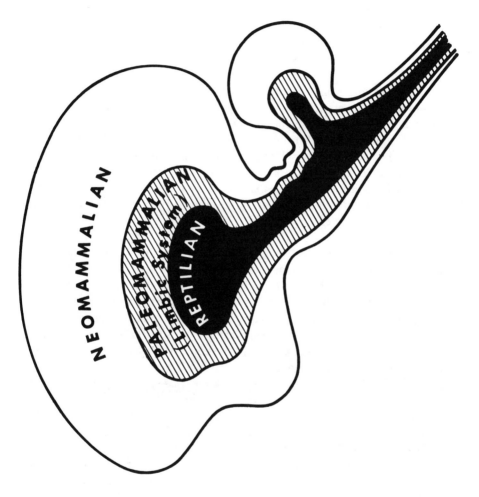

Figure 2.1

In its evolution the human brain has expanded along the lines of three basic patterns which may be characterized as reptilian, paleomammalian, and neomammalian. From Ref. 25.

in an essay on the contributions of molecular biology,[39] is equally insistent on applying the "principle of objectivity" in the life sciences. "The cornerstone of the scientific method," he writes, "is the postulate that nature is objective." Even in the world of fiction one finds a book reviewer saying, "Humanity is likely to be saved, if it is at all, by a search for an objective reality we can all share--for truths like those of science."[52]

Early in this century, John B. Watson and others of the behaviorist school sought to revive the spirit of the Helmholz tradition and to establish psychology as an exact science on an equal footing with physics and the other natural sciences.[45] In their study of animals and human beings they advocated a completely objective approach that dispensed with the consideration of consciousness, subjectivity, and introspection.[51] The irony of all such "objective" attitudes is that every behavior selected for study, every observation and interpretation, requires subjective processing by an introspective observer.

Logically, there is no way of circumventing this subjectivity or the more disturbing conclusion that the cold, hard facts of science, like the firm pavement underfoot, are all derivatives of a "soft" brain. No measurement or computation obtained by the hardware of the exact sciences enters our comprehension without undergoing subjective transformation by the "software" of the brain. The implication of Spencer's statement[47] that objective psychology owes its origins to subjective psychology could apply to the whole realm of science.

For such reasons it is important to consider how a fifth dimension [in addition to the capacities for learning, memory, problem solving, and the transmissions of culture], the subjective brain, affects our relative view of the world. In considering this problem, I do not intend to deal with the familiar Cartesian topic of perceptual illusions. Rather, I focus on brain research concerned with the origins of other forms of experience and attitudes that may be of more basic significance for "epistemics" and epistemology, giving particular attention to forebrain mechanisms underlying "paleopsychic" processes and "prosematic" (nonverbal) behavior.

Subjective Experience. For each one of us as individuals there is nothing so vital as our subjective experience. Without the essence of subjectivity, there would be no means of realizing our existence. Subjectivity represents a form of information. As Wiener stated more succinctly than Berkeley or Hume, "Information is information, not matter or energy."[53] At the same time, it is empirically evident that there can be no communication of information without the intermediary of what we recognize as physical behaving entities. This invariance might be considered a law of communication.

"*Facts.*" I should also mention at this point my conclusion that facts apply only to those things that can be agreed upon publicly as entities behaving in a certain way. The term validity does not apply to the facts themselves, which are neither true nor false *per se*, but rather to what is agreed upon as true by subjective individuals after a public assessment of the facts. What is agreed upon as true or false by one group may be quite contrary to the conclusions of another group.

COMMUNICATIVE BEHAVIOR

Next in importance to our subjective experience is the ability to share what we feel and think with other beings. Such communication must be accomplished through some form of behavior. Human communicative behavior can be broadly categorized as verbal and nonverbal.

Like P.W. Bridgman, the physicist-philosopher, the great majority of people would probably conclude that "most communication is verbal."[3] Since we are so accustomed to think of ourselves as verbal beings, we have given less attention to the analysis of nonverbal behavior. This neglect is evidenced by our lack of a specific word for nonverbal behavior; we refer to it negatively by stating what it is not.

It is an everyday experience that in spite of all kinds of talk--no matter how well documented--we are never quite sure how we develop attitudes or reach decisions regarding all manner of human relationships. Who would feel confident in trying to identify the nonverbal factors affecting one's choice of spouse, friends, associates; a vote for a particular candidate; one's judgments as a member of a committee or jury? In an article on nonverbal communication in Japan, Morsbach[40] illustrates the bewilderment commonly felt in trying to reconstruct human decisions. In an anecdote conjuring a feeling of *deja vu* he describes two professors who after a faculty meeting found themselves in agreement that everyone had spoken positively about a particular proposal that was subsequently voted down. "Don't you agree," one asked the other, "that everyone was in favor?" "Yes," was the reply, "but you did not hear the silences."

Contrary to the popular view, many behavioral scientists would be inclined to give greater importance to nonverbal than verbal behavior in day-to-day human activities. For example, when a psychologist, a behavioral ecologist, a specialist in environmental design, and an ethologist were asked to draw two squares representative of the weight that they would give verbal and nonverbal communication in everyday human activity, there was a striking similarity in their responses. In each case, the square for nonverbal behavior was about three times bigger than the one for verbal behavior. It must be admitted, however, that we are so ignorant of the hidden aspects of nonverbal behavior that it would be impossible to make quantitative assessments of their influence.

Nonverbal ("Prosematic") Behavior. Nonverbal behavior mirrors in part what Freud (1900) called primary processes. In drawing a distinction between verbal and nonverbal behavior it is easier to see differences than similarities. But in a very real sense, nonverbal behavior like verbal behavior, has its semantics and syntax--in other words, *meaning* and *orderly arrangement* of specific acts.

It is nonverbal behavior that we possess in common with animals. Since it is hardly appropriate to refer to nonverbal behavior of animals,[19] it is desirable to use some other term for this kind of behavior. The Greek word "*sema*" pertains to a sign, mark, or token. By adding the prefix "*pro*" in the particular sense of "rudimentary" one obtains the word "prosematic" which would be appropriate for referring to any kind of nonverbal signal--vocal, bodily, chemical.[34,36]

It has been the special contribution of ethology to provide the first systematic insights into the semantics and syntax of animal behavior.[21,48]

An analysis of prosematic behavior of animals reveals that somewhat parallel to words, sentences, and paragraphs, it becomes meaningful in terms of its components, constructs, and sequences of constructs. Since the patterns of behavior involved in self-preservation and survival of the species are generally similar in most terrestrial vertebrates, it is rather meaningless to speak, as in the past, of species-specific behavior. But since various species perform these behaviors in their own typical ways, it is both correct and useful to refer to species-typical behavior.

Introspectively, we recognize that prosematic communication may be either active or passive. When two or more individuals are within communicative distance, there is the possibility for either active ("intentional") or passive ("unintentional") communication to occur with respect to the "sender" or "receiver." Even when an individual is alone a sound, utterance, movement, or odor emanating from the self may have self-communicative value as it originates either actively or passively.

SYNOPSIS OF EXPERIMENTAL WORK

For the past 25 years, my research has been primarily concerned with identifying and analyzing forebrain mechanisms underlying prosematic forms of behavior, which on phylogenetic and clinical grounds might be inferred to represent expressions of "paleopsychic" processes. In this work, I have taken a comparative evolutionary approach which has the advantage that it allows one to telescope millions of years into a span that can be seen all at once, and as in plotting a curve makes it possible to see trends that would not otherwise be apparent. It also shows the usefulness of research on animals for obtaining insights into brain mechanisms underlying human prosematic behavior.

Since animal experimentation provides us our only systematic knowledge of brain functions, I should comment briefly on the justification of using findings on animals for drawing inferences about the workings of the human brain. At the molecular or cellular levels, there is general enthusiasm for applying findings on animals to human biology. In the field of psychiatry, neurochemical and neuropharmacological discoveries in animals have radically changed the treatment of certain neuropsychiatric disorders. But many people believe that behavioral and neurological observations on animals have little or no human relevance.

Such a bias perhaps stems from a failure to realize that in its evolution, the human brain expands in hierarchic fashion along the lines of three basic patterns which were mentioned earlier and characterized (figure 2.1) as reptilian, paleommmammalian, and neomammalian. It deserves reemphasis that the three formations are markedly different in chemistry and structure and in an evolutionary sense eons apart. Extensively interconnected, the three basic formations represent an amalgamation of three-brains-in-one, or what may be appropriately called a *triune* brain.[28,32,33] The word triune also serves to imply that the "whole" is greater than the sum of its parts, because with the exchange of information among the three formations each derives a greater amount of information than if it were operating alone. Stated in popular terms, the amalgamation amounts to three interconnected biological computers, with each inferred to have its own special intelligence, its own subjectivity, its own sense of time and space, and its own memory, motor, and other functions.

This scheme for subdividing the brain may seem simplistic, but thanks to improved anatomical, physiological, and chemical techniques, the three basic formations stand out in clearer detail than ever before. Moreover, it should be emphasized that despite their extensive interconnections, there is evidence that each brain type is capable of operating somewhat independently. Most important in regard to the "verbal-nonverbal" question, there are clinical indications that the reptilian and paleomammalian formations lack the neural machinery for verbal communication. To say that they lack the power of speech, however, does not belittle their intelligence, nor does it relegate them subjectively to the realm of the "unconscious."

The basic neural machinery required for self-preservation and the preservation of the species is built into the neural chassis contained in the midbrain, pons, medulla, and spinal cord. As shown by the early experiments of Ferrier[12] and others, an animal with only its neural chassis is as motionless and aimless as an idling vehicle without a driver. But this analogy stops short because with the evolution of the forebrain, the neural chassis acquires three drivers, all of different minds and all vying for control.

THE REPTILIAN-TYPE BRAIN

Let us look first at the reptilian "driver." In mammals, the major counterpart of the reptilian forebrain is represented by a group of large

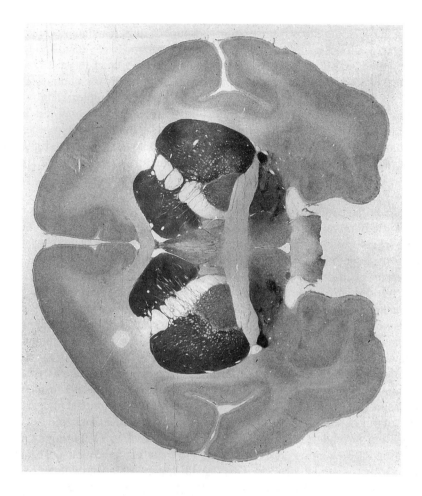

Figure 2.2

This section from the brain of a squirrel monkey shows how the greater part of the R-complex is selectively colored (black areas) by a stain for cholinesterase. From Ref. 29.

ganglia including the olfactostriatum, corpus striatum (caudate nucleus and putamen), globus pallidus, and satellite gray matter. Since there is no name that applies to all of these structures, I shall refer to them in this synopsis as the R-complex. As shown in figure 2.2, the stain for cholinesterase reveals a remarkable chemical contrast between the R-complex and the two other cerebrotypes. The shaded areas in figure 2.3 show how this stain sharply demarcates the R-complex in animals ranging from reptiles to humans. In using the flourescent technique of Falck and Hillarp (1959), it is striking to see how the structures corresponding to those in the figure glow a bright green because of large amounts of dopamine.[20]

From an evolutionary standpoint it is curious that ethologists have paid little attention to reptiles, focusing instead on fishes and birds. Some authorities believe that of the existing reptiles, lizards would bear the closest resemblance to the mammal-like reptiles believed to be the forerunners of mammals. At all events, lizards and other reptiles provide illustrations of complex prototypical *patterns* of behavior commonly seen in mammals, including humans. One can quickly list more than 20 such behaviors that may primarily involve self-preservation or the survival of the species[36:] (1) selection and preparation of homesite; (2) establishment of domain or territory; (3) trail making; (4) "marking" of domain or territory; (5) showing place-preferences; (6) ritualistic display in defense of territory, commonly involving the use of coloration and adornments; (7) formalized intraspecific fighting in defense of territory; (8) triumphal display in successful defense; (9) assumption of distinctive postures and coloration in signaling surrender; (10) routinization of daily activities; (11) foraging; (12) hunting; (13) homing; (14) hoarding; (15) use of defecation posts; (16) formation of social groups; (17) establishment of social hierarchy by ritualistic display and other means; (18) greeting; (19) "grooming"; (20) courtship, with displays using coloration and adornments; (21) mating; (22) breeding and, in isolated instances, attending offspring; (23) flocking; and (24) migration.

Five Interoperative Behaviors. There is an important *pentad* of prototypical forms of behavior of a general nature that may be variously operative in the activities above. In anticipation of some later comments, I name and briefly characterize them. They may be denoted as: (1) isopraxic, (2) perseverative, (3) reenactment, (4) tropistic, and (5) deceptive behavior.

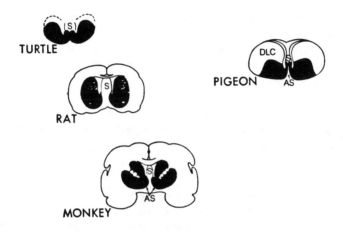

Figure 2.3

Shaded areas indicate how a stain for cholinesterase demarcates the greater part of the R-complex in animals ranging from reptiles to primates. With the fluorescent technique of Falck and Hillarp, the same areas shown above would glow a bright green because of the high content of dopamine. The pallidal part of the striatal complex does not fluoresce. No existing reptiles represent the forerunners of mammals. Birds are an offshoot from the *Archosauria* ("ruling reptiles"). Adapted from Ref. 42.

The word "isopraxic" will be used to refer to behaviors in which two or more individuals engage in the same kind of activity. Purely descriptive, it avoids preconceptions and prejudices commonly attached to such terms as social facilitation and imitation. Perseverative behavior applies to repetitious acts, such as occur in displays or in conflictive situations. Reenactment behavior refers to the repetition on different occasions of behaviors seeming to represent obeisance to precedent as, for example, following familiar trails or returning year-after-year to the same breeding grounds. Tropistic behavior is characterized by positive or negative responses to partial or complete representations of animate or inanimate objects and includes what ethologists refer to as "imprinting" and "fixed action patterns." Deceptive behavior involves the use of artifice and deceitful tactics such as are employed in stalking a prey or evading a predator.

Except for altruistic behavior and most aspects of parental behavior, it is remarkable how many *patterns of behavior* seen in reptiles are also found in human beings.

As yet, hardly any investigations have been conducted on reptiles in an attempt to identify specific structures of the forebrain involved in the various behaviors listed above. All that is known thus far is that the neural guiding systems for species-typical complex forms of behavior lie forward of the neural chassis.

In contrast to reptiles, the R-complex of mammals has been subjected to extensive investigation. Curiously enough, however, 150 years of experiementation have revealed remarkably little about its functions. The finding that large destructions of the mammalian R-complex may result in no obvious impairment of movement speaks against the traditional clinical view that it subserves purely motor functions. At our Laboratory of Brain Evolution and Behavior, we are conducting comparative studies of reptiles, birds, and mammals in which we are testing the hypothesis that the R-complex plays a basic role in species-typical prosematic behavior.

In the work thus far, crucial findings relevant to prosematic behavior have developed from experiments on more than 100 squirrel monkeys

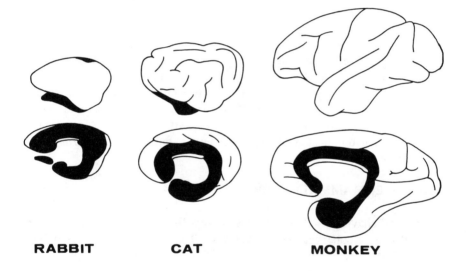

RABBIT   **CAT**   **MONKEY**

Figure 2.4

The limbic lobe of Broca (shaded) is found as a common denominator in the brains of all mammals. It contains the greater part of the cortex representative of the paleomammalian brain. The cortex of the neomammalian brain (shown in white) mushrooms late in evolution. After Ref. 25.

(*Saimiri sciureus*). Animals of this species perform a characteristic display of the erect phallus in a show of aggression, in courtship, and as a form of greeting.[25,44] Members of one subspecies consistently display to their reflections in a mirror, providing a means of systematically testing the effects of brain ablations on the incidence and manifestations of the display.[26] I have found that large bilateral lesions of the paleo- and neomammalian parts of the forebrain may have either no effect or only a transitory effect on the display. After bilateral lesions of the pallidal part of the R-complex,[29,31] however, or interruption of its main pathways,[35] monkeys may no longer show an inclination to display. Without a test of the innate display behavior, one might conclude that they were unaffected by the loss of brain tissue.

These experiments provide the first evidence in mammals that the R-complex and its major pathways are basically involved in the performance of genetically constituted, species-typical, prosematic behavior. Such work represents a necessary first step for a more detailed analysis of forebrain mechanisms underlying "territorial" assertiveness, courtship, and social deportment. Since the mirror display also involves isopraxic factors, the experiments also indicate that the R-complex is implicated in *natural* forms of imitation.

THE PALEOMAMMALIAN BRAIN

There are behavioral indications that the reptilian brain is poorly equipped for learning to cope with new situations. The reptilian brain has only a rudimentary cortex. In the lost transitional forms between reptiles and mammals--the so-called mammal-like reptiles--it is presumed that the primitive cortex underwent further elaboration and differentiation.

The primitive cortex might be imagined as comparable to a crude radar screen, providing the animal a better means of viewing the environment and learning to survive. In all existing mammals the phylogentically old cortex is found in a large convolution which the nineteenth century anatomist, Broca[4] called the great limbic lobe because it surrounds the brain stem. Limbic means "forming a border around." As illustrated in figure 2.4, the limbic lobe forms a *common denominator* in the brains of *all mammals*. In 1952, I suggested the term limbic system as a designation for the limbic cortex and structures of the brain stem with which it has primary connections.[22]

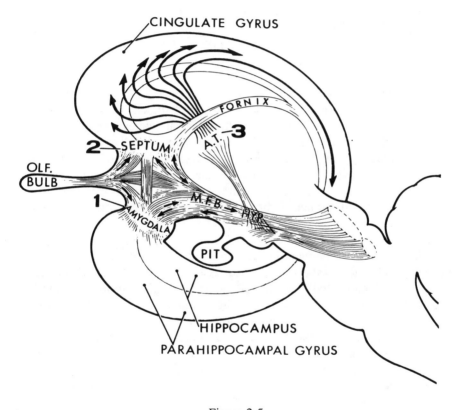

Figure 2.5

Diagram of three main subdivisions of the limbic system and their major pathways. See text for summary of their respective functions. Abbreviations: AT, anterior thalamix nuclei; HYP, hypothalamus; MFB, medial forebrain bundle; PIT, pituitary; OLF, olfactory. After Ref. 24.

The limbic cortex is structurally less complicated than the new cortex. Although it was once believed to receive information mainly from the olfactory and visceral systems, we have shown by recording from single nerve cells in awake, sitting monkeys that signals also reach it from the visual, auditory, and somatic senses.[33] There are clinical indications that the combined reception of information from the inside and outside worlds is essential for a feeling of individuality and personal identity.[30]

Also in contrast to the new cortex, the limbic cortex has large cablelike connections with the hypothalamus which has long been recognized to play a central role in integrating the performance of mechanisms involved in self-preservation and the procreation of the species.

Although the limbic system undergoes considerable expansion in the brains of higher mammals, the basic pattern of organization remains the same as in lower mammals. Electrophysiological studies have shown that this basically paleomammalian brain is functionally, as well as anatomically, an integrated system. In the past 40 years, clinical and experimental investigations have provided evidence that the limbic system derives information in terms of emotional feelings that guide behavior with respect to the two basic life principles of self-preservation and the preservation of the species.

Before further comment on limbic functions, it should be noted that many people maintain that it is inadmissible to make sharp distinction between "emotion" and "reason." Raphael Demos,[8] in an introduction to the dialogues of Plato, expresses a traditional philosophical view: ". . . we are apt to separate reason from emotion. Plato does not. Reason is not merely detached understanding; it is conviction, fired with enthusiasm." Piaget, the founder of the Center for Genetic Epistemology, is quite vehement, saying that "nothing could be more false or superficial" than to attempt "to dichotomize the life of the mind into emotion and thoughts." ". . . Affectivity and intelligence," he insists, "are indissociable and constitute the two complementary aspects of all human behavior" (p.15).[43]

Granted the complementary aspects of "emotion" and "thought," we are faced with evidence from the study of "psychomotor" epilepsy that the two may occur independently because they are products of different cerebral mechanisms. Clinical observations provide the best evidence of the role of the limbic system in emotional behavior. Epileptic discharges in or near the limbic cortex result in a broad spectrum of vivid emotional feelings. It is one of the wonders of the brain that limbic discharges tend to spread in and be confined to the limbic system, not directly involving the neocortex. I have referred to this condition as a "schizophysiology"[23] and have suggested that the underlying factors may contribute to inexplicable conflicts between "what we feel" and "what we know."

In regard to structures possibly involved in mental illness, it is significant that limbic discharges may result in symptoms characteristic of the toxic and endogenous psychoses, such as feelings of depersonalization, distortions of perception, paranoid delusions, and hallucinations.[33] I referred earlier to the striking chemical differences of the three basic cerebrotypes. An accumulation of evidence indicates that many of the psychotherapeutic drugs owe their salutary effects to a selective action on the limbic system and the R-complex.

It is of special epistemological interest that at the beginning of a limbic discharge, a patient may have an intense free-floating feeling of what is real, true, and important or experience eureka-type feelings like those associated with discovery. There may be oceanic feelings such as occur in mystical revelation or under the influence of psychedelic drugs. Ironically, it seems that the ancient limbic system has the capacity to generate strong affective feelings of conviction that we attach to our beliefs, regardless of whether they are true or false!

Three Subdivisions of the Paleomammalian Brain. The limbic system comprises three subdivisions.[24] The two older ones (see figure 2.5) are closely related to the olfactory apparatus. Our experimental work has provided evidence that these two divisions are involved respectively in oral and genital functions. The findings are relevant to orosexual manifestations in feeding situations, in mating, and in aggressive behavior and violence. The close relationship between oral and genital functions seems to be due to the olfactory sense which, dating far back in evolution, is involved in both feeding and mating.

The main pathway to the third subdivision bypasses the olfactory apparatus. In evolution, this subdivision reaches its greatest development in the human brain. An assortment of evidence suggests that this remarkable expansion reflects a shift from olfactory to visual and other influences in sociosexual behavior. It is also possible that this subdivision, together with the prefrontal cortex of the neomammalian brain, has provided a neural substrate for the evolution of human empathy.

Avenues to the Basic Personality. The major pathways to and from the reptilian-type and paleomammalian-type brains pass through the hypothalamus and subthalamic region. If the majority of these pathways are destroyed in monkeys, they are greatly incapacitated, but with careful nursing may recover the ability to feed themselves and move around. The most striking characteristic of these animals is that although they look like monkeys, they no longer behave like monkeys. Almost everything characteristic of species-typical simian behavior has disappeared.

If one were to interpret these experimental findings in the light of certain clinical case material, one might say that these large connecting pathways between the reptilian and paleomammalian formations provide the avenues to the basic personality. Here, certainly, would seem to be the pathways to the expression of prosematic behavior.

THE NEOMMAMMLIAN BRAIN

Compared with the limbic cortex, the neocortex (shown in white in figure 2.4) is like an expanding numerator. As C. Judson Herrick has commented, "Its explosive growth late in phylogeny is one of the most dramatic cases of evolutionary transformations known to comparative anatomy."[18] The massive proportions achieved by the neocortex in higher mammals explains the designation of "neomammalian brain" applied to it and structures of the brain stem with which it is primarily connected. The neocortex culminates in the human brain, affording a vast neural screen for the portrayal of symbolic language and the associated functions of reading, writing, and arithmetic.

Mother of invention and father of abstract thought, the new cortex promotes the preservation and procreation of ideas.[32] As opposed to the limbic cortex, the sensory systems projecting to the neocortex are primarily those giving information about the external environment--namely, the visual, auditory, and somatic systems. It therefore seems that the neocortex is primarily oriented toward the outside world. Here, perhaps, is a clue to what was mentioned earlier regarding the traditional emphasis of the sciences on the external environment.

THREE FORMS OF MENTATION

A brief discussion of questions relevant to brain research requires me to use the expressions protomentation, emotomentation, and ratiomentation.

Protomentation applies to rudimentary mental processes underlying complex, prototypical forms of behavior mentioned above, as well as to propensions, a term used to cover mental states variously alluded to by such words as drives, impulses, compulsions, and obsessions. Emotomentation (emotional mentation) will refer to cerebral processes underlying what are popularly recognized as "emotions", ignoring at this time an important semantic distinction between "emotions" and "affects", as well as the classification of three species of affects that are subject to emotional expression.[28] Paleopsychic processes are understood to cover those aspects of protomentation and emotomentation that are manifest by prosematic behavior. The meaning of ratiomentation (ratiocination) is assumed to be self-evident.

QUESTIONS RELEVANT TO BRAIN RESEARCH

In the past there has been the tendency to lump together many of the psychological processes that have just been alluded to in regard to protomentation and emotional mentation. Originally the German word "Trieb" which Freud (1900) used to refer to drive, impulse, or urge was inappropriately translated into English as "instinct." This twist apparently led to the commonly used expression "instinctual drives." Instincts were regarded as the biological driving forces that, analogous to the pressure head in a hydraulic system, impelled an individual to action. The pressure of the instinctive forces was believed to result in emotional feelings of an unpleasant sort, while the reduction of tension gave rise to pleasurable feelings. Freud used the impersonal word "id" (i.e., "it") to apply to the instinctual forces of the so-called "unconscious" part of the "mental personality." In 1933, at the age of 77, he stated in his *New Introductory Lectures*, "In popular language . . . we may say that the id stands for the untamed passions."[15]

Since the disposition to equate the "instincts" and "emotions" has continued to the present day, it is timely to point out developments in the study of the brain and behavior that bring into better focus some distinctions between protomentation and emotional mentation. In addition to the role of protomentation in special prototypical behaviors such as are observed in the establishment of territory, we want to give consideration to the part it plays in the *pentad* of general prototypical behaviors as they become manifest in obsessive-compulsive behavior; day-to-day rituals of which we are hardly aware; the tendency to seek and give obeisance to precedent as in legal and other matters; superstitious actions; deceptive behavior; and "imitation" (isopraxis).

Because of their subjective obtrusiveness, perhaps a disproportionate emphasis has been given to the importance of "emotions" in influencing our day-to-day activities, but we should keep in mind the possibility that "emotions" may oftentimes be passive reflectors of psychic states rather than determinants of action, and that under many circumstances propense forms of protomentation may play a more basic role.

The world's literature provides abundant evidence that because of moral customs and society's numerous ways of meting out punishment for wrongdoing, we tend to give greater weight to the role of "emotions" in unpleasant affairs than in situations of joy and gratification. This biased attitude carries over into the scientific literature where one finds an authority on brain mechanisms of emotion referring to anger and fear as the "major emotions."[1]

Some Medical and Legal Aspects. The negative role assigned to the "emotions" in medical and legal matters has a long history. Miss Grange[6] points out that in the eighteenth century "moral" insanity was the equivalent of "emotional" insanity. In an article on Pinel, the well-known eighteenth-century psychiatrist, she explains how he helped to popularize the use of the word "moral" to describe emotional factors in mental experience. He believed that the chief cause of insanity was "moral," and his treatment of insanity was based on Aristotle's theory of "balancing the passions." Grange also describes how Pinel's writings inspired others to examine the emotions "in relation to health, to education, to politics, to crime, to urban and rural environments, to organic disease, and to the welfare of groups and individuals" (p. 452).[16]

Today, just as two centuries ago, "emotions" are commonly believed to be the root of psychoneuroses, several forms of psychoses, "psychosomatic disease," alcoholism, narcotic addiction, implacable domestic situations, juvenile deliquency, and crime. But in all these conditions, developing insights require that we keep in mind that protomentation may be more fundamentally involved than emotomentation, recalling, symbolically, that "the reptiles does what it has to do."

There is another side of the "emotions" that has received less attention, possibly because it is considered an unalterable part of human nature. I refer now to the paradoxical capacity of emotional mentation to find support for opposite sides of any question. We take it for granted that the "emotions" will generate divisiveness in every field of discourse whether it is religious, ethical, artistic, sociological, legal, economic, political, educational, or scientific. However much this may be lamented, there is the potential benefit that argument and conflict may stir up the gene pool of ideas and lead to new and constructive concepts.

All such concerns about the "emotions" seem insignificant, however, compared with those deeply personalized feelings experienced when the utter isolation of death separates us from a loved one, or finally, after long prospect, forces itself upon each one of us.

Some Scientific Implications. After the presentation of behavioral and experimental data, it is of interest to consider how in scientific affairs protomentation and protoreptilian propensities may be influential in regard to the establishment of intellectual domain ("territory"), the *idee fixe* of such a scientist as Kepler, obeisance to precedent, adherence to doctrine, and intolerance of new ideas.

As regards emotional mentation, it seems a particular irony that in science, as in politics, the "emotions" make it possible to stand on any platform. How does it happen that different groups of reputable scientists presented with the same data often find themselves at opposite poles--and sometimes in bitter, acrimonious debate--because of diametric views of what is true?

It is equally puzzling--and intellectually incongruous--that for years, and even centuries, the world order of science may emotionally cling to, and champion, "suspect" beliefs that are destined to crumble. What makes it psychologically possible for wise individuals to build higher and higher on foundations of such beliefs without fear of their sudden collapse?

It is also curious that the emotional investment of some scientists is such that they remain convinced of the truth of a theory long after it has proven to be false. As the late E.G. Boring commented in paraphrasing a statement of Max Planck, "Important theories, marked for death by the discovery of contradictory evidence, seldom die before their authors."[2] In two essays, Washburn[49] and Washburn and Ciochon[50] have made an instructive analysis of how emotional factors seem to have been instrumental in solidifying the thinking of proponents of divergent views of human evolution despite the admitted lack of sufficient data. They suggest some insightful correctives.

Why Brain Research?   Why is it so necessary to investigate brain mechanisms to understand the various forms of paleopsychic processes under consideration?   After all, the laws of formal thought have been derived without an understanding of the underlying machinery of the brain.

It is the peculiarity of ratiomentation that it lends itself, as in the case of logic, to symbolic representation in the form of words or other signs which, when semantically specified and syntactically related according to certain rules, result in inevitable conclusions. A parallel situation applies to numerical procedures in which the steps of calculation can be so interlocked as to assure an outcome as predictable as the movements of a geartrain. Within a generation, we have seen the evolution from simple calculating machines to giant computers which, when programmed according to the laws of logic, can reach the solution of a problem in but a small fraction of the time formerly required.

In formal ratiomentation, we have the advantage of being able to specify the inputs into our own brains or the prosthetic brains of computers. But the situation is quite different in the case of protomentation and emotomentation. Here the known input is so obscured by an indefinable input from the person's ancestral past and personal life history that there is no means of ascertaining what the outcome will be. The successive mentational processes have neither been identified nor shown to obey laws that allow predictable conclusions.

Because of the inability to specify and control internal input for paleopsychic processes, there is the hope that insights may be gained from an investigation of underlying mechanisms. Until the restrictions of the mechanisms are known, there can be as many explanations of paleopsychic processes as there are explicators.

Many learning theorists and behaviorists would take exception to this point of view, contending that the cranium and its contents may be regarded as a black box. Some adherents to operant conditioning claim that in utilizing the principle of reinforcement, any form of behavior can be shaped and predicted. Until it can be demonstrated, however, that neuroses in animals and human beings can be regularly induced and alleviated by operant techniques, one may reserve judgment about such claims.

Jeans has stated that "physics gives us exact knowledge because it is based on exact measurements." But if the ultimate scientific instrument, the human brain, is for one reason or another predisposed to artifactual interpretations, where does confidence lie in any field?

Time and Space. Although nuclear physicists are quick to point out the "evaporation" of the material world at the atomic level, many of them seem to retain an abiding faith in the existence of time and space. They would contend that if all particles were to disappear from the universe, space and time would still remain. There is an evident inconsistency in such an argument when we relook at what Kant said about the "transcendental aesthetic." In view of the tripartite division of the brain under consideration, we want to keep in mind the question whether there exist "reptilian time," "paleomammalian time," and "neomammalian time." A parallel question applies to space. Recently, students of environmental design have begun to consider the latter question in connection with urban planning and the desirable uses of space.[10,17,37]

CONCLUDING COMMENT

In these introductory remarks on the evolution of three mentalities, it has been the implication that the reptilian, paleomammalian, and neomammalian formations provide three underlying neural mechanisms for what have been provisionally referred to as protomentation, emotomentation, and ratiomentation. At the same time, I have used the expression *triune brain* to symbolize that no hard and fast boundaries exist between the three formations and their respective functions. With these provisions, I use a metaphor to summarize.

In the field of literature it is recognized that there is an irreducible number of basic plots and associated emotions. *In describing the functions of the triune brain metaphorically, one might imagine that the reptilian brain provides the basic plots and actions; that the limbic brain influences emotionally the developments of the plots; while the neomammalian brain has the capacity to expound the plots and emotions in as many ways as there are authors.*

With respect to epistemics, particular attention will be given to an analysis of clinical and experimental findings (some of which have been mentioned) that indicate that the two older evolutionary formations of the brain are fundamentally involved in the psychogenesis of propense and affective states and that their projecting pathways are essential for the prosematic expression of the basic personality.

Other problems to be considered include the major one concerning mechanisms of intercommunication of three evolutionary formations which are so radically different in anatomy and chemistry. A discussion of this problem requires our delving not only into anatomical questions, but also into the nature of biochemical and bioelectrical signaling devices. Whatever these intersignaling devices are, it must be inferred that they involve nonverbal coding.

Stated otherwise, there are indications that with the evolution of the forebrain structures underlying the three mentalities in question, no provision was made for intercommunication by the use of words. Expressed in phrases from the introductory quotation, this situation may help to explain "the insufficiency . . . of the laws of the understanding, to resolve these problems which lie nearer to our hearts. . . ."

*A slightly edited version from Chapter Fifteen *New Dimensions in Psychiatry*: A World View, Volume 2, edited by Silvano Arieti and Gerald Chrzanowski (New York: John Wiley & Sons, Inc., 1972).

**The wording of this passage follows closely that of MacLean, 1970.

NOTES

1. Bard, P.: A diencephalic mechanism for the expression of rage with special reference to the sympathetic nervous system. *Amer. J. Physiol.* 84:490-513, 1928.
2. Boring, E.G.: Cognitive dissonance: Its use in science. *Science*, 145:680-685, 1964.
3. Bridgman, P.W.: *The Way Things Are*, Harvard University Press, Cambridge, Mass., 1959, 333 pp.
4. Broca, P.: Anatomie comparee des circonvolutions cerebrales. Le grand lobe limbique et la scissure limbique dans la serie des mammiferes. *Rev. Anthropol.* 1:385-498, 1878.
5. Calhoun, J.B.: Population density and social pathology. *Sci. Amer.* 206:139-146, 1962.
6. Calhoun, J.B.: Space and the strategy of life. In *Behavior and Environment*, A.H. Esser, (Ed.), Plenum Press, New York, 1971, pp.329-387.
7. Chance, M.: Towards the biological definition of ethics. In *Biology and Ethics*, J. Ebling, (Ed.), Academic Press, New York and London, 1969.
8. Demos, R.: Introduction. In *The Dialogues of Plato*, Transl. B. Jowett, Random House, New York, 2 vols., 1937, 879 pp. and 939 pp.
9. Descartes, R.: *The Philosophical Works of Descartes*, Transl. E.S. Handane and G.R. T. Ross, Cambridge University Press, Cambridge, Mass., 2 vols., 1967, 452 pp. and 380 pp.
10. Esser, A.H.: Environment and mental health. *Sci. Med. Man*, 1:181-193, 1974.
11. Falck, B. and Hillarp, N.A.: On the cellular localization of cathecholamines in the brain. *Acta Anat.*, 38:277-279, 1959.
12. Ferrier, D.: *The Functions of the Brain*, Smith, Elder, and Company, London, 1876.
13. Foerster, H. von, Mora, P.M., and Amiot, L.W.: Doomsday: Friday 13 November. A.D. 2026. *Science*,132:1291-1295, 1960.
14. Freud, S.: *The Interpretation of Dreams*, (1900) Standard Edition, Hogarth Press, London, 1953.
15. Freud, S.: *New Introductory Lectures on Psychoanalysis*, Transl. W.J.H.

42

Sprott, The Hogarth Press and The Institute of Psycho-Analysis, London, 1949, 239 pp.

16. Grange, K.M., Pinel and eighteenth-century psychiatry. *Bull. Hist. Med.* 35:442-453, 1961.

17. Greenbie, B.: *Design for Diversity*, Elsevier Scientific Publishing Company, Amsterdam, in press.

18. Herrick, C.J.: The functions of the olfactory parts of the cerebral cortex. *Proc. Nat. Acad. Sci. USA*, 19:7-14, 1933.

19. Hinde, R.A.: *Non-Verbal Communication*, The University Press, Cambridge, Mass., 1972, 443 pp.

20. Juorio, A.V., and Bogt, M.: Monoamines and their metabolites in the avian brain. *J. Physiol.* 189:489-518, 1967.

21. Lorenz, K.Z.: The companion in the bird's world. *Auk*, 54:245-273, 1937.

22. MacLean, P.D.: Some psychiatric implications of physiological studies on frontotemporal portion of limbic system (visceral brain). *Electroenceph. Clin. Neurophysiol.* 4:407-418, 1952.

23. MacLean, P.D.: The limbic system and its hippocampal formation. Studies in animals and their possible application to man. *J. Neurosurg.* 11:29-44, 1954.

24. MacLean, P.D.: Contrasting functions of limbic and neocortical systems of the brain and their relevance to psychophysiological aspects of medicine. *Amer. J. Med.* 25:611-626, 1958.

25. MacLean, P.D.: New findings relevant to the evolution of psychosexual functions of the brain. *J. Nerv. Ment. Dis.* 135:289-301, 1962.

26. MacLean, P.D.: Mirror display in the squirrel monkey, Saimiri sciureus. *Science*, 146:950-952, 1964.

27. MacLean, P.D.: The brain in relation to empathy and medical education. *J. Nerv. Ment. Dis.* 144:374-382, 1967.

28. MacLean, P.D.: The triune brain, emotion, and scientific bias. In *The Neurosciences: Second Study Program*, F.O. Schmitt, (Ed.), The Rockefeller University Press, New York, 1970, pp.336-349.

29. MacLean, P.D.: Cerebral evolution and emotional processes: New findings on the striatal complex. *Ann. N.Y. Acad. Sci.* 193:137-149, 1972.

30. MacLean, P.D.: Implications of microelectrode findings on exteroceptive inputs to the limbic cortex. In *Limbic System Mechanisms and Autonomic Function*, C.H. Hockman, (Ed.), Charles C. Thomas, Springfield, 1972, pp. 115-136.

31. MacLean, P.D.: Effects of pallidal lesions on species-typical display behavior of squirrel monkey. *Fed. Proc.* 32:384, 1973.

32. MacLean, P.D.: The brain's generation gap: Some human implications. *Zygon J. Relig. Sci.*, 8:113-127, 1973.

33. MacLean, P.D.: A triune concept of the brain and behavior, Lecture I. Man's reptilian and limbic inheritance; Lecture II. Man's limbic brain and the psychoses; Lecture III. New trends in man's evolution. In *The Hincks Memorial Lectures*, T. Boag, and D. Campbell, (Eds.), University of Toronto Press, Toronto, 1973, pp. 6-66.

34. MacLean, P.D.: The triune brain. In *Medical World News*, Special Supplement on "Psychiatry," New York, October, 1974a, Vol. 1, pp.55-60.

35. MacLean, P.D.: Role of pallidal projections in species-typical behavior of squirrel monkey. *Trans. Amer. Neurol. Assoc.*, 100, 1975, 110-113.

36. MacLean, P.D.: An evolutionary approach to brain research on "prosematic" (nonverbal) behavior. In *The Daniel S. Lehrman Memorial Symposium on Reproductive Behavior and Evolution*, Institute of Animal Behavior, Rutgers University, 1974, (to be published)

37. Mallows, E.W.N.: Urban planning and the systems approach. (I.B.M. System & Engineering Symposium, October, 1969) *Plan* (Successor to *S.A. Archit. Rec.*), 55:11-24, 1970.

38. Meadows, D.H., Meadows, D.L., Randers, J., and Behrens, III, W.W.: *The Limits to Growth*, Universe Books, New York, 1972, 205 pp.

39. Monod, J.: *Chance and Necessity*, A.A. Knopf, New York, 1971.

40. Morsbach, H.: Aspects of nonverbal communication in Japan. *J. Nerv. Ment. Dis.* 157:262-277, 1973.

41. Myers, K., Hale, C.S., Myktowycz, R., and Hughes, R.L.: The effects of varying density and space on sociality and health in animals. In *Behavior and Environment*. A. H. Esser, (Ed.), Plenum Press, New York, 1971, pp.148-187.

42. Parent, A. and Olivier, A.: Comparative histochemical study of the corpus striatum. *J. Hirnforsch.* 12:75-81, 1970.

43. Piaget, J.: *Six Psychological Studies*, Transl. A. Tenzer, Random House, New York, 1967, 169 pp.

44. Ploog, D.W., and MacLean, P.D.: Display of penile erection in squirrel monkey (Saimiri sciureus). *Anim. Behav.* 11:32-39, 1963.

45. Shakow, D., and Rapaport, D.: The influence of Freud on American psychology. In *Psychological Issues*, International Universities Press, New York, 1964, Vol. 4, Monograph 13, 243 pp.

46. Snow, C.P.: *Variety of Men*, Charles Scribner's Sons, New York, 1967, 270 pp.

47. Spencer, H.: *Principles of Psychology*, D.Appleton and Company, New York, 2 vols., 1896.

48. Tinbergen, N.: *The Study of Instinct*, The Clarendon Press, Oxford, 1951, 228 pp.

49. Washburn, S.L.: The evolution game. *J.Hum. Evol.* 2:557-561, 1973.

50. Washburn, S.L., and Ciochon, R.L.: Canine teeth: Notes on controversies in the study of human evolution. (in press)

51. Watson, J.B.: *Behaviorism*, The People's Institute Publishing Company, New York, 1924, 251 pp.

52. Weisberger, B.A.: Book Review of "Black Mountain," *The Washington Post*, Washington, D.C., November 19, 1972.

53. Wiener, N.: *Cybernetics, or Control and Communication in the Animal and the Machine*, Wiley, New York, 1948, 194 pp.

Chapter Three

THE MYTH-RITUAL COMPLEX; A BIOGENETIC

STRUCTURAL ANALYSIS*

by

Eugene G. d'Aquili

Abstract. The structuring and transformation of myth is presented as a function of a number of brain "operators." Each operator is understood to represent specifically evolved neural tissue primarily of the neocortex of the brain. Mythmaking as well as other cognitive processes is seen as a behavior arising from the evolution and integration of certain parts of the brain. Human ceremonial ritual is likewise understood as the culmination of a long phylogenetic evolutionary process, and a neural model is presented to explain its properties. Finally, the mechanism by which ritual is used to resolve the antinomies of myth structure is explored.

The thesis of this paper is that the generation of myth, its structure and transformations, as well as the resolution of the myth problem via ceremonial ritual are derived from the functioning of neural structures, which evolved and became progressively elaborated because of the adaptive advantage they conferred on their bearers. For our purposes we shall refer to such organization of neural tissue as neural operators. Each operator shall be considered as having a specific functional capacity accounting for one of the operations of the neocortex of the brain. Thus each structure or connected set of structures which forms a single operator will be viewed as an independent functional unit.

We shall proceed, first, by describing the probable neuroanatomical structures of the major cognitive operations involved in generating myth. Second, we will present a model which derives the nature and necessity of myth formation from certain of these operations as well as from the neurobiology underlying the transformations of the surface structure of myths. Third, we will present a model based on recent neurophysiological research that explains the resolution of mythic antinomies by the integration of ritual behavior into myths.

COGNITIVE STRUCTURES, OPERATORS, AND THEIR NEURAL SUBSTRATES

A cognitive structure may be defined as all the possible primary logical or affective relationships which obtain between elements comprising a single semantic domain. It is important to realize that any given individual can, under the proper circumstances, rearrange the elements of the structure bringing to consciousness alternate surface manifestations of the deep structure. This rearranging of elements of a semantic domain may or may not represent a stable configuration upon which behavior is based. It is only the *stable structural reorganizations* that we refer to when we speak of a transformation of cognitive structure. The relationship of structural reorganizations--transformations--to mythology will be discussed below.

The very existence of cognitive structures such as myth themes presupposes the ability to abstract dimensions of meaning from the universe, by which we can define the elements contained with a semantic field. Such abstraction is performed by what we have termed cognitive operators. To understand the generation of myth we must understand the function of cognitive operators.

When we use the term "cognitive operator," we are using the term "operator" analogously to the way it is used in mathematics. For example, a mathematical operator can be looked upon as the means by which certain mathematical elements are made to relate to one another in specific ways. Similarly, a cognitive operator represents a neural structure which processes sensory input by relating various elements in ways specific to that operator. For the purposes of this discussion we will describe six operators in their simplest forms:

> (1) the *holistic operator* permits reality to be viewed as a whole or as a gestalt;

> (2) the *causal operator* permits reality to be viewed in terms of causal sequences of abstract elements;

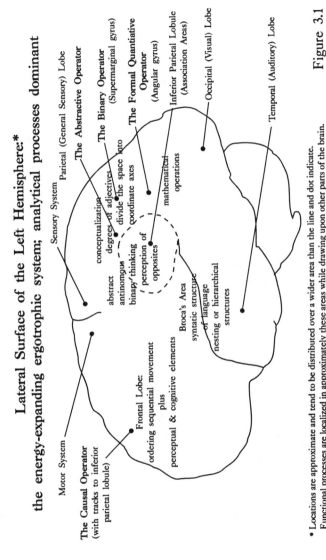

Lateral Surface of the Left Hemisphere:*
the energy-expanding ergotrophic system; analytical processes dominant

Motor System

Sensory System

Parietal (General Sensory) Lobe

The Abstractive Operator

The Binary Operator
(Supermarginal gyrus)

The Formal Quantiative Operator
(Angular gyrus)

Inferior Parietal Lobule
(Association Areas)

Occipital (Visual) Lobe

Temporal (Auditory) Lobe

The Causal Operator
(with tracks to inferior parietal lobule)

Frontal Lobe:
ordering sequential movement
plus
perceptual & cognitive elements

Broca's Area
syntatic structure
of language
nesting or hierarchical
structures

conceptualization
degrees of adjectives
divide the space into
coordinate axes

mathematical
operations

abstract
antinomous
binary thinking
perception of
opposites

* Locations are approximate and tend to be distributed over a wider area than the line and dot indicate. Functional processes are localized in approximately these areas while drawing upon other parts of the brain.

Figure 3.1

Figure 3.1

(3) the *abstractive operator* permits the formation of a general concept from the perception of empirical individuals;

(4) the *binary operator* permits the extraction of meaning by ordering abstract elements into dyads involving varying degrees of polarity so that each pole of the dyad derives meaning from contrast with the other pole (this operator is particularly important in the generation of myth);

(5) the *formal quantitative operator* permits the abstraction of quantity per se from the perception of empirical individuals, generating arithmetic and mathematics; and

(6) the *value operator* permits an affective valence to be assigned to various elements of perception and cognition.[1]

We shall now present an anatomical model for each of these six operators, based on recent neurophysiological research. In terms of each model we shall attempt to localize these operators in terms of specific neuroanatomical structures. This permits a consideration of the morphological evolution of these structures in a phylogenetic perspective.

The Holistic Operator. Recent experiments with animals, as well as observations of humans who have had their corpus callosum and anterior commissure sectioned to prevent the interhemispheric spread of epilepsy, have strongly supported the early clinical observations of neurologists that the parietal lobe on the *nondominant* side of the brain is intimately involved in the perception of spatial relations. Indeed most of the recent evidence indicates that this perception is of a holistic or gestalt nature (see figure 3.1).

It is of more than passing interest that specific areas on the opposite or *dominant* side (specifically the angular gyrus) are related to the performance of mathematical operations. Other areas on this side are involved in the performance of certain basic logical-grammatical operations, particularly the perception of opposites and the ability to set one object over against another to emphasize its full semantic properties.[2] These and other basic logical-grammatical functions are related to areas of the parietal lobe adjacent to the angular gyrus and proximate to the anterior margin of the occipital lobe on the dominant side.[3] N. Geschwind has called this area the inferior parietal lobule. Lesions of this area in humans prevent the generation of antonyms as well as the use of the comparative degree of adjectives.[4]

In short, such lesions prevent the formation of abstract dyadic oppositions or polarities. This is a function basic to human cognition, one which we will consider below in relation to the generation of myths.

The Abstractive, Binary, and Quantitative Operators. The inferior parietal lobule is comprised of the supramarginal and angular gyri as well as certain adjacent areas. It can best be visualized as the area of overlap between the somaesthetic, visual, and auditory association areas. As an association area of association areas, it allows for direct transfer across sensory modalities without involvement of the limbic or affective system. It is as if three computer systems, one for each of the three major sensory modalities mentioned, were hooked into each other and the information from each became available to all. Such a complex system allows classes of objects to be set up which are vastly more inclusive than any classificatory system possible within each individual sensory modality.

That this area of the brain may subserve conceptualization became powerfully supported by the evidence of Geschwind in his now classic monograph "Disconnection Syndromes in Animals and Man."[5] Soviet researchers refer to roughly the same area as simply the parieto-occipital area, and A.R. Luria also notes that it is intimately involved in the formation of basic logical-grammatical categories.[6] Luria and others have shown that destruction of parts of this area of the brain inhibits the use of the comparative degree of adjectives: a person is not able to be set off [as] one object against another in one-to-one comparison.

Therefore, such statements as "larger than," "smaller than," "better than," and so on, become impossible for patients with lesions in portions of this area. Furthermore, such patients are not able to name the opposite of any word which is presented to them.

Although not conclusive, this kind of evidence indicates that the inferior parietal lobule on the dominant side not only may underlie conceptualization but may be responsible for the human proclivity for abstract antinomous or binary thinking, which underlies the basic structure of myth.

Such considerations lead us to postulate that the formal quantitative, binary, and abstractive operators can be localized to the dominant hemisphere, roughly in the area that Geschwind calls the inferior parietal lobule. The more specific areas in this region are intimately interconnected and might be viewed as a single region, as Geschwind proposes[7] (see figure 3.2).

It is probably no coincidence that those neural structures which appear to generate gestalt spatial perception on the nondominant side are homologous, in terms of the "geography" of the brain, to those structures on the dominant side which underlie mathematical, logical, and grammatical relationships. It is certainly no news that mathematical operations appear to derive from the quantification of spatial properties. It is our contention that basic logical-grammatical operations are likewise so derived. If one considers the holistic perception of spatial relationships as the more primitively evolved or more basic function of the parietal lobe, one could easily postulate that this has been preserved or even elaborated in humans on the nondominant side. Modification on the contralateral or dominant side has been in the opposite direction, that is, breaking down the spatial gestalt into various composite units and relationships.

This goes along with our contention that *the evolution of humanity is most characteristically marked by the evolution of analytic cognitive processes*; this permitted the evolution of abstract thought and problem solving, of which myth formation and resolution is a prime example. Such analytic processes most probably involved a modification and elaboration of the more basic gestalt operations in what we now call the nondominant side into the analytic functions which we associate with the dominant hemisphere of the brain. Such elaboration of function, and probably also of microstructure, is just that, namely, a modification of more primitive functions. The analytic functions of the dominant side do not arise *de novo* but are intimately related to the more primitive operations preserved on the nondominant side.

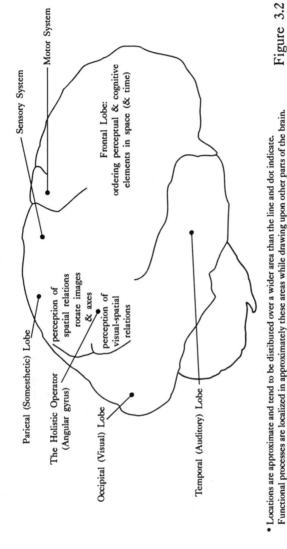

Lateral Surface of the Right Hemisphere:*
the energy-stabilizing trophotropic system; holistic-gestalt processes dominant

Sensory System

Motor System

Frontal Lobe:
ordering perceptual & cognitive
elements in space (& time)

Parietal (Somesthetic) Lobe

The Holistic Operator
(Angular gyrus)

perception of
spatial relations
rotate images
& axes

perception of
visual-spatial
relations

Occipital (Visual) Lobe

Temporal (Auditory) Lobe

Figure 3.2

* Locations are approximate and tend to be distributed over a wider area than the line and dot indicate.
Functional processes are localized in approximately these areas while drawing upon other parts of the brain.

Figure 3.2

Thus, one can postulate the parieto-occipital area on the dominant side developed not so much to perceive spatial relationships in their total configuration but rather to perform the operation we now call the division of space into coordinate axes.

G. Ratcliff has confirmed the findings of L. Franco and R.W. Sperry, G. Cohen and N. Betters et al. that the ability to rotate images (and axes) has evolved in humans as a function of the parietal and parieto-occipital regions on the nondominant side.[8] The ability to mentally rotate images and axes is the first step in the spatial breakdown necessary for quantitative analysis, which evolved in the homologous areas on the dominant side. Furthermore, the elaboration of function on the dominant side generates the capability of defining axes in terms of the polar termini of each axis. In this second operation one can perceive the basis of conceptual dyadic opposition beginning to derive from the evolution of an analytic perception of space.

We have proposed the loci of the analytic operations (i.e., binary, abstractive, and formal quantitative operators) to reside in various areas of the parietal lobe on the dominant side. Similar evidence leads us to localize the synthetic or holistic operator in the parietal region of the nondominant side.[9] As noted earlier, this operator permits the perception of reality as a whole or single perceived unity. As we shall see later, the function of the parietal lobe on the nondominant side (i.e., the holistic operator) becomes crucially important as a means of resolving the antinomies of myth, and the most important mechanism activating the holistic operator is ceremonial ritual.

The Causal Operator. There is considerable neurophysiological evidence that the ordering of events in time or more properly into a temporal sequence (since time may have no ontological reality outside the neural events which constitute the perception of it) is a result of the reciprocal interrelationship between the anterior convexity of the frontal lobe on the dominant side and the inferior parietal lobule via evolved fiber tracts.[10] It has long been known that the anterior portions of the frontal lobes, particularly on the dominant side, are involved in ordering not only sequential movement but also perceptual and cognitive elements in both space and time. We have attempted to show elsewhere that this basic

The Medial Surface of the Right Hemisphere,
with special note of Mammalian-Limbic Features of the Value Operator

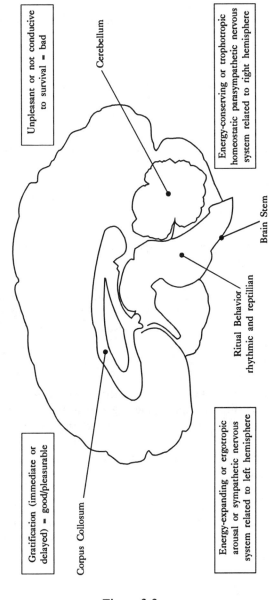

Unpleasant or not conducive
to survival = bad

Cerebellum

Energy-conserving or trophotropic
homeostatic parasympathetic nervous
system related to right hemisphere

Brain Stem

Ritual Behavior
rhythmic and reptillian

Corpus Collosum

Gratification (immediate or
delayed) = good/pleasurable

Energy-expanding or ergotropic
arousal or sympathetic nervous
system related to left hemisphere

Affective or emotional relationships contribute to moral and value judgement.

Figure 3.3

Figure 3.3

temporal ordering of conceptual material underlies the faculty of abstract causal thinking.[11]   This view is consistent with clinical data which confirm that lesions of the anterior convexity of the frontal lobe and/or its connection with the inferior parietal lobule interfere drastically with causal thinking. W. Grey Walter's work tends to confirm the importance of the frontal lobes in the process of abstract causal thinking.[12] Furthermore, the research of M.N. Livanov, N.A. Gavrilova, and A.S. Aslanov[13] supports the position that the areas of the frontal lobes are intimately related to processing information in terms of what we have called abstract causality.

Thus, we would locate the causal operator in the interrelationship of the anterior convexity of the frontal lobe on the dominant side and the inferior parietal lobule (see figure 3.1).

The Value Operator. The value operator resides in the interconnections of the neocortex with the limbic system (see figure 3.3).

Considerable evidence beginning with J.W. Papez implicates the limbic system as the modulator of emotions.[14]   The connections between the neocortex and the limbic system for visual and tactile learning have been demonstrated by M. Mishkin, J. Sunshine and M. Mishkin, and B. Jones and M. Mishkin.[15] Thus, for example, for visual learning they have demonstrated a sequential hierarchy of structures involving the striate, prestriate, inferior temporal, and ventromedial frontotemporal regions. These areas act as links mediating the neocortical-limbic pathway for visual-affective associations. These and similar neocortical-limbic connections for other sensory modalities, we have collectively called the value operator. The value operator attaches an affective valence to various cognitions and perceptions thereby powerfully enriching them.

It appears that, phylogenetically, with the evolution of the inferior parietal lobule, the anterior convexity of the frontal lobes, and their reciprocal interconnections humans began to develop as "culture bearers" and "myth makers."

It is interesting that ontogenetically these areas of the brain are the last to myelinate, and their myelinization corresponds with the development of J. Piaget's formal operations and the perfection of linguistic ability. We are not claiming these areas are the sole explanations for spoken language. Other areas of the brain needed to evolve as well in order for spoken language to develop. But these areas (anterior convexity of the frontal lobe, the inferior parietal lobule and their interconnections) appear to be involved in the critical elements of myth structuring, that is, in conceptualization, abstract causal thinking, and abstract antinomous thinking.

COGNITIVE STRUCTURES

At this point one can see that cognitive operators--or, if one wishes to be more precise, the neural structures which operate on quanta of experience to organize them in specific ways--produce what we have called cognitive structures such as myth themes. *Cognitive structures are simply the subjective manifestation of ways in which reality is organized by the operators. In other words, depending on which operator is functioning, the world is perceived in terms of synthetic unity, abstract causal relationships, relationships of binary opposition, and so on.*

We must emphasize that in ordinary day-to-day cognitive functioning all these operators function in concert, each relating its function to that of the others in order to abstract maximal meaning from experience. In other words, *the brain operates as a functional unit.* The predominant function of any single operator to the exclusion of the others is a rare event, although as we shall see it is not altogether impossible.

These operators allow us to propose that the most sophisticated mathematical, logical, or grammatical operation can ultimately be reduced to the simplest spatial and spatio-temporal analysis, which itself can be understood as an evolutionary elaboration of the more gestalt operation of the nondominant hemisphere of the brain.

Consequently we would argue that the apparent multiplicity of relationships between elements of a cognitive structure such as a myth theme can be reduced to a relatively small list of ultimately basic analytic relationships including (1) inside-outside, (2) above-below, (3) left-right, (4) in front-behind, (5) all-nothing, (6) before-after, and (7) simultaneous-sequential. These relatively few basic spatio-temporal relationships can be enriched by combining them with affective or emotional valence. Thus, "within" is usually identified with good and "without" with bad, "above" with good and "below" with bad, "right" with good and "left" with bad, "in front" with good and "behind" with bad, "all" with good and "nothing" with bad, and so on. These affective valences are *not* absolute and the reverse of any of them may occur.

It is interesting, however, to note how frequently the relationships just mentioned do in fact culturally receive the affective valence stated. We feel there is a reason for this association which involves issues of simple preservation. For example, "above" is usually safer than "below" and is therefore good; "within" is usually safer than "without" and is therefore good. Nevertheless we must reiterate that these associations are not absolute and the reverse associations can theoretically occur and occasionally, in fact, do occur.

Instead of embarking on the impossible task of listing all the possible complex relationships that can exist between elements of a cognitive structure, we have chosen rather to attempt to reduce them to a handful of simple spatio-temporal relationships. We feel it can be practically demonstrated that all complex relationships (whether they be mathematical, local, or grammatical) can be reduced to either one or a combination of the basic spatio-temporal relationships we have just considered, with one exception: affective or emotional relationships.

Affective relationships represent feeling states of crucial importance. In one way or another, they enter into moral and value judgments and underlie the emotional impact of myths. On the most primitive level they can be resolved into whether a stimulus is positive or aversive for an organism. Simply put, that which provides either immediate or delayed gratification is good; that which the organism experiences as unpleasurable or not conducive to survival is bad. As with the spatio-temporal relationships the basic affective relationships can be elaborated into a number of subtle feeling states and can be related to perception and cognition in various ways. The neurophysiological substrate for such affective-cognitive-perceptual linkages is the numerous connections alluded to above which exist between various limbic structures and either the secondary sensory association areas (in the case of perceptions) or the inferior parietal lobule (in the case of cognitions) (see figure 3.4).

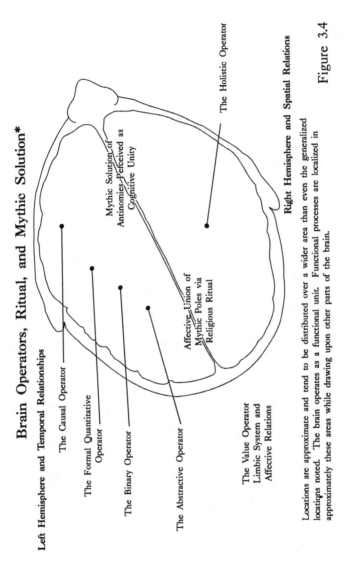

Brain Operators, Ritual, and Mythic Solution*

Left Hemisphere and Temporal Relationships

The Causal Operator

The Formal Quantitative Operator

The Binary Operator

The Abstractive Operator

Mythic Solution of Antinomies Perceived as Cognitive Unity

Affective Union of Mythic Poles via Religious Ritual

The Holistic Operator

Right Hemisphere and Spatial Relations

The Value Operator Limbic System and Affective Relations

Locations are approximate and tend to be distributed over a wider area than even the generalized locations noted. The brain operates as a functional unit. Functional processes are localized in approximately these areas while drawing upon other parts of the brain.

Figure 3.4

Figure 3.4

Thus far we have attempted to delineate the basic classes of relationships--spatial, temporal, and affective--which obtain between elements of a cognitive structure such as a myth theme. We have presented theoretical neurophysiological models for the evolution of such relationships. All this brings us to the problem of transformation of cognitive structures. As we have noted above, the transformation of cognitive structures presents the rearrangement of the relationships of cognitive elements and underlies the various mutations of the surface forms of myths.

THE NEUROBIOLOGY OF TRANSFORMATIONS

The issue of the biological base of transformations within a structural system is one which has received little or no attention by structuralists whether they be anthropologists (e.g., C. Levi-Strauss), linguists (e.g., N. Chomsky), or developmental psychologists (e.g., Piaget). A comprehensive meaning of transformation is the one most often suggested by developmental psychologists. In this sense more complex cognitive structures such as myth themes (in which are embedded potential models of the world) evolve from simpler structures.

More specifically, developmental psychology is viewed as the progressive elaboration of a series of nesting structures of increasing complexity. The relationship of the more complex to the less complex structures involves rules of transformation which include: (1) possible alteration or substitution of one element for another as in the case of the fully open structures; (2) addition of new elements of content which were not previously present in the simpler structures; and (3) specific rules of reorganization of all the elements of content such as is conveyed in the Levi-Straussian understanding of transformation.[16]

Such a complex system of transformation allows for the classical Piagetian model of nesting structures, which often has been described as the form of the simpler structure becoming the content of the more complex. Recent evidence suggests that the human capacity to organize data in terms of nesting or hierarchical structures may involve the inferior frontal convolution known as Broca's area.[17] It has been known for some time that the syntactic structure of language is organized by this area of the brain, and it has been presumed that the nesting structures which generate language in Chomsky's model likewise reside in this area (see figure 3.2).

What is exciting about this new evidence is that it seems to indicate the inferior frontal convolution on the dominant side may be generally responsible for any organization of thought into hierarchical structures (not just for linguistic organization). Such a structural system may be called a "semiclosed" system. We choose to call such structures semiclosed because we feel this term emphasizes the fact that they are highly stable neural and cognitive systems, not easily changed, but not absolutely and permanently fixed in either an ontogenetic or a phylogenetic sense, as the Levi-Straussian model would seem to imply.

The major question with which we are concerned here is: under what circumstances does the surface manifestation of a structure (myth) undergo a transformation?

Considering the work of Levi-Strauss and his followers, as well as the findings of a number of cognitive psychologists, it seems that structures such as myths are composed of relationships between dyads of cognitive elements, such relationships setting one element off against another for semantic clarity. Furthermore, the relationships *themselves* can be grouped into dyads involving the opposing of spatial, temporal, or affective relationships we have considered above, such as up-down, left-right, before-after, or good-bad.[18] Thus, every pair of relationships involves three or four cognitive elements: four cognitive elements if each pole of the two relationships is separate, or three elements if one cognitive element is common to two polar dyads.

One of the few ways in which the work of cognitive psychologists and of anthropologists such as Levi-Strauss can be made to make sense is if we postulate that it is inherent within the machinery of the brain to relate the cognitive elements of a structure (again in this case a myth) in such a way that for every pair related by one aspect of a relationship such as "up" *at least* one other pair must be related by the opposite relationships such as "down."[19] Furthermore, one must postulate that these relations obtain in such a way that, if the elements related by "up" are changed so that they are now related by "down," then at least some of the elements formerly related by "down" must now become related by "up"--unless, of course, the reciprocal change would result in nonsense. If one does not postulate some such system of reciprocal change attendant upon transformation, one simply cannot explain, for example, the almost algebraic neatness of Levi-Strauss's famous solution of the problem of affective valence between son-father and sister's son-mother's brother.[20]

Note that, according to the postulate of reciprocal change, such change is operative only when it involves a new surface structure that has meaning. Certain combinations can obviously involve nonsense. It would appear at this point that we are invoking the subjective entity of meaning to be the constraint within which basic neurophysiological processes operate. If this were true, then the phenomenon would be dependent upon the epiphenomenon, and we would be reduced to absolute idealism.

On the contrary, we affirm the physicalistic perspective that those constellations of relationships between cognitive elements of a structure which we consider meaningful possess the quality of "meaningfulness" simply because they are the subjective manifestations of inherently stable relationships within the neural microstructure. The locus of such relationships probably resides in various configurations as being adaptive and thus conducive to survival. It is only in this sense of the word meaning that we will say that meaning imposes constraints upon the postulate of reciprocal change during a transformation.

Thus any given cognitive (and by extension social) structure is limited in the number of its possible transformations not by the theoretical total of all the permutations generated by the postulate of reciprocal change but rather to a number which represents a subset of that total set, that is, those possible transformations which also are meaningful subjectively or, in other words, those which have adaptive properties and represent a high degree of isomorphism with the external world.

The answer to why any given constellation (surface structure) of relationships among elements of a semantic field (myth) is present and stable at all at a given time is simply because it is adaptive psychophysiologically for an individual or socio-ecologically for a group. It is the environment, therefore, which ultimately imposes the constraints that define exactly which surface manifestation of a deep structure will obtain, either cognitively or socially, at any given time. It is change in the environment, ultimately, which causes a disconfirmation of a given surface structure as representing the external world and which permits a change in one or more relationships between cognitive elements. Once one change takes place the entire system becomes rearranged according to the postulate of reciprocal change; a number of possible configurations are generated until one which is more adaptive to the circumstances becomes fixed (either for the individual or for the group).

It seems to us that when Anthony Wallace speaks of mazeway resynthesis, what he is essentially talking about is the rearrangement of relationships between multiple dyads (usually under the influence of intense limbic arousal) of a superordinate structure involving the relationship of the individual to the universe as a whole.[21] Thus, mazeway resynthesis can be seen as a transformation of the most encompassing superordinate cognitive structure under conditions of intense stress. It is a testimony to the stability of cognitive structures that only the most severe stresses, the most intense states of limbic arousal, are able to facilitate the transformation of important superordinate structures.

We must deny the charge that has often been made that biogenetic structuralism tends to ignore the influence of the environment. As we have seen, it is the environment and only the environment which is responsible for both the content of cognitive elements which comprise structures such as myth and for the fixing of a given constellation of relationships between cognitive elements at any point in time. Furthermore, it is the environment which ultimately governs the time when either an individual cognitive structure or a social structure (which can be seen as the social projection of a cognitive structure) will undergo transformation.

RESOLUTION OF THE MYTH PROBLEM COGNITIVELY AND RITUALLY

For the purpose of this discussion we *consider a myth as performing two distinct but related functions*. First, a myth presents a problem of ultimate concern to a society. This problem is always presented in antinomous form in the surface structure, that is, in terms of juxtaposed opposites such as

life-death, good-evil, and heaven-hell.[22]   Second, once the existential
problem is presented in the myth, it is solved by some resolution or
unification of the seemingly irreconcilable opposites which constitute the
problem. As we shall see, the most meaningful resolution of the problem
presented in the surface structure of a myth is usually achieved by
expressing the myth in the form of ceremonial ritual.

The ability to structure a mythic problem and its resolution involves the
operators we have discussed, especially the abstractive, causal, binary, and
holistic operators. In other words, myths, first, are couched in terms of
named categories of objects which we call concepts or ideas and which
serve as the elements of the surface structure. Second, myths, like all other
rational thoughts, involve causal sequences. Third, myths involve the
orientation of the universe into multiple dyads of polar opposites. Fourth,
the resolution of the problem presented by these antinomies is accomplished
most effectively by ritual.

The Mythic Problem. Human beings have no choice but to construct myths
to explain their world.[23] The myths may be social in nature, or they may
be individual in terms of dreams, daydreams, or other fantasy aspects of the
individual person. Nevertheless, as long as human beings are aware of the
contingency of their existence in the face of what often appears to be a
capricious universe, they must construct myths to orient themselves within
that universe. This constructive orientation is inherent in the obligatory
functioning [of] the neural structures or operators we have considered
above. Since it is highly unlikely that human beings will ever know the
first cause of every strip of reality observed, it is highly probable that we
will always generate gods, powers, principles, or other entities as first
causes to explain what we observe. Indeed we cannot do otherwise.

Myth problems, therefore, are structured either socially or individually,
primarily according to the analytic and verbal mode of consciousness of the
dominant hemisphere. They codify unexplained reality in terms of
antinomies or polar oppositions such as good-evil, change-permanence, and
so on, and in terms of causal explanatory sequences.

Thus far we have only presented a neural model explaining the
mechanism and necessity for structuring input from the external world into

causal sequences and mythic antinomies, that is, into dyadic structures of ultimate existential concern to humanity. The second aspect of myth is to resolve these antinomies and hence to solve the problem.

The Mythic Solution. Mythic solutions are exemplified by the cognitive resolution of the god-human antinomy by a solar hero, a Christ figure, or a divine king. These resolutions are effected by a subtle shift in cognitive dominance from the major hemisphere to the minor hemisphere of the brain. The cognitive functions we have been considering up to now [conceptualization, abstract, causal thinking, and antinomous thought] represent the evolution of major hemisphere function. As we have noted in previous sections, the minor hemisphere is related to gestalt perceptions, that is, to the perception of incoming sensory input as a whole rather than as a string of associated elements. We propose that *the cognitive assimilation of logically irreconcilable polar opposites presented in the myth structure*--such as god and human in a solar hero or a Christ figure-- *represents a shift of predominating influence from the major hemisphere to a predominant influence of the minor hemisphere, which allows the antinomies to be perceived as a cognitive unity.*

Thus, for example, the concepts of a Christ figure or a solar hero represent cognitive solutions within the myth to the problem presented by the basically antinomous myth structure. Although this is undoubtedly so, we feel that classical structuralists have tended to overemphasize the resolution in terms of the internal dialectic of structures. We contend that the only resolutions which are psychologically powerful to both individuals and groups are those which have an aspect of existential reality. We will attempt to show in what follows that such a powerfully affective resolution arises primarily from ritual and rarely from a cognitive fusion of antinomies alone, although such a cognitive fusion may be a necessary precursor in human religious ritual.

The Ritual Resolution. Religious ritual aims at existentially uniting opposites in an effort to gain control over an essentially unpredictable universe. The ultimate union of opposites is that of contingent and vulnerable humanity with a powerful, possibly omnipotent, force. In other words, we propose that humanity and superhuman power are the ultimate poles of much mythic structure, and that this polarity is the basic problem ritual must resolve existentially.

Side by side with this basic antinomy are usually other correlative antinomies which frequently must be resolved according to the specific myth before the basic god-human antinomy can be resolved. Such polar opposites include heaven-hell, sky-earth, good-bad, left-right, strong-weak, as well as an almost endless series of other polarities recurring in myths. Before we consider what it is about ritual that allows such a powerfully affective union of mythic poles, let us first consider why it is that human beings tend to act out their myths at all.

There is some evidence that whatever is present in one neural system tends to be present in other neural systems, even if its manifestation in other systems is inhibited. We consider five major neural systems: visual, auditory, tactile, conceptual-cognitive, and motor.

Thus, for example, it has been known for some time that whatever is heard tends to be repeated. In normally functioning individuals the actual physical repetition of whatever is heard is inhibited by mechanisms within the frontal lobe leaving only an internal repetition within our heads. When the frontal inhibitory mechanisms are released in certain pathological states, the phenomenon of echolalia occurs in which individuals obligatorily repeat whatever they hear.

Likewise, there is an inbuilt tendency to have a representation in the motor system of whatever movement appears in the visual system. As one might suspect, such imitation is ordinarily inhibited in fact, except in a few pathological conditions in which the patient exhibits echopraxia. Such individuals necessarily perform any action they see.

In a recent article in *Science*, T.M. Field et al. demonstrated this visual-motor connection in the imitation by neonates of facial expressions presented to them.[24] The auditory motor connection is seen in the rare condition of *latah* in which the patients obligatorily obey whatever they hear.

For our purpose here we are interested in the cognitive-verbal-motor connection.

The motor manifestation of cognitive-verbal expression is ordinarily inhibited. However, it tends to break through in normal individuals when we "talk with our hands." I propose there is a powerful inbuilt mechanism encouraging us to act out our thoughts. This proclivity is especially powerful when our thoughts and words form a learned, closed cognitive system as in the recitation of a myth. Because of the reciprocal representation of the content of the major neural systems, human beings are naturally disposed to act out their myths, but not by using ordinary motor behavior. This propensity to enact a myth in rhythmic motor form is responsible for the myth-ritual complex. Humans reach far into their evolutionary past and graft an ancient motor behavior onto the product of their neocortexes, that is, myth. Why should we do so? The answer lies in the consideration of the nature of ritual behavior itself.

Ritual Behavior. At this point one must ask what is meant by ritual behavior. We define ritual behavior as a sequence of behavior which:

(1) is structured or patterned;

(2) is rhythmic and repetitive (to some degree at least), that is, tends to recur in the same or nearly the same form with some regularity;

(3) acts to synchronize affective, perceptual-cognitive, and motor processes within the central nervous system of individual participants; and

(4) most particularly, synchronizes these processes among the various individual participants.

G.H. Manley has considered in some detail this synchronizing function of ritual in the black-headed gull.[25] From the work of M.W. Schein and E.B. Hale with the domestic turkey, N. Tinbergen with three-spined sticklebacks and queen butterflies, and J.S. Rosenblatt with cats--it appears there is something about the repetitive or rhythmic emanation of signals from a conspecific which generates a high degree of arousal of the limbic system of the brain.[26] With respect to this rhythmic quality of ritual, K. Lorenz notes: "The display of animals during threat and courtship furnishes an abundance of examples, and so does the culturally developed ceremonial of humans. The deans of the university walked into the hall with a 'measured step'; pitch, rhythm and loudness of the Catholic priests chanting during mass are all strictly regulated by liturgic prescription. The unambiguity of the communication is also increased by its frequent repetition. Rhythmical repetition of the same movement is so characteristic of very many rituals, both instinctive and cultural, that it is hardly necessary to describe examples."[27]

V.J. Walter and W.G. Walter as well as E.Gellhorn and W.F. Kiely have shown that such repetitive auditory and visual stimuli can drive cortical rhythms and eventually produce an intensely pleasurable, ineffable experience in humans.[28] Furthermore, Gellhorn and Kiely cite evidence that such repetitive stimuli can bring about simultaneous intense discharges from both the human sympathetic and parasympathetic nervous systems.[29] When one considers the evidence taken from the literature on animal studies together with the limited studies that have been done on humans, one can infer that there is something about repetitive rhythmic stimuli which may, under proper condition, bring about the unusual neural state of simultaneous high discharge of both autonomic subsystems.

In reaching this state of high arousal, three stages of tuning of the sympathetic-parasympathetic subsystems are recognized.

In the first stage, reactivity in one system increases while at the same time it decreases in the other system.

If augmented reactivity of the sensitized system continues, the second stage of tuning is reached after stimuli exceed a certain threshold; at this point not only is inhibition of the nonsensitized system complete, but also stimuli which usually elicit a response in the nonsensitized system instead evoke a response in the sensitized system. Behaviors resulting from this second stage of tuning are termed reversal phenomena.

If stimulation continues beyond this stage, increased sensitization can lead to a third stage in which the reciprocal relationship fails and simultaneous discharges in both systems result.

Normally, either the sympathetic or the parasympathetic system predominates, and the excitation of one subsystem normally inhibits the other. In the special case of prolonged rhythmic stimuli, it appears that the simultaneous strong discharge of both autonomic systems creates a state of stimulation of the median forebrain bundle generating not only a pleasurable sensation but, under proper conditions, a sense of union with conspecifics and a blurring of cognitive boundaries. We suggest that *such driving of the autonomic subsystems by rhythmic stimuli powerfully activates the holistic operator allowing various degrees of gestalt perception.* The simplest paradigm to explain the situation in humans is the feeling of union that occurs during orgasm. During orgasm, as during other states we shall consider later, there is intense simultaneous discharge from both the autonomic subsystems.

Hence, we are postulating that the various ecstasy states, which can be produced in humans after exposure to rhythmic auditory, visual, or tactile stimuli, produce a feeling of union with other members participating in that ritual. In fact, the oneness of all participants is the theme running through the myth of most human rituals. It is probably the sense of oneness and the vagueness of boundaries, which are experienced at certain nodal points in ritual, which allow the symbol to be experienced as that for which it stands itself. The fusion of symbols and their referents at various points in human religious ritual is undoubtedly accomplished by the general feeling of oneness or unity which obtains when a ritual triggers the holistic operator. Although it is very difficult to extrapolate from humans to animals, it is probable that some sort of analogous affective state is produced by rhythmic, repeated ritual behavior in other species. This state may vary in intensity, but it always has the effect at least of unifying the social group.

Put simply, there is increasing evidence that rhythmic or repetitive behavior synchronizes the limbic discharges (i.e., the affective states) of a group of conspecifics. It can generate a level of arousal which is both pleasurable and reasonably uniform among the individuals so that necessary group action is facilitated.

Thus far we have said nothing about the communication aspect of this rhythmic signaling. There is a great body of evidence that many of these rhythmic stimuli serve as communications. The position of most ethologists is that rhythmicity evolved in lower animal species in the service of communication. However, many ethologists maintain that the rhythmicity evolved an autonomous effect of its own, separate from its signaling function. Thus, Lorenz states: "Both instinctive and cultural rituals become independent motivations of behavior by creating new ends or goals toward which the organisms strive for their own sake. It is in their character of independent motivating factors that rituals transcend their original function of communication and become able to perform their equally important secondary tasks of controlling aggression and of forming a bond between certain individuals."[30]

Simultaneous Cortical Functioning. Let us see how the recent discoveries of differential hemispheric functioning, discussed earlier in this paper, fit into this line of thinking. Permit me to recapitulate in two or three sentences the recent discoveries concerning the functions of the nondominant hemisphere (see figure 3.1).

What is new is the discovery that the so-called nondominant or minor hemisphere has extremely important nonverbal, nonanalytic functions. First, it is related to the perception of visual-spatial relationships. Over and above this, there is good evidence that it perceives the world not in terms of discrete entities but in terms of gestalts, or nondiscrete, holistic perceptions. The perception of wholeness or unity, which this hemisphere controls, is extremely important to this discussion as we have seen. Furthermore, there is evidence that the minor hemisphere may be chiefly responsible for creative or artistic ability.

J. Levy and C. Trevarthen are obtaining evidence that in the normally functioning individual both hemispheres operate in solving problems via a mechanism of reciprocal inhibition controlled at the brainstem level.[31] Put simply, the world is approached by a rapid alternation pattern of functioning of each hemisphere. In other words, one hemisphere is flashed on and then turned off, the second flashed on and then turned off, the first flashed on again, and so on, in rapid alternation. The rhythm of this process, and whether one side or the other tends to predominate in this process, may account for various cognitive styles--from the extremely analytic and scientific to the extremely artistic and synthetic. There is some evidence reviewed by B. Lex that this duality of cerebral functioning may parallel the duality of autonomic functioning which we have just considered.[32]

Actually, it is easier conceptually to integrate the two modes of consciousness into a more general duality of patterning within the central nervous system. Lex does this by utilizing Hess's model of an energy-expending or ergotropic system and an energy-conserving or trophotropic system operating in a complementary fashion within the human organism (see figure 3.3).

In this model, the ergotropic system consists of not only the sympathetic nervous system, which governs arousal states and fight or flight responses, but also any energy-expanding process within the central nervous system.

Conversely, the trophotropic system includes not only the parasympathetic peripheral nervous system, which governs basic vegetative and homeostatic functions, but also any central nervous system process which maintains the baseline stability of the organism.

Thus, the ergotropic-trophotropic model represents an extension to the central nervous system of sympathetic-parasympathetic peripheral nervous functioning. Further extending this model, we can identify the minor or nondominant hemisphere with the trophotropic or baseline energy state system and the dominant or major hemisphere, which governs analytical verbal and causal thinking, with the ergotropic or energy-expanding system.

Alteration in the tuning of these systems from the peripheral autonomic level to the cerebral level has been offered as an explanation for various altered states of consciousness by a number of investigators, including E.Gellhorn, Gellhorn and W.F. Kiely, and R.E. Ornstein.[33]   These investigators present evidence that at maximal stimulation of either the trophotropic or ergotropic system there is, as it were, a spillover into the opposite, complementary system. It has been postulated that the rhythmic activity of ritual behavior supersaturates the ergotropic or energy-expending system to the point that not only is the trophotropic system simultaneously excited by a kind of spillover but, on rare occasions, may achieve nearly maximal stimulation of the trophotropic system as well so that, briefly at least, both systems are intensely stimulated. The positive, ineffable affect which this state produces was alluded to above.

In humans we propose that, *concomitant with the simultaneous stimulation of the lower aspects of both systems, their cerebral representations, that is, both hemispheres of the brain, also may function simultaneously.* Cognitively, this is manifested by the presentation of polar opposites by the analytic hemisphere (i.e., the presentation of a problem to be solved in terms of the myth structure) and the simultaneous experience of their union via the excitation or stimulation of the minor hemisphere, specifically the holistic operator. This could explain the often reported experience of the resolution of unexplainable paradoxes by individuals during certain meditation states on the one hand or during states induced by ritual behavior on the other.

In one of the few experiments carried out in any kind of controlled manner on the experiences of meditation, A.J. Deikman notes that one of the phenomena common to all subjects is what appears to be simultaneity of conflicting perceptions during relatively advanced meditation states:

The subjects' reports indicated that they experienced conflicting perception. For example, in the third session, subject B stated, about the vase, "it certainly filled my visual field" but a few minutes later stated "it didn't fill the field by any means." In the seventh session referring to the landscape he commented," . . . a great deal of agitation . . . but it isn't agitating . . . it's . . . pleasurable." In general, subjects found it very difficult to describe their feelings and perceptions during the meditation periods -- "it's very hard to put into words," was a frequent comment. This difficulty seemed due in part to the difficulty in describing their experience without contradictions.[34]

It appears that during certain meditation states and ritual states, logical paradoxes or the awareness of polar opposites as presented in a myth appear simultaneously both as antinomies and as unified wholes. This experience is coupled with the intensely affective, oceanic experience, which has been described during various meditation states as well as at certain nodal points of ritual. During intense meditative experiences, such as yogic ecstasy and the *unio mystica* of the Christian tradition, the experience of the union of opposites, or *conjunctio oppositorum*, is expanded to the experience of the total union of self and other, or, as it is expressed in the Christian tradition, the union of the self with God.

Ritual is always performed to solve a problem presented by and to the verbal analytic consciousness. The problem may be between good and evil, life and death, or the disparity between God and humanity. The problem may be as simple as the disparity between human beings and a capricious rain god or as subtle as the disparity between humanity's existential contingent state and the state of an all-knowing, all-powerful, unchangeable ground of being. In any case, the problem is presented in the analytic mode which involves ergotropic excitation.

Like all other animals, humans attempt to cope with the environmental situation via motor behavior. The motor behavior goes back far into our phylogenetic past. It is usually a repetitive motor activity with visual, auditory, or other sensory stimulus feedback; as we have just seen, this strongly drives the ergotropic system. Even the cadence and chanting of words contributes to this repetitive quality. The slow rhythmicity of a religious procession or the fast beat of drums or rattles all serve to drive the ergotropic system.

With prayers and chanting, this system is often driven in two ways. The myth may be presented within the ritual prayer, thus exciting by its meaning the cognitive ergotropic functions of the dominant hemisphere. The rhythmicity of the prayer or chant, by its very rhythmicity, drives the ergotropic system independent of the meaning of words. If the ritual works, the ergotropic system becomes, as it were, supersaturated and spills over into excitation of the trophotropic system, resulting in the same end state as meditation but from the opposite neural starting point. In any case the holistic operator is activated.

This unusual physiological state, produced by both approaches (meditation and ritual), produces other aesthetic-cognitive effects besides a sense of union of opposites. Numerous reports from many religious traditions point to the fact that such states yield a feeling not only of union with a greater force or power, but also an intense awareness that death is not to be feared, accompanied by a sense of harmony of the individual with the universe. This sense of harmony with the universe may be the human cognitive extrapolation from the more primitive sense of union with other conspecifics, which ritual behavior also excites in prehuman animals.

Thus, we see that the phylogenetic origins of ritual carry through in an unbroken line to the most complex human religious rituals. However, onto these primitive functions are grafted other adaptive functions, namely, those of higher cognition. Humans are not simply the sum of neural mechanisms, independently evolved under various selective pressures. Rather, each of us functions as an integrated whole. Although our higher cognition may have evolved as a very practical, adaptive, problem-solving process, it carried with it--indeed it requires--the formation of myths that present problems for which the ancient rhythmic motor behaviors help generate solutions.

In other words, when ritual works (and it by no means works all the time), it powerfully relieves our existential anxiety, and, when it is most powerful, it relieves us of the fear of death and places us in harmony with the universe. It allows individual humans to become incorporated in myth, and, conversely, allows for the very incarnation of myth. Is it no wonder then that any behavior so powerful has persisted throughout the ages? Indeed, ritual is likely to persist for some time to come.

*An edited copy of the paper presented at a symposium on "Ritual in Human Adaptation" in Chicago on 12-13 November 1982, sponsored by the Institute on Religion in an Age of Science in association with the Center for Advanced Study in Religion and Science, the Chicago Theological Seminary, the Disciples Divinity House, and the Lutheran School of Theology at Chicago.

NOTES

1. Eugene G. d'Aquili, "The Neurobiological Bases of Myth and Concepts of Deity," *Zygon 13* (December 1978):257; idem, "Senses of Reality in Science and Religion: A Neuroepistemological Perspective," *Zygon 17* (December 1982):361.

2. A.R. Luria, *Higher Cortical Functions in Man* (New York: Basic Books, 1966); idem, "The Frontal Lobes and the Regulation of Behavior," in *Psychophysiology of the Frontal Lobes*, ed. K.H. Pribram and A.R. Luria (New York: Academic Press, 1973); idem, *The Working Brain* (New York: Basic Books, 1973).

3. N. Geschwind, "Disconnection Syndromes in Animals and Man," *Brain 88* (1965):237-94, 585-644; A. Basso et al., "Neuropsychological Evidence for the Existence of Cerebral Area Critical to the Performance of Intelligence Tasks," *Brain 96* (1973):715-28; A.G. Friederici and P.W. Schoenle, "Computational Dissociation of Two Vocabulary Types: Evidence from Aphasis," *Neuropsychologia 12* (1980):11-20.

4. Luria, *Higher Cortical Functions*; idem, "Frontal Lobes"' idem, *Working Brain*.

5. Geschwind, "Disconnection Syndromes."

6. Luria, *Higher Cortical Functions*.

7. Geschwind, "Disconnection Syndromes."

8. G. Ratcliff, "Spatial Thought, Mental Rotation and the Right Cerebral Hemisphere," *Neuropsychologia 17* (1979):49-54; L. Franco and R.W. Sperry, "Hemisphere Lateralization for Cognitive Processing of Geometry." *Neuropsychologia 15* (1977):104-14; G. Cohen, "Hemispheric Differences in the Utilization of Advance Information," in *Attention and Performance*, ed. P.M.A. Rabbit and S. Dornic, vol.5 (London: Academic Press, 1975); N. Butters, M. Barton, and B.A. Brody, "Role of the Right Parietal Lobe in the Mediation of Cross-Modal Associations and Reversible Operations in Space," *Cortex 6* (1970):174-90.

9. R.W. Sperry, M.S. Gazzaniga, and J.E. Bogen, "Interhemispheric Relationships: The Neocortical Commissures; Syndromes of Hemisphere Disconnection," in *Handbook of Clinical Neurology*, ed. P.J. Vinken and C.W. Bruyn, vol. 4 (Amsterdam: North Holland Publishing Co., 1969); R.D.Nebes and R.W. Sperry, "Hemispheric Deconnection Syndrome with Cerebral Birth Injury in the Dominant Arm Area," *Neuropsychologia 9* (1971):249-59; M.S. Gazzaniga, *The Bisected Brain* (New York: Appleton Century Crofts, 1970); M.S. Gazzaniga and S.A. Hillyard, "Language and Speech Capacity of the Right Hemisphere," *Neuropsychologia 9* (1971):273-80; J.E. Bogen, "The Other Side

74

of the Brain, II: An Appositional Mind," *Bulletin of Los Angeles Neurological Society 34* (1969):135-62; J. Levy-Agresti and R.W. Sperry, "Differential Perceptual Capacities in Major and Minor Hemispheres," *Proceedings of the National Academy of Science 61* (1968):1151; C. Trevarthen, "Brain Bisymmetry and the Role of the Corpus Callosum in Behavior and Conscious Experience," presented at the International Colloquium on Interhemispheric Relations, Czechoslovakia, 1-13 June 1969.

10. Luria, *Higher Cortical Functions*; K.H. Pribram and A.R. Luria, eds., *The Psychophysiology of the Frontal Lobes* (New York: Academic Press, 1973); L. Mills and G.B. Rollman, "Hemispheric Asymmetry for Auditory Perception of Temporal Order," *Neuropsychologia 18* (1980):41-47; L. Swisher and I. Hirsch, "Brain Damage and the Ordering of Two Temporally Successive Stimuli," *Neuropsychologia 10* (1971):137-52.

11. E.G. d'Aquili and C. Laughlin, "The Biopsychological Determinants of Religious Ritual Behavior," *Zygon 10* (March 1975):32-58.

12. W.G. Walter, "Human Frontal Lobe Functions in Sensory-Motor Association," in *Psychophysiology of the Frontal Lobes*, ed. K.H. Pribram and A.R. Luria (New York: Academic Press, 1973).

13. M.N. Livanov, N.A. Gavrilova, and A.S. Aslanov, "Correlations of Biopotentials in the Frontal Parts of the Human Brain," in *Psychophysiology of the Frontal Lobes*, ed. K.H. Pribram and A.R. Luria (New York: Academic Press, 1973).

14. J.W. Papez, "Reticulospinal Tracts in the Cat," *Journal of Comparative Neurology 41* (1926):364; idem, *Comparative Neurology* (New York: Hafner, 1961).

15. M. Mishkin, "Analogous Neural Models for Tactual and Visual Learning," *Neuropsychologia 17* (1979):139-51; J. Sunshine and M.A. Mishkin, "A Visual-Limbic Pathway Serving Visual Associative Functions in Rhesus Monkeys," *Federation Proceedings 34* (1975):440; B. Jones and M. Mishkin, "Limbic Lesions and the Problem of Stimulus-Reinforcement Associations," *Explorations in Neurology 36* (1972):362-77.

16. C. Levi-Strauss, *Structural Anthropology* (New York: Anchor Books, 1963).

17. M. Grossman, "A Central Processor for Hierarchically-Structured Material: Evidence from Broca's Aphasia," *Neuropsychologia 18* (1980):299-308.

18. Levi-Strauss, *Structural Anthropology*; C.Levi-Strauss, *The Savage Mind* (Chicago: University of Chicago Press, 1963); J. Piaget, *Structuralism* (New York: Basic Books, 1970); O.J. Harvey, D.E. Hunt, and H.M. Schroder, *Conceptual Systems and Personality Organization* (New York: John Wiley & Sons, 1961).

19. Levi-Strauss, *Structural Anthropology*; idem, *Savage Mind*; C. Levi-Strauss, *Mythologiques: Le Cru et le Cuit* (Paris: Plon, 1964).

20. Levi-Strauss, *Structural Anthropology*.

21. A.F.C. Wallace, *Culture and Personality* (New York: Random House, 1961).

22. Levi-Strauss, *Structural Anthropology*; idem, *Mythologiques*; C.G. Jung, *Psyche and Symbol* (New York: Doubleday Anchor Books, 1958); C.G. Jung, "The Psychology of Transference," in *The Practice of Psychotherapy*, Bollingen series 20, 2nd ed. (New York: Pantheon Books, 1966).

23. d'Aquili and Laughlin (n.11 above); d'Aquili, "Neurobiological Bases of Myth (n.1 above).

24. T.M. Field et al., "Discrimination and Imitation of Facial Expressions by Neonates," *Science 218* (1982):179-81.

25. G.H. Manley, Ph.D. dissertation on the displays of the Black-headed Gull, Oxford University, 1960.

26. M.W. Schein and E.B. Hale, "Stimuli Eliciting Sexual Behavior," in *Sex and Behavior*, ed. F.A. Beach (New York: John Wiley & Sons, 1965); N. Tinbergen, *The Study of Instinct* (London: Oxford University Press, 1951); J.S. Rosenblatt, "Effects of Experience on Sexual Behavior in Male Cats," in *Sex and Behavior*, ed. F.A. Beach (New York: John Wiley & Sons, 1965).

27. Konrad Lorenz, *On Aggression* (New York: Bantam Books, 1966), p.72.

28. V.J. Walter and W.G. Walter, "The Central Effects on Rhythmic Sensory Stimulation," *Electroencephalography and Clinical Neurophysiology* 1 (1949):57-85; E. Gellhorn and W.F. Kiely, "Mystical States of Consciousness: Neurophysiological and Clinical Aspects," *Journal of Nervous and Mental Disease 154* (1972):399-405; idem, "Autonomic Nervous System in Psychiatric Disorder," in *Biological Psychiatry*, ed. J. Mendels (New York: John Wiley & Sons, 1973).

29. Gellhorn and Kiely, "Mystical States"; idem, "Autonomic Nervous System."

30. Lorenz, *On Aggression*, p.72.

31. Levy-Agresti and Sperry (n.9 above); Trevarthen (n.9 above).

32. B. Lex, "The Neurobiology of Ritual Trance," in *The Spectrum of Ritual: A Biogenetic Structural Analysis*, ed. E.G.d'Aquili et al. (New York: Columbia University Press, 1979).

33. Gellhorn, *Principles*; Gellhorn and Kiely, "Mystical States"; idem, "Autonomic Nervous System"; R.E. Ornstein, *The Psychology of Consciousness* (San Francisco: Calif." W.H. Freeman, 1972).

34. A.J. Deikman, "Experimental Meditation," in *Altered States of Consciousness*, ed. C.T.Tart (Garden City, N.Y.: Doubleday, 1969), pp.208-9.

Chapter Four

BODY, BRAIN, AND CULTURE*

by

Victor Turner

Abstract. Recent work in cerebral neurology should be used to fashion a new synthesis with anthropological studies. Beginning with Paul D. MacLean's model of the triune brain, we explore Ralph Wendell Burhoe's question whether creative processes result from a coadaptation, perhaps in ritual itself, of genetic and cultural information. Then we examine the division of labor between right and left cerebral hemispheres and its implications for the notions of play and "ludic recombination." Intimately related to ritual, play may function in the social construction of reality analogous to mutation and variation in organic evolution. Finally, we consider how our picture of brain functioning accords with some distinctive features of the religious systems dominant in human cultures.

The present essay is for me one of the most difficult I have ever attempted. This is because I am having to submit to question some of the axioms anthropologists of my generation--and several subsequent generations--were taught to hallow. These axioms express the belief that all human behavior is the result of social conditioning. Clearly a very great deal of it is, but gradually it has been borne home to me that there are inherent resistances to conditioning.

As Anthony Stevens has recently written in an interesting book which seeks to reconcile ethological and Jungian approaches: "Any attempt to adopt forms of social organization and ways of life other than those which are *characteristic of our species* must lead to personal and social disorientation" (italics added).[1] In other words, our species has distinctive features, genetically inherited, which interact with social conditioning, and set up certain resistances to behavioral modification from without.

Further, Robin Fox has argued: "If there is no human nature, any social system is as good as any other, since there is no base line of human needs by which to judge them. If, indeed, everything is learned, then surely people can be taught to live in any kind of society. Humanity is at the

77

mercy of all the tyrants who think they know what is best for it. And how can humanity plead that they are being inhuman if it doesn't know what being human is in the first place?"[2]

One of those distinctive human features may be a propensity to the ritualization of certain of our behaviors, from smiling and maternal responsiveness onwards.

THEORIES OF RITUALIZATION

In June 1965, I took part in a discussion on "ritualization of behavior in animals and man" organized by Sir Julian Huxley for the Royal Society and held--perhaps appropriately--in the lecture hall of the Zoological Society of London, near the Mappin Terraces, where the monkeys revel. The "hard core" of the conference consisted of zoologists and ethologists: Huxley, Konrad Lorenz, R.A. Hinde, W.H. Thorpe, Desmond Morris, N.M. Cullen, F.W. Braestrup, I. Eibl-Eibesfeldt, and others. Sir Edmund Leach, Meyer Fortes, and I spoke up for British anthropology in defining ritual, but by no means as unanimously as the ethologists did in defining ritualization.

Other scholars represented other disciplines: psychiatrists included Erik Erikson, R.D. Laing, and G. Morris Carstairs. Sir Maurice Bowra and E.H. Gombrich spoke about the ritualization of human cultural activities, dance, drama, and art. Basil Bernstein, H. Elvin and R.S. Peters discussed ritual in education and David Attenborough shared his ethnographic films on the Kava ceremony in Tonga and land-diving in Pentecost, New Hebrides.

As Culturally Transmitted. The nonethologists generally accepted Leach's position that "it cannot be too strongly emphasized that ritual, in the anthropologist's sense, is in no way whatsoever a genetic endowment of the species."[3] I took up no public position at that time, since I was secretly, even guiltily impressed by the ethologists' definition of "ritualization" which seemed to strike chords in relation to human ritual, summed up by Huxley as follows:

Ritualization is the adaptive formalization or canalization of emotionally motivated behavior, under the teleonomic pressure of natural selection so as:

(a) to promote better and more unambiguous signal function, both intra- and inter-specifically; (b) to serve as more efficient stimulators or releasers of more efficient patterns of action in other individuals; (c) to reduce intra-specific damage; and (d) to serve as sexual or social bonding mechanisms.[4]

Actually, much of Huxley's definition is better applied analogically to those stylized human behaviors we might call "communicative," such as manners, decorum, ceremony, etiquette, polite display, the rules of chivalry (which inhibit the infliction on one another of damage by conspecifis) than to ritual proper.

In various publications I have suggested that ritual was "a *transformative* performance revealing major classifications, categories, and contradictions of cultural processes." In these respects it might conceivably fulfill Huxley's fourth function, that of "serving as sexual or social bonding mechanisms," by transforming social and personal life-crises (birth, initiation, marriage, death) into occasions where symbols and values representing the unity and continuity of the total group were celebrated and reanimated. The cultural rituals which seem most to embody something resembling Huxley's definition of "ritualization" are "seasonal, agricultural, fertility, funerary, and healing ones, because they make explicit the interdependence of people with their physical environments and bodies."[5]

But as I have written elsewhere, ritual is not necessarily a bastion of social conservatism; its symbols do not merely condense cherished sociocultural values. Rather, through its liminal processes, it holds the generating source of culture and structure. Hence, by definition ritual is associated with social *transitions* while *ceremony* is linked with social *states*. Performances of ritual are distinctive phases in the social process, whereby groups and individuals adjust to internal changes and adapt to their external environment.

As Genetically Programmed. Meyer Fortes, William Wyse Professor of Anthropology and Archaeology at Cambridge, influenced by Sigmund Freud, defined ritual at the London conference as "procedure for prehending the occult, that is, first, for grasping what is, for a particular culture, occult (i.e., beyond everyday human understanding, hidden, mysterious) in the events and incidents of people's lives, secondly, for binding what is so grasped by means of the ritual resources and beliefs available in that culture, and thirdly, for thus incorporating what is grasped and bound into the normal existence of individuals and groups."[6]

This formulation might well identify psychoanalytical clinical procedure as ritual process. Fortes makes his Freudian affiliation quite clear when he goes on to write that "ritual is concerned with prehending the unconscious (in the psychoanalytical sense) forces of individual action and existence, and their social equivalents, the irreducible factors in social relations (e.g., the mother-child nexus, at one end of the scale, the authority of society at the other). By bringing them, *suitably disguised*, or symbolized in tangible material objects and actions, into the open of social life, ritual binds them and makes them manageable" (italics added).[7]

Unlike Leach, Fortes sees ritual more as the handling of otherwise unmanageable power than the communication of important cultural knowledge. For Fortes irreducible ambiguities and antinomies are made visible and thus accessible to public and legitimate control--a position to which with important modifications I myself have subscribed--while for Leach the emphasis in ritual is cognitive and classificatory. As he writes,

> it is characteristic of many ritual and mythical sequences in primitive society that the actors claim to be recapitulating the creation of the world and that this act of creation is mythologized as a list of names attached to persons, places, animals, and things. The world is created by the process of classification and the repetition of the classification of itself perpetuates the knowledge which it incorporates.[8]

Ritual's multicoded redundancies inscribe its "messages" on the minds of the participants.

Clearly, the main difference between anthropologists of the Leachian persuasion and the ethologists in their concept of ritualization or ritual lay in the emphasis of the former on ritual as learned, culturally transmitted behavior, intrinsically linked with the development of language, and of the latter on ritual as genetically programmed behavior with important nonverbal components.

THE NEUROBIOLOGY OF THE BRAIN: CULTURETYPE
AND GENOTYPE

The years passed. I continued to treat ritual essentially as a cultural system. Meanwhile exciting new findings were coming from genetics, ethology, and neurology, particularly the neurobiology of the brain.

I found myself asking a stream of questions more or less along the following lines. Can we enlarge our understanding of the ritual process by relating it to some of these findings? After all, *can we escape from something like animal ritualization without escaping our own bodies and psyches, the rhythms and structures of which arise on their own*? As Ronald Grimes has said, "They flow with or without our conscious assent; they are uttered-exclamations of nature and our bodies."[9]

I also asked myself many of the questions raised by Ralph Wendell Burhoe[10]--especially following Edward O. Wilson, what is the nature of the alleged "chain," and how long is it, by which genes hold cultural patterns, including ritual patterns, to use the idiom of sociobiology, "on leash"? This, it seemed to me, is where the neurobiology of the human brain begins to be relevant.

We shall have occasion to look at the findings of Paul MacLean, the neuroanatomist, again later, but something should be said now about his work on what might be called "archaic" structures of the human brain. His early work dealt with what is called the limbic system, an evolutionarily ancient part of the brain concerned with the emotions, cradled in or near the fringes of the cortex. In a 1949 paper he suggested that the limbic system is "the major circuit that would have to be involved in psychosomatic diseases, such as gastronintestinal ulcers caused by social or psychological stress, a now widely accepted hypothesis since it has been demonstrated that this system controls the pituitary gland at the base of the brain and the autonomic nervous systems, which in turn control the viscera."[11] MacLean further proposed in 1952 that the frontal lobes of the cerebral hemispheres, shown to be "the seat of the highest human faculties, such as *foresight and concern for the consequences and meaning of events*, may have these functions and others *by virtue of intimate connections between the frontal lobes and the limbic system*" (italics added). Here we see that the highest and newest portion of the cerebral cortex has by no means detached itself from an ancient, "primitive" region, but functions as it does precisely "by virtue of its relationship to the old emotional circuitry."[12]

Later, Walle Nauta, a celebrated neuroanatomist, has referred to the frontal lobes as "the neocortex of the limbic system."[13] As Melvin Konner concludes: "Just as other parts of the cortex have been identified as the highest report-and-control centers for vision, hearing, tactile sensation, and movement, so the frontal lobes have emerged as the highest report-and-control center for the emotions."[14] Thus evolutionarily recent and archaic patterns of innervation interarticulate, and the frontal lobes are pliant to conditioning while the limbic system is quite resistant.

Paul MacLean's work and related studies by Jason Brown raise the question neatly formed by Burhoe:

What is the role of the brain as an organ for the appropriate mixing of genetic and cultural information in the production of mental, verbal, or organic behavior?

Burhoe raises further important questions:

To what extent is the lower brain, including the limbic system and its behavior (to continue the metaphor), "on a very short leash" under the control of the genotype? (Konner uses the term genetically "hard wired.") In other words is genetic inheritance a definitive influence here?

The corollary would seem to run as follows:

To what extent is the upper brain, especially the neocortex, which is the area responsible in mammals for coordination and for higher mental abilities, on a longer leash in terms of control by the genotype or genome, the fundamental constitution of the organism in terms of its hereditary factors?

Does socioculturally transmitted information *take over* control in humankind and, if so, what are the limits, if any, to its control?

Does the genotype take a permanent back seat, and is social conditioning now all in all?

The picture thus built up for me was of a kind of *dual control* leading to what Burhoe calls a series of symbiotic coadaptations between what might be called culturetypes and genotypes. MacLean's hypothesis about the anatomical relations of the frontal lobes to the limbic system is certainly suggestive here. Subsequently, MacLean went further and gave us his model of the "triune brain." (As we shall see later, J.P. Henry and P.M. Stephens have recently argued that the dominant or left cerebral hemisphere represents a fourth and phylogenetically most recent system peculiar to our species.[15])

According to his model, MacLean sees us as possessing three brains in one, rather than conceiving of the brain as a unity. Each has a different phylogenetic history, each has its own distinctive organization and make-up, although they are interlinked by millions of interconnections, and each has its own special intelligence, its own sense of time and space, and its own motor functions.[16] MacLean postulates that the brain evolved in three stages, producing parts of the brain which are still actively with us though modified and intercommunicating.

The Instinctual Brain. The first to evolve is the *reptilian brain.* This is the brain stem, an upward growth of the spinal cord and the most primitive part of the brain, which we share with all vertebrate creatures and which has remained remarkably unchanged throughout the myriads of years of evolution. In lizards and birds this brain is the dominant and controlling circuitry. It contains nuclei which control processes vital to the sustenance of life (i.e., the cardiovascular and respiratory systems). Whereas we can continue to exist without large portions of our cerebral hemispheres, without our reptilian brain we would be dead!

What MacLean did was to show that this "structure" or "level," as some term the reptilian brain, whether in reptiles, birds, or mammals, is not only concerned with control of movement, but also with the storage and control of what is called "instinctive behavior"--the fixed action patterns and innate releasing mechanisms so often written about by the ethologists, the genetically preprogrammed perceptual-motor sequences such as emotional displays, territorial defense behaviors, and nest-building. According to

Brown, reptilian consciousness at the sensory-motor level is centered on the body itself and not differentiated from external space; yet it constitutes, I suppose, a preliminary form of consciousness.

The reptilian brain also has nuclei which control the reticular activating system, which is responsible for alertness and the maintenance of consciousness. It is a regulator or integrator of behavior, a kind of traffic control center for the brain. Reptiles and birds, in which the *corpus striatum* seems to be the most highly developed part of the brain, have behavioral repertoires consisting of stereotyped behaviors and responses; a lizard turning sideways and displaying its dewlap as a threat, or a bird repeating again and again the same territorial song. I am not suggesting that mammals have no such behavior--clearly many have much--but rather that birds and reptiles have little else.

The Emotional Brain. MacLean's "second brain" is the one he calls the *palaeo-mammalian* or "old mammalian brain." This seems to have arisen with the evolution of the earliest mammals, the monotremata, marsupials, and simpler placentals such as rodents. It is made up of those subcortical structures known as the midbrain, the most important components of which are the limbic system, including the hypothalamus (which contains centers controlling homeostatic mechanisms associated with heat, thirst, satiety, sex, pain and pleasure, and emotions of rage and fear), and the pituitary gland (which controls and integrates the activities of all the endocrine glands in the body).

The old mammalian brain differs from the reptilian brain generally in that it is, as the neuroanatomist James Papez defines it, "the *stream of feeling*," while the older "level" is the "*stream of movement.*" The hypothalamic and pituitary systems are homeostatic mechanisms *par excellence*; they maintain normal, internal stability in an organism by coordinating the responses of the organ systems that compensate for environmental changes.

Later we shall refer to such equilibrium-maintaining systems as "trophotropic," literally, "responding to the 'nourishing' (*trophe*) maintenance of organic systems," "keeping them going," as opposed to the "ergotropic" or aroused state of certain systems when they do "work" (*ergon*), "put themselves out," so to speak. These trophotropic systems, in

Stevens's words,

> not only maintain a critical and supremely sensitive control of hormone levels [hormones, of course, being substances formed in some organ of the body, usually a gland, and carried by a body fluid to another organ or tissue, where it has a specific effect], but also balance hunger against satiation, sexual desire against gratification, thirst against fluid retention, sleep against wakefulness. By this evolutionary stage, the primitive mammalian, the major emotions, fear and anger, have emerged, together with their associated behavioral responses of flight or fight. Conscious awareness is more in evidence and behavior is less rigidly determined by instincts, though these are still very much apparent. The areas concerned with these emotions and behaviors lie in the limbic system, which includes the oldest and most primitive part of the newly evolving cerebral cortex-the so-called *palaeocortex*. . . . In all mammals, including homo sapiens, the midbrain is a structure of the utmost complexity, controlling the psychophysical economy and many basic responses and attitudes to the environment. An animal deprived of its cerebral cortex can still find its way about, feed itself, slake its thirst, and avoid painful stimuli, but it has difficulty in attributing function or "meaning" to things: a natural predator will be noticed, for example, but not apparently perceived as a threat. Thus, accurate perception and the attribution of meaning evidently requires the presence of the cerebral hemispheres.[17]

The Cognitive Brain. The *neo-mammalian* or "new mammalian" brain, the third in MacLean's model, corresponds to "the stream of thought" proposed by Papez and achieves its culmination in the complex mental functions of the human brain. Structurally, it is the *neocortex* -- the outer layer of brain tissue or that part of the cerebrum which is rich in nerve-cell bodies and synapses. Some estimate there to be 10,000 million cells[10]. Functionally, it is responsible for cognition and sophisticated perceptual processes as opposed to instinctive and affective behavior. Further quesions are triggered by MacLean's model of the triune brain.

For example, how does it fit with Freud's model of the id, ego, and superego, with Carl Jung's model of the collective unconscious and archetypes, with neo-Darwinian theories of selection, and especially with cross-cultural anthropological studies and historical studies in comparative religion?

One might further ask with Burhoe: to what extent is it true that human feelings, hopes, and fears of what is most sacred are a necessary ingredient in generating decisions and motivating their implementation? This question is connected with the problem of whether it is true that such information is necessarily filtered through the highly genetically programmed areas in the lower brain, the brain stem, and the limbic systems.   Further   questions now arise. For example, if ritualization, as discussed by Huxley, Lorenz, and other ethologists, has a biogenetic foundation, while meaning has a neocortical learned base, does this mean that creative processes, those which generate new cultural knowledge, might result from a coadaptation, perhaps in the ritual process itself, of genetic and cultural information?

We also can ask whether the neocortex is the seat of programs largely structured by the culture through the transmission of linguistic and other symbol systems to modify the expression of genetic programs.   How far, we might add, do these higher symbols, including those of religion and ritual, derive their meaning and force for action from their association with earlier established neural levels of animal ritualization? I will discuss this later in connection with my field data on Central African ritual symbols.

HEMISPHERIC LATERALIZATION

Before I examine some recent conjectures about the consequences for the study of religion of a possible coadaptation of cultures and gene pools, I should say something about the "lateralization" (the division into left and right) of the cerebral hemispheres and the division of control functions between the left and right hemispheres.

The work of the surgeons P.Vogel, J.Bogen, and their associates at the California Institute of Technology in the early sixties, in surgically separating the left hemisphere from the right hemisphere to control epilepsy by cutting the connections between the two, particularly the inch-long, quarter-inch thick bundle of fibers called the *corpus callosum*, led to the devising of a number of techniques by R.W.Sperry (who won a Nobel Prize in 1981), Michael Gazzaniga, and others, which gained unambiguous evidence about the roles assumed by each hemisphere in their patients. In 1979, an important book appeared, *The Spectrum of Ritual*, edited and partly authored by Eugene G. d'Aquili, Charles D. Laughlin, and John McManus.[18]

In an excellent overview of the literature on ritual trance from the neurophysiological perspective, Barbara Lex summarizes the findings of current research on hemispheric lateralization. She writes: "In most human beings, the left cerebral hemisphere functions in the production of speech, as well as in linear, analytic thought, and also assesses the duration of temporal units, processing information sequentially. In contrast, the specializations of the right hemisphere comprise spatial and tonal perception, recognition of patterns--including those constituting emotion and other states in the internal milieu--and holistic, synthetic thought, but its linguistic capability is limited and the temporal capacity is believed absent. Specific acts involved complementary shifts between the functions of the two hemispheres."[19]

Howard Gardner, following Gazzaniga, suggests that

at birth we are all split-brained individuals. This may be literally true, since the corpus callosum which connects the hemispheres appears to be nonfunctional at birth. Thus, in early life, each hemisphere appears to participate in all of learning. It is only when, for some unknown reason, the left side of the brain takes the lead in manipulating objects, and the child begins to speak, that the first signs of asymmetry are discernible. At this time the corpus callosum is gradually beginning to function. For a number of years, learning of diverse sorts appears to occur in both hemispheres, but there is a gradual shift of dominant motor functions to the left hemisphere, while visual-spatial functions are presumably migrating to the right. . . . The division of labor grows increasingly marked, until, in the post-adolescent period, each hemisphere becomes incapable of executing the activities that the other hemisphere dominates, either because it no longer has access to its early learning, or because early traces have begun to atrophy through disuse.[20]

d'Aquili and Laughlin hold that both hemispheres operate in solving problems "via a mechanism of mutual inhibition controlled at the brain stem level." The world "is approached by a rapid functional alternation of each hemisphere. One is, as it were, flashed on, then turned off; the second flashed on, then turned off. The rhythm of this process and the predominance of one side or the other may account for various cognitive styles [one thinks of Pascal's contrast between 'l'esprit de geometrie' and 'l'esprit de finesse'], from the extremely analytic and scientific to the extremely artistic and synthetic."[21] These authors and Lex then make an

interesting attempt to link the dual functioning of the hemispheres with
W.R.Hess' model of the dual functioning of what are termed the ergotropic
and trophotropic systems within the central nervous system, as a way of
exploring and explaining phenomena reported in the study of ritual behavior
and meditative states.[22]

Let me explain these terms.

As its derivation from the Greek *ergon* ("work") suggests, ergotropic is
related to any energy-expending process within the nervous system. It
consists not only of the sympathetic nervous system, which governs
arousal states and fight or flight responses, but also such processes as
increased heart rate, blood pressure, sweat secretion as well as increased
secretion of catabolic hormones, epinephrine (a hormone secreted by the
medulla of the adrenal gland, which stimulates the heart and increases
muscular strength and endurance) and other stimulators. Generally
speaking, the ergotropic system affects behavior in the direction of
arousal, heightened activity, and emotional responsiveness, suggesting
such colloquialisms as "warming up" and "getting high."

The trophotropic system (*trophe*, in Greek, means nourishment--here the
idea is of system-sustaining) includes not only the parasympathetic
nervous system, which governs basic vegetative and homeostatic
functions, but also any central nervous system process that maintains the
baseline stability of the organism, for example, reduction in heart rate,
blood pressure, sweat secretion, pupillary constriction as well as
increased secretion of insulin, estrogens, androgens, and so on. Briefly,
the trophotropic system makes for inactivity, drowsiness, sleep "cooling
down" and trance-like states.[23]

Developing the work of Hess, d'Aquili and Laughlin propose an
extended model "according to which the minor or nondominant hemisphere
[usually the right hemisphere] is identified with the trophotropic or baseline
energy state system, and the dominant or major hemisphere [usually the
left] that governs analytical verbal and causal thinking is identified with the
ergotropic or energy-expending system."[24] They present evidence which
suggests that when either the ergotropic or trophotropic system is
hyperstimulated, there results a "spillover" into the opposite system after
"three stages of tuning," often by "driving behaviors" employed to facilitate

ritual trance. They also use the term "rebound" from one system to the other; they find that when the left hemisphere is stimulated beyond a certain threshold, the right hemisphere is also stimulated.

In particular, they postulate that the rhythmic activity of ritual, aided by sonic, visual, photic, and other kinds of "driving," may lead in time to simultaneous maximal stimulation of both systems, causing ritual participants to experience what the authors call "positive, ineffable affect." They also use Freud's term "oceanic experience," as well as "yogic ecstasy," also the Christian term *unio mystica*, an experience of the union of those cognitively discriminated opposites, typically generated by binary, digital left-hemispherical ratiocination. I suppose one might also use the Zen term *satori* (the integrating flash), and one could add the Quakers' "inner light," Thomas Merton's "transcendental consciousness," and the yogic *samadhi*.[25]

d'Aquili and Laughlin believe that though the end point of simultaneous strong discharge of both the ergotropic and trophotropic systems is the same in meditation and ritual, the former begins by intensely stimulating the trophotropic system through techniques for reducing thought and desire in order to maintain "an almost total baseline homeostasis."[26] This results in "spillover" to the ergotropic side, and eventually to strong excitation of both systems. Ritual, on the other hand, involves initial ergotropic excitation.

The authors have previously speculated that *causal* thinking arises from the reciprocal interconnections of the inferior parietal lobule and the anterior convexity of the frontal lobes, particularly on the dominant, usually left side, and is an inescapable human propensity. They call this brain nexus "the causal operator" and claim that it "grinds out the initial terminus or first cause of any strip of reality."[27] They argue that "gods, powers, spirits, personified forces, or any other causative ingredients are automatically generated by the causal operator."[28]   Untoward events particularly cry out for a cause. Hence "human beings have *no choice* but to construct myths to explain their world," to orient themselves "in what often appears to be a capricious universe." Cause-seeking is "inherent in the obligatory functioning of the neural structures."

We are, indeed, back, via neurobiology it would seem, to Aristotle's "first cause that is uncaused" or "Prime Mover unmoved"! We humans cannot do otherwise than postulate first causes to explain what we observe. They write, "since it is highly unlikely that humankind will ever know the first cause of every strip of reality observed, it is highly probable that humankind will always create gods, powers, demons, or other entities as first causes."[29]

Myths present problems to the verbal analytic consciousness. Claude Levi-Strauss has made us familiar with some of these problems: life and death, good and evil, mutability and an unchangeable "ground of being," the one and the many, freedom and necessity, and a few other perennial "posers."[30] Myths attempt to explain away such logical contradictions, but puzzlement remains at the cognitive left-hemispherical level. d'Aquili and Laughlin argue that *ritual* is often performed situationally to resolve problems posed by myth to the analytic verbalizing consciousnes. This is because like all other animals, humanity attempts to master the environmental situation by means of motor behavior, in this case ritual, a mode going back into its phylogenetic past and involving repetitive motor, visual, and auditory driving stimuli, kinetic rhythms, repeated prayers, mantras, and chanting, which strongly activate the ergotropic system.[31]

Ergotropic excitation is appropriate because the problem is presented in the "mythical" analytical mode, which involves binary thinking, mediations, and causal chains arranging both concepts and percepts in terms of antinomies or polar dyads. These are mainly left-hemispheric properties and connect up, in the authors' view, with the augmented sympathetic discharges mentioned earlier: increased heart rate, blood pressure, sweat secretion, pupilary dilation, increased secretion of catabolic hormones, and so on. If excitation continues long enough the trophotropic system is triggered too, with mixed discharges from both sides, resulting often in ritual trance. Lex writes that "driving techniques [also] facilitate right-hemisphere dominance, resulting in gestalt, timeless, nonverbal experiences, differentiated and unique when compared with left-hemisphere functioning or hemisphere alternation."[32]

One solution, if it can so be termed, of the Sphinxian riddles posed by myth, according to d'Aquili and Laughlin, is that "during certain ritual and meditation states, logical paradoxes or the awareness of polar opposites as presented in myth appear simultaneously, *both* as antinomies and as unified wholes" (italics added).[33] There is an ecstatic state and a sense of union, brief in ritual, prolonged in meditation, where culturally transmitted techniques and intense personal discipline sustain the peak experience. One is aware of paradox, but rejoices in it, reminding one of Soren Kierkegaard's joyous celebration of the paradox of the cross as the heart of Christianity.

The problem, therefore, is resolved in d'Aquili and Laughlin's view not at the cognitive, left-hemispheric level but directly by an experience which is described by the authors as ineffable, that is, literally beyond verbal expression. Presumably the frequent embodiment or embedment of the myth in the ritual scenario, either verbally in prayer or song, or nonverbally in dramatic action or visual symbolism, continues to arouse within the ritual context the "cognitive ergotropic functions of the dominant hemisphere."[34] If the experiences of participants have been rewarding--and ritual devices and symbolic actions may well tune a wide range of variant somatic, mental, and emotional propensities in a wide range of individuals (amounting to the well-known redundancy of ritual with its many sensory codes and multivocal symbols)--faith in the cosmic and moral orders contained in the myth cycle will obviously be reinforced. A.J. Mandell argues, in "Toward a Psychobiology of Transcendence," that "transcendent consciousness, suggested by William James to be the primary religious experience, is a neurochemically and neurophysiologically definable state, an imperturbable hypomania . . . blissful, empathic, and creative."[35]

PLAY

It is clear that all this refers to the serious work of the brain as distinct from "play." Full ergotropic, left-hemisphere behavior tends to be dramatic, agonistic behavior. I am not too happy about some authors' tendency to localize mental functions somewhat specifically in cortical regions rather than in interrelational networks, but there does seem to be, broadly speaking, something in the division of labor between the hemispheres, in the different work they do.

The term "ergotropic," as we have seen, is derived from the Greek *eron*, "work" and *tropos*, "a true, way, manner." It represents the autonomic nervous system in the mode of work, as a sympathetic subsystem, whereas the trophotropic system (from the Greek *trophe*, "food, nourishment") represents the autonomic nervous system in the mode of sustentation, as a parasympathetic subsystem responsible for producing a balance of functions and of chemical composition within an organism. This, too, is a kind of diffused work, less focused and mobilized, less intense than the ergotropic functions.

But where does "play" play a part in this model? One seldom sees much mention of play in connection with brain neurophysiology. Yet play is a kind of dialectical dancing partner of ritual, and ethologists give play behavior equal weight with ritualization. d'Aquili and Laughlin hardly mention the word.

The hemispheres clearly have their *work* to do, and the autonomic nervous system has its *work* to do. The one [i.e., the hemispheres] makes for social dramas, the other [i.e., the autonomic system] for social routines. Whether normally functioning or intensely stimulated, the components of the central nervous system seem to have clearly assigned, responsible, interdependent roles to perform. One might speculate that at the neurobiological level play might have something to do with the sensitization of neural structures of an interface type, like the limbic system at the core of the brain, which is known to be intimately associated with the expression of emotion, particularly with the experience of pleasure, pain, and anger. We will return to this later.

Transient. As I see it, play does not fit in anywhere particular; it is a transient and is recalcitrant to localization, to placement, to fixation--a joker in the neuroanthropological act. Johann Huizinga, and Karl Groos before him, dubbed it a free activity, but Huizinga, Roger Caillois, and many afterwards have commented on the enclosure of playing within frames of "arbitrary, imperative, and purposely tedious conventions."[36]

Playfulness is a volatile, sometimes dangerously explosive essence, which cultural institutions seek to bottle or contain in the vials of games of competition, chance, and strength, in modes of simulation such as theater, and in controlled disorientation, from roller coasters to dervish dancing-- Caillois' "ilinx" or vertigo. Play could be termed dangerous because it may subvert the left-right hemispheric regular switching involved in maintaining social order. Most definitions of play involve notions of disengagement, of free-wheeling, of being out of mesh with the serious, "bread-and-butter," let alone "life-and-death" processes of production, social control, "getting and spending," and raising the next generation.

The neuronic energies of play, as it were, lightly skim over the cerebral cortices, sampling rather than partaking of the capacities and functions of the various areas of the brain. As Don Handelman and Gregory Bateson have written, that is possibly why play can provide a metalanguage (since to be "meta" is to be both beyond and between) and emit metamessages about so many and varied human propensities, and thus provide, as Handelman has said, "a very wide *range* of commentary on the social order."[37] Play can be everywhere and nowhere, imitate anything, yet be identified with nothing.

Play is "transcendent" (to use Edward Norbeck's term), though only just so, brushing the surfaces of more specialized neural organizations rather than existing apart from them or looking down from a godlike height on them. Play is the supreme *bricoleur* [indirect or unexpected move] of frail transient constructions, like a caddis worm's case or a magpie's nest in nature. Its metamessages are composed of a potpourri of apparently incongruous elements: products of both hemispheres are juxtaposed and intermingled. Passages of seemingly wholly rational thought jostle in a Joycean or surrealist manner with passages filleted of all syntactical connectedness. Yet, although "spinning loose" as it were, the wheel of play reveals to us (as Mihaly Csikszentmihalyi has argued[38]) the possibility of changing our goals and, therefore, the restructuring of what our culture states to be reality.

Liminal. You may have guessed that play is, for me, a liminal or liminoid mode, essentially "elusive"--a term derived from the Latin *ex* for "away" plus *ludere*, "to play"; hence the Latin verb *eludere* acquired the sense of "to take away from someone at play," thus "to cheat" or "to deceive." As such, play cannot be pinned down by formulations of left-hemisphere thinking--such as we all must use in keeping with the rhetorical conventions of academic discourse. Play is neither ritual action nor meditation, nor is it merely vegetative, nor is it just "having fun"; it also has a good deal of ergotropic and agonistic aggressivity in its odd-jobbing, *bricolage* style.

As Roger Abrahams has remarked, play makes fun of people, things, ideas, ideologies, institutions, and structures; it is partly a mocker as well as a mimic and a tease, arousing hope, desire, or curiosity without always giving satisfaction.[39] It is as much a reflexive interrupter as an inciter of what Csikzsentmihalyi has described as flow states. Like many Trickster figures in myths (or should these be"antimyths," if myths are dominantly left-hemisphere speculations about causality?), play can deceive, betray, beguile, delude (another derivation of *ludere* "to play"), dupe, hoodwink, bamboozle, and gull--as that category of players known as "cardsharps" well know! Actually, Walter Skeat derives the English verb "play" itself from the Anglo-Saxon *plegian*, "to strike or clap"; the Anglo-Saxon noun *plega* means not only "a game, sport," but also, commonly, "a fight, battle" (here again with ergotropic implications).

Play, as stated earlier, draws its materials from all aspects of experience, both from the interior milieu and the external environment. Yet, as Handelman writes, it has no instrumental potency; it is, we might put it, a "shadow warrior," or *Kagemusha*.[40] For this very reason, its range of metacommunication is great; nothing human escapes it. Still, in its own oxymoronic style, it has a dangerous harmlessness, for it has no fear. Its lightness and fleetingness protect it. It has the powers of the weak, an infantine audacity in the face of the strong. To ban play is, in fact, to massacre the innocents. If humanity is a neotenic species [i.e., capable of becoming sexually mature in a preadult state], play is perhaps its most appropriate mode of performance.

Educative. More than that, it is clear, as Konner points out, play is educative. The most intelligent and long-lived mammals have developed it most fully--the primates, the cetecea, and the terrestrial and aquatic carnivores. "It serves the functions of exercise, of learning about the environment and conspecifics, and, in some species, of sharpening or even acquiring fundamental subsistence and social skills." Opportunity for observation of a task in the frame of "play," while or before trying to do it, has been "shown to improve the rate of learning it in a number of mammals in experimental settings."[41]

Play, then, is probably related to the higher cerebral centers--not forgetting its connection also with arousal and pleasure--particularly in rough and tumble games, where the limbic system is clearly engaged.

Yet serious violence is usually controlled objectively and culturally by rules and subjectively by inhibitory mechanisms of perhaps a different type from the Freudian superego or ego-defense mechanisms, although perhaps play does defend consciousness from some of the more dangerous unconscious drives.

As-If Subjunctivity. Finally, play like other liminal phenomena, is in the subjunctive mood. What does this mean?

The subjunctive designates a verb form or set of forms used in English to express a contingent or hypothetical action. A contingent action is one that may occur but that is not likely or intended. Subjunctivity is possibility. It refers to what may or might be. It is also concerned with supposition, conjecture, and assumption, with the domain of "as-if" rather than "as-is". (Hence, there must be a good deal of left-hemispheric activity in play, linguistic and conceptual activity, but done for its own sweet sake.) "As-is" refers to the world of what culture recognizes as factuality, the world of cause and effect, expressed in the "indicative mood"--which indicates that the denoted act or condition is an objective fact. This is *par excellence* the world of the left cerebral hemisphere.

The world of the right hemisphere is, nevertheless, not identical with the world of play either, for its gestalt grasp of things holds for it the sense of a higher reality, beyond speculation or supposition. Play is a light-winged, light-fingered sceptic, a Puck between the day world of Theseus and the night world of Oberon, putting into question the cherished assumptions of both hemispheres, both worlds. There is no sanctity in play; it is irreverent and is protected in the world of power struggles by its apparent irrelevance and clown's garb. It is almost as though the limbic system were itself endowed with higher intelligence, in a kind of carnivalesque reversal of the indicative situation.

However, since play deals with the whole gamut of experience, both contemporary and stored in culture, it can be said perhaps to play a similar role in the social construction of reality as mutation and variation in organic evolution. Its flickering knowledge of all experience possible to the nervous system and its detachment from that system's localizations enable play to perform the liminal function of ludic recombination of familiar elements in unfamiliar and often quite arbitrary patterns. Yet it may happen that a light, play-begotten pattern for living or social structuring, once thought whimsical, under conditions of extreme social change may prove an adaptive, "indicative mood" design for living.

Here early theories that play arises from excess energy have renewed relevance. Part of that surplus fabricates ludic critiques of presentness, of the status quo, undermining it by parody, satire, irony, slapstick; part of it subverts past legitimacies and structures; part of it is mortgaged to the future in the form of a store of possible cultural and social structures, ranging from the bizarre and ludicrous to the utopian and idealistic, one of which may root in a future reality, allowing the serious dialectic of left- and right-hemispherical functions to propel individuals and groups of individuals from earth to heaven and heaven to earth within a new indicative mood frame. But it was the slippery Trickster who enabled them to do it, and he/she modestly, in Jacques Derrida's ludic words, "erases the trace."

The experiments of James Olds and Peter Milner, at the California Institute of Technology from 1953 onwards, on stimulating (by implanted electrodes) the hypothalamus of the brains of rats, including the parts radiating from the hypothalamus like spokes (neural pathways to the olfactory and limbic systems, the septal areas, amygdala, etc.), seem to have a bearing on the pleasures of play, but I have not followed up this avenue of enquiry.[42]

FURTHER QUESTIONS ON THE BRAIN: RELIGION, ARCHETYPES, AND DREAMING

By indirections we seek out directions. This long digression on hemispherical lateralization, play, and cultural subjunctivity brings me back to some of Burhoe's questions that have been vexing me.

Religion. One is: How does this picture of brain functioning and of the central nervous system accord with distinctive features of the varied religious systems that have survived to this point in time and exerted paradigmatic influence on major societies and cultures?

Here we could profitably compare Eastern and Western religions and their variations. Can some be described as emphasizing in their cosmologies, theologies, rituals, meditative techniques, pilgrimages, and so on, right-hemispherical properties or left-hemispherical dominance? Do some emphasize rituals, while others stress modes of meditation and contemplation as their central processes of worship? Again how does this picture fit with descriptions of the varieties of religious experience that have been noted by William James and his successors? Would it be a fruitful enterprise to foster experimental work on the varied genetic and experiential structurings of human brains which might throw light on aspects of religious experience and motivation? We will take a brief look later in this essay at some interesting guesswork by Jungians in relation to this problem.

Conversely, can we illuminate, through cross-cultural comparison, the capacity of culturally shaped systems of ritual, symbols, myths, and rational structures to produce viable types of religious experience in the genetically varied population of brains? Here much more detailed descriptive work in the study of different kinds of ritual in a single religious system, as well as cross cultural and transhistorical studies of ritual systems, is imperative.

So many questions; so few answers. But we can only do fruitful research if we first ask the right questions.

Naturally, the findings of neurophysiologists have provoked many speculations from members of other disciplines not directly concerned with the brain and its workings. The notion of the triune brain propounded by MacLean, for instance, has encouraged Jungian psychologists to claim that a neurological basis has been found for the collective unconscious and its archetypes. One Jungian, Anthony Stevens, has been impressed by the work of P.Flor-Henry and of G.E.Schwartz, R.J.Davidson, and F.Maer.[43] The latter showed that human emotional responses are dependent on neuronal pathways linking the limbic system of the midbrain (the old mammalian brain) with parietal and frontal areas of the right hemisphere. Flor-Henry found that this whole complicated right-hemisphereic/limbic affectional system is under the surveillance and control of the left, I repeat, of the *left* frontal cortex.

This lends additional testimony to the view that the left hemisphere (via the corpus callosum or the large cable of nerve fibers which connect the two cerebral hemispheres, functioning to transmit information between the hemispheres and to coordinate their activities) can repress or inhibit the activities, especially the emotionally toned activities (which are the vital concern of psychiatrists), of the right. In my discussion of the possible neuronal base of play, you will recall, I guessed at a connection between the midbrain and human upper brain. If Flor-Henry is correct in supposing a left-hemisphere inhibiting effect, might not the propensity to play result from a temporary relaxation of the inhibitory effect, perhaps through the focused cultural means of framing and arousal?

Archetypes. All this leads Stevens to speculate rather interestingly about the relationship of various psychical processes recognized by depth psychology to what is known about the neurophysiology of the brain.

His views also bear on the questions I have been raising about the possible nature of religion as at once a supergenetic and a superindividual agency developed from the coadaptation or integration of two semiautonomous systems. These are, in Burhoe's terms, first, basic genetic information and its biological expression, particularly in the lower levels of the brain, whose genetic programs are not so very different from those in protohuman hominids, and, second, the specifically human generation of a living sociocultural system where the learning powers of the upper brain radically modify the common human gene pool, resulting in enormous cultural and phenotypical variation, that is, variation in manifest characteristics.

Stevens argues, "while it may well be that psychic processes belonging to the personal 'Freudian' unconscious proceed in the right hemisphere, it seems probable that Jung was right when he guessed that the archetypal systems, if they could be given a local habitation and a name, must have their neuronal substrate located in the phylogenetically much older parts of the brain."[44]

For those who are unfamiliar with Jungian terminology, archetypes (according to Stevens's definition) are "innate neuropsychic centers possessing the capacity to initiate, control, and mediate the common behavioral characteristics and typical experiences of all human beings irrespective of cultural differences."[45] Jung himself, who rejected the view that humankind was a blank slate or a *tabula rasa* on which experience was prenatally[46] and postnatally inscribed, held that our species is *born* with numerous predispositions for perceiving, feeling, behaving, and conceptualizing in particular ways.

As Jung put it:

> There is no human experience, nor would experience be possible at all without the intervention of a subjective aptitude. What is this subjective aptitude? Ultimately it consists of an innate psychic structure which allows [humanity] to have experiences of this kind. Thus the whole nature of the human male presupposes woman, both physically and spiritually. His system is tuned in to woman from the start, just as it is prepared for a quite definite world where there is water, light, air, salt, carbohydrates, etc. The form of the world into which he is born is already inborn in him as a virtual image. Likewise parents, wife, children, birth, and death are inborn in him as virtual images, as psychic aptitudes. These *a priori* categories have by nature a collective character; they are images of parents, wife, and children in general, and are not individual predestinations. [This is perhaps Jung's clearest formulation of what he means by archetypes.] We must therefore think of these images as lacking in solid content, hence as unconscious. They only acquire solidity, influence, and eventual consciousness in the encounter with empirical facts which touch the unconscious aptitude and quicken it to life. They are, in a sense, the deposits of all our ancestral experiences, but they are not the experiences themselves.[47]

Archetypes manifest themselves subjectively in such things as dreams, fantasies, writing, poetry, painting and objectively in such collective representations as myths, rituals, and cultural symbols--and in many other modalities. Jung speaks of the Family archetype, the Feminine archetype, the God archetype, the Hero archetype, the Mother archetype, the Masculine archetype, the Wise Old Man archetype, using capital letters to distinguish them from the identically named roles occupied by actual, historical individuals.

Stevens thinks it is impossible to locate any of the archetypes in any precise neurological fashion. Each must have "an extremely complex and widely ramifying neurological substrate involving millions of neurones in the brain stem and limbic system (the instinctive or biological pole) and *both* cerebral hemispheres (the psychic or spiritual pole)."[48] However, E. Rossi another Jungian psychologist, argues that it is the right hemisphere which principally processes archetypal components, since "Jung's concepts of archetype, collective, unconscious, and symbol are more closely associated with the use of the imagery, gestalt, and visuospatial characteristics of right hemisphere functioning."[49] Rossi also insists that, although the archetype is an imprint or pattern--perhaps a "trace"--which exists independently of the conscious ego, it constantly comes under left hemispheric processing in the form of words, concepts, and language. But when this happens the archetypes, he writes, "take their color from the individual consciousness in which they happen to appear."[50] Thus they are, so to speak, superficially denatured and clothed in the vestments provided by individual memory and cultural conditioning.

Dreaming. It is because of the difficulty of translating right-hemispherical processes into the logical, verbal formulations of the left brain that some emissions into ego consciousness of archetypal images are perceived as numinous, awesome and mysterious or uncanny, preternaturally strange. They seem to be clad in primordial authority undetermined by anything known or learned. Henry and Stephens consider that both hemispheres are able to suppress communication from the limbic system.[51] We have seen how the left hemisphere may inhibit communication from the right.

Henry and Stephens believe that psychic health and personality integration depend as much on the maintenance of open communication between limbic system and cortex as on interhemispheric communication. *They suggest that the neurophysiological function of dreaming is to facilitate integration of processes occurring in the limbic system with those of the cerebral hemisphere.* This would fit well with Jung's views as well as with the French sleep expert Michel Jouvet's findings that the low voltage, high frequency EEG waves characteristic of dreaming sleep originate in the brain stem and spread upward through the midbrain to the cortex--perhaps bringing information from various levels of the unconscious.[52]

Perhaps dreams, like the ritual symbols I have analyzed, are laminated, accreting semantic layers, as they move from brain stem through limbic system to the right hemisphere before final processing or editing by left-hemispheric processes.

THE COMPOSITE BRAIN AND THE BIPOLAR SYMBOL

These findings are interesting when related to my fieldwork among the Ndembu, a matrilineal society of northwest Zambia, during the 1950s. I discovered that what I called dominant or pivotal symbols in their ritual processes were not only possessors of multiple meanings but also had the property of polarization.

For example, a tree which exuded a milky white latex was the dominant symbol of the girls' puberty ritual (the novice was laid under a consecrated "milk tree" wrapped in a blanket, where she had to lie motionless throughout a whole long day while initiated women danced around her and the tree). The whole milk tree site, almost *mise-en-scene* was called *ifwilu*, which means "place-of-dying," for it was there that she died from her childhood. At this point she was separated from her own mother, who took a minimal part in the ritual. But the milk tree (*mudyi*) was intimately connected with motherhood.

I pieced together its many meanings from talking to many informants during many performances at which my wife and I were present, and have written about this research in several books, including *The Forest of Symbols* and *The Drums of Affliction*.[53] Briefly, the milk tree was said to "be" (more than merely to "represent") mother's milk, lactation, breasts, and nubility, at what could be called the physiological or orectic pole of its meaning. "Orectic" is a term used by philosophers, and was formerly quite popular among psychologists, meaning "of or characterized by appetite or desire."

But the milk tree also "was" the matrilineage of the girl novice; it was where the "ancestress slept, where they initiated her and another ancestress and then another down to the grandmother and the mother and ourselves the children. It is a place where our tribe (*muchidi*) began--and also the men in just the same way."[54] Thus it was more than a particular matrilineage; it was the principle of matriliny itself. It was even the whole Ndembu nation, one of whose distinctive features was its matrilineal organization. At some episodes of the long complex ritual, the milk tree was also said to stand for women and for womanhood.

Another meaning, indexical rather than iconic, represented the milk tree as the relationship between the novice and her own mother in that place and at that time. It indicated that the relationship would be transformed by the performative action, since the daughter was no longer a dependent child but would become, like her mother, a married woman after the ritual seclusion and the coming-out rites were over and was potentially a mother herself. I called this more abstract set of meanings the normative or ideological pole, since it referred to principles of social organization, social categories, and values.

The milk tree also has other denotations and connotations, but it has struck me recently that these layers of meaning might well relate to what is being discovered about the functions of the brain. The orectic pole, referring to physical mothering and lactation, and charged with desire--the novice's desire to be fully a woman, the desire of the mature women to add a recruit to their number, the desire of a lineage for replenishment, the future bridegroom's desire for the novice (represented by the insertion of an arrow presented by the bridegroom into the ground among the roots of the milk tree) and many other modalities of desire--the orectic pole, then, surely has some connection with the functions of the limbic system, the old mammalian brain.

This system MacLean calls the visceral brain because of its close connections to control centers for drive and emotion. Structures in the limbic system are believed to be the sites of action of many psychotropic drugs, including antipsychotic tranquilizers (elgl, Thorazine) and hallucinogens (elgl, LSD). In the ritual itself, with its powerful drumming and insurgent singing in which the women lampoon and deride the men, we observe ways of arousing the ergotropic system and the left-hemispheric functions of critical, linear thought. We can also see a triggering of the right-hemispheric apprehensions of pattern and holism by finally including the men in the ritual action and making them part of a scenario in which the novice is borne off to a newly made seclusion hut on the margin of the village, where she will undergo liminal instruction by female elders for many months, before "coming out" in a ritual which is also the precursor of her marriage.

Clearly, too, the normative pole of meaning including the references to matriliny, womanhood, tribal unity and continuity, and the mother-child bond, has connections with upper brain activities involving both hemispheres. One might speculate that the Jungian archetype of the Great Mother and the difficulty, resolved among the Ndembu by prolonged and sometimes painful initiation ritual, of separation from the archetypal power of the Great Mother is in some way connected with the milk tree symbolism and with the ritual behavior associated with it. It is interesting to me that a dominant symbol--every ritual system has several of them--should replicate in its structural and semantic make-up what are coming to be seen as key neurological features of the brain and central nervous system.

CONCLUSION

Does the new work on the brain further our species' self understanding?

Clearly an extreme ethological view of human society as rigidly genetically determined is as uninformative as an extreme behaviorist view of the human brain as a *tabula rasa* written on by experience. According to the extreme ecologists, we are "innately aggressive, acquisitive, nationalistic, capitalistic, and destructive."[55] Some of them announce our doom by overcrowding or urge the space race as a means of channelling aggressiveness. Some even give veiled approval to limited war or natural population control by drought, famine, or plague, as the means of securing ecological balance. Hence the vogue for doom talk about such inevitabilities as ecocide, population explosion, and innate aggressiveness. Surely, a middle path is possible.

Cannot we see those modalities of human perception and conceptualization, the lower brain and the upper brain, the archaic and recent systems of innervation as having been for at least several millions of years in active mutual confrontation?

It seems to me that *religion may be partly the product of humanity's intuitions of its dual interiority and the fruitful creative Spirit generated by the interplay of the gene pool, as the Ancient of Days, and the upper brain, as Logos*, to use the intuitive language of one historical religion, Christianity. The Filioque principle (the Spirit proceeding from the Father *and* the Son), Western Christians might say! Since culture is in one sense, to paraphrase Wilhelm Dilthey, objectivated and crystallized mentality

(Geist), it *may well be that some cultures reinforce one or another semiautonomous cerebral system at the expense of others through education and other modes of conditioning. This results in conflict between them or repression of one by another, instead of free interplay and mutual support-- what is sometimes called love.*

As you can see, I have been asking questions and making guesses in this paper rather than coming up with answers. My career focus mostly has been on the ritual process, a cultural phenomenon, more than on brain neuroanatomy and neurophysiology. But I am at least half convinced that there can be genuine dialogue between neurology and culturology, since both take into account the capacity of the upper brain for adaptability, resilience, learning, and symbolizing, in ways perhaps neglected by the ethologists *pur sang*, who seem to stop short in their thinking about ritualization at the more obviously genetically programmed behaviors of the lower brain. It is to the dialectic, and even contradiction at times, between the various semiautonomous systems of the developed [neocortex] and archaic structures of innervation [of the older cortex], particularly those of the human brain, that we should look for the formulation of testable hypotheses about the ritual process and its role as performing noetic functions in ways peculiar to itself, as a *sui generis* mode of knowing.

Let me conclude by reassuring those who may have obtained the impression that all I am saying is that ritual is nothing but the structure and functioning of the brain writ large, or that I am reducing ritual to cerebral neurology, that I am really speaking of a global population of brains inhabiting an entire world of inanimate and animate entities, a population whose members are incessantly communicating with one another through every physical and mental instrumentality. But if one considers the geology, so to speak, of the human brain and nervous system, we see represented in its strata--each layer still vitally alive--not dead like stone, the numerous pasts and presents of our planet.

Like Walk Whitman, we "embrace multitudes." And even our reptilian and palaeomammalian brains are human, linked in infinitely complex ways to the conditionable upper brain and kindling it with their powers. Each of us is a microcosm, related in the deepest ways to the whole life-history of that lovely deep blue globe, swirled over with the white whorls, first photographed by Edwin Aldrin and Neil Armstrong from their primitive space chariot, the work nevertheless of many collaborating human brains. The meaning of that living macrocosm may not only be found deep within us but also played from one mind to another as history goes on--with ever finer tuning--by the most sensitive and eloquent instrument of Gaea the Earth-spirit--the cerebral organ.

*An edited copy of the paper presented at a symposium on "Ritual in Human Adaptation" in Chicago on 12-13 November 1982, sponsored by the Institute on Religion in an Age of Science in association with the Center for Advanced Study in Religion and Science, the Chicago Theological Seminary, the Disciples Divinity House, and the Lutheran School of Theology at Chicago.

REFERENCES

1. Anthony Stevens, *Archetypes: A Natural History of the Self* (New York: Morrow, 1982), p.24.

2. Robin Fox, *Encounter with Anthropology* (New York: Harcourt Brace Jovanovich, 1973), p.13.

3. E.R. Leach, "Ritualization in Man in Relation to Conceptual and Social Development," in *A Discussion on Ritualization of Behaviours in Animals and Man*, ed. Julian Huxley, Philosophical Transactions of the Royal Society of London, series B., vol.251, Biological Sciences (London: Royal Society, 1966), p.403

4. Julian Huxley, "Introduction," in *A Discussion on Ritualization of Behaviours in Animals and Man*, ed. Julian Huxley, Philosophical Transactions of the Royal Society of London, series B., vol.251, Biological Sciences (London, Royal Society, 1966), p.250.

5. Ronald Grimes, *Beginnings in Ritual Studies* (Washington, D.C.: University Press of America, 1982), p.34.

6. Meyer Fortes, "Religious Premises and Logical Technique in Divinatory Ritual," in *A Discussion on Ritualization of Behaviours in Animals and Man*, ed. Julian Huxley, Philosophical Transactions of the Royal Society of London, series B., vol.251, Biological Sciences (London: Royal Society, 1966), p.411.

7. Ibid., p.413.

8. Leach, p.405.

9. Grimes, p.36.

10. Quoted in Melvin Konner, *The Tangled Wing: Biological Constraints on the Human Spirit* (New York: Holt, Rinehart, & Winston, 1982), p.147.

11. Ibid.

12. Ibid.

13. Walle Nauta elaborated this outlook in "The Problem of the Frontal Lobe: A Reinterpretation," *Journal of Psychiatric Research* 8 (1971):167-87.

14. Konner, p.147.

15. J.P. Henry and P.M. Stephens, *Stress, Health and the Social Environment* (New York: Springer-Verlag, 1977).

16. Paul D. MacLean, "Sensory and Perceptive Factors in Emotional Functions of the Triune Brain," in *Biological Foundations of Psychiatry*, ed. R.G. Grenell and S. Gabay, 2 vols. (New York: Raven Press, 1976), 1:177-98. See also idem, "A Triune Concept of the Brain and Behavior," in *The Hincks Memorial Lectures*, ed. T. Boag and D. Campbell (Toronto: University of Toronto Press, 1973), pp.6-66; "On the Evolution of Three Mentalities," *Man-Environment Systems* 5 (1975):213-24, reprinted in *New Dimensions in Psychiatry: A World View*, ed. S.Ariete and G. Chrzanowski, 2 vols. (New York: John Wiley & Sons, 1977), 2:305-28; and "Evolution of the Psychencephalon," *Zygon* 17 (June 1982): 187-211. Cf. J. Brown, *Mind, Brain, and Consciousness* (New York: Academic Press, 1977).

17. Stevens (n.1 above), pp.264-65.

18. Eugene G. d'Aquili et al., *The Spectrum of Ritual: A Biogenetic Structural Analysis* (New York: Columbia University Press, 1979).

19. Barbara Lex, "Neurobiology of Ritual Trance," in *The Spectrum of Ritual: A Biogenetic Structural Analysis*, ed. Eugene G. d'Aquili et al. (New York: Columbia University Press, 1979), p.125.

20. Howard Gardner, *The Shattered Mind* (New York: Vintage, 1975), p.386.

21. Eugene G. d'Aquili and Charles D. Laughlin, Jr., "The Neurobiology of Myth and Ritual," in *The Spectrum of Ritual: A Biogenetic Structural Analysis*, ed. Eugene G. d'Aquili et al. (New York: Columbia University Press, 1979), p.174.

22. W.R. Hess, *On the Relationship Between Psychic and Vegetative Functions* (Zurich: Schwabe, 1925).

23. E. Gellhorn and W.F. Kiely, "Mystical States of Consciousness: Neurophysiological and Clinical Aspects," *Journal of Mental and Nervous Diseases 154* (1972):339-405.

24. d'Aquili and Laughlin, p.175.

25. See Arnold J. Mandell, "Toward a Psychobiology of Transcendence," in *The Psychobiology of Consciousness*, ed. J.M. Davidson and J.R. Davidson (New York: Olenum, 1978), p.80.

26. d'Aquili and Laughlin, p.176.

27. Ibid., p.170.

28. Ibid.

29. Ibid., p.171.

30. C.Levi-Strauss, *Structural Anthropology* (New York: Anchor Books, 1963); idem, *The Savage Mind* (Chicago: University of Chicago Press, 1963); idem, *Mythologiques: Le cru et le cuit* (Paris: Plon, 1964).

31. d'Aquili and Laughlin, p.177.

32. Lex (n.19 above), p.146.

33. d'Aquili and Laughlin, p.176.

34. Ibid., p.177.

35. Mandell (n.25 above), p.1.

36. Roger Caillois, *Men, Play, and Games* (New York: Schocken Books, 1979), p.13.

37. Don Handelman, "Play and Ritual: Complementary Frames of Meta-communication," in *It's A Funny Thing, Humor*, ed. A.J. Chapman and H. Fort (London: Pergamon, 1977), p.189.

38. Mihaly Csikszentmihalyi, *Beyond Boredom and Anxiety* (San Francisco: Jossey-Bass, 1975).

39. Roger Abrahams, personal communication both in a letter and in an essay.

40. See Akira Kurasawa's film, *Kagemusha*.

41. Konner (n.10 above), pp.246-47.

42. James Olds, "Behavioral Studies of Hypothalamic Functions," in *Biological Foundations of Psychiatry*, ed. R. Grenell and S. Gabay, vol.1 (New York: Raven, 1976).

43. P. Flor-Henry, "Lateralized Temporal-Limbic Dysfunction and Psychopathology," *Annals of the New York Academy of Science 380* (1976):777-97; G.E. Schwartz, R.J. Davidson, and F. Maer, "Right Hemisphere Lateralization for Emotion in the Human Brain: Interaction with Cognition," *Science* 190 (1975):286-88.

44. Stevens (n.1 above), pp.265-66.

45. Ibid., p.296.

46. Experience begins in the womb, and child psychologists hold that communication between mother and child correlates with the development of neuronal pathways in the foetal brain. See for example Colwyn Trevarthen, "Cerebral Embryology and the Split Brain," in *Hemispheric Disconnection and Cerebral Function*, ed. M. Kinsbourne and W.L. Smith (Springfield, Ill.: Charles C. Thomas, 1974), pp.208-36.

47. Carl Jung, *Collected Works*, vol. 7, *Two Essays on Analytical Psychology* (Princeton, N.J.: Princeton University Press, 1972), para.300.

48. Stevens (n.1 above), p.266.

49. Cited in Stevens (n.1 above), p.266.

50. Ibid.

51, Henry and Stephens (n.15 above).

52. Michel Jouvet, "The Function of Dreaming: A Neurophysiologist's Point of View," in *Handbook of Psychology*, ed. M.S. Gazzaniga and C. Blakemore

(New York: Academic Press, 1975).

53. Victor Turner, *The Forest of Symbols* (Ithaca, N.Y.: Cornell University Press, 1967); idem, *The Drums of Affliction* (Oxford: Clarendon Press, 1968).

54. Turner, *Drums of Affliction*, pp.198-268.

55. A point well made by Steven Rose, *The Conscious Brain* (New York: Vintage Books, 1976), p.351.

Chapter Five

PSYCHOLOGY'S MENTALIST PARADIGM and
the RELIGION/SCIENCE TENSION*

R.W. Sperry
California Institute of Technology

ABSTRACT. Science traditionally has favored a strictly objective, value-free description of brain function and behavior that ultimately excludes freedom of will, conscious purpose, subjective value, morality, and other subjective phenomena that are vital to religion. The consequent incompatibility of science even with liberal theology no longer holds for psychology's new mentalist (cognitive) paradigm in which the formerly excluded subjective mental states now have become legitimate, ineliminable explanatory constructs as interactive emergent properties of brain processing. These mentalistic revisions invoke emergent forms of causal control that transform conventional scientific descriptions of both human and nonhuman nature, presenting a new fundamental philosophic position that integrates positivistic thought with phenomenology and opens the way for a consistent naturalistic foundation for both scientific and religious belief. It is suggested that the new mentalist outlook, which combines macro- with microdeterminism, represents a more valid determinist framework for all science.

Long-standing differences in the kinds of beliefs upheld by science and religion concerning the nature and origins of humankind and the universe and the kinds of forces in control go to the central foundations of human value priorities wherein are said to lie the sources, and possibly answers, to some of the most ominous problems of our times. It is a privilege and no small challenge to help explore these critical and timely issues.

As a scientist, my world outlook with regard both to human and nonhuman nature underwent a major conversion during the mid 1960s. Long-trusted principles in neuroscience and behaviorist doctrine had proclaimed a full account of brain function and behavior to be possible in strictly objective physicochemical and physiological terms, with no reference to conscious experience. The physiological account was taken to be complete within itself, leaving no place for conscious subjective

109

influences. These principles, which always had seemed to be airtight and irrefutable, were discovered to have a logical flaw or shortcoming and to be outweighed by a new "emergent interactionist" reasoning with wide application throughout nature (Popper, 1965/1972; Sperry, 1965).

A modified formula for mind-brain interaction was perceived in which conscious mental states, as emergent properties of brain processes, could interact functionally at their own level and also exert downward causal control over brain physiology in a supervenient sense. It meant a radical turnaround in accepted notions in science regarding the relation of the conscious mind to the physical brain. As a result, I renounced my earlier views in favor of a new *mentalist* position in which the traditionally rejected subjective mental qualities of inner experience were conceived to play an active, causal control role in conscious behavior and evolution.

SCIENTIFIC TURNABOUT ON CONSCIOUSNESS

The new reasoning was later presented to the National Academy of Sciences and to psychology and neuroscience (Bindra, 1970; Sperry, 1969, 1970). By the mid-1980s, mainstream psychology had also revised its earlier views concerning consciousness and the subjective, replacing long dominant behaviorist theory with a new mentalist or cognitive paradigm. This changeover, impelled by a large complex of cognitive, linguistic, computer, and related theoretic and sociologic developments (Chomsky, 1959; Dember, 1974; Gardner, 1985; Hilgard, 1980; Matson, 1971; Miller, Galanter, & Pribram, 1960; Neisser, 1967; Sperry, 1987), has now legitimized the contents of inner experience, such as sensations, percepts, mental images, thoughts, feelings, and the like, as ineliminable causal constructs in the scientific explanation of brain function and behavior.

In what follows, I discuss religion and science from the standpoint of this recent paradigm shift in behavioral science as a whole, not from the standpoint of personal philosophy. It is important for present purposes to emphasize this paradigm's basis in mainstream psychology, not personal opinion. The arguments have support in the working conceptual framework of a whole scientific discipline--the discipline that specializes in mind and behavior. What we are dealing with essentially, I believe, is a shift in science to a different and more valid form of causal determinism equally applicable in all the sciences, not just psychology.

The answer to the question, "Is there convergence between science and religion?" seems from the standpoint of psychology to be a definite and emphatic "yes." Over the past 15 years, changes in the foundational concepts of psychology instituted by the new cognitive or mentalist paradigm have radically reformed scientific descriptions of human nature and the conscious self. The resultant views today are less atomistic, less mechanistic, and more mentalistic, contextual, subjectivist, and humanistic. From the standpoint of theology, these new mentalistic tenets, which no longer exclude on principle the entire inner world of subjective phenomena, are much more palatable and compatible than were those of the behaviorist-materialist era.

Whereas science and religion had formerly stood in direct conflict on this matter, to the point even of being mutually exclusive and irreconcilable, one sees now a new compatibility, potentially even harmony with liberal religion--defined as religion that does not rely on dualistic or supernatural beliefs, forms of which have become increasingly evident in contemporary theology (e.g., Burhoe, 1970; Kaufman, 1985; Starr, 1984). A similar reconciliation applies in respect to the growing gulf between scientists and humanists in the two cultures described by C.P. Snow (1959) and rooted in basic contradictions between the worldview of science and that upheld in the humanities (W.T. Jones, 1965).

Before proceeding further, it may help to say a little more about the theoretical turnabout in psychology on which these alleged convergences directly depend. The mentalistic developments in question are not vague, abstract, or obscure, nor are they a matter of wishful thinking. The swing in behavioral science during the 1970s away from long dominant, rigorously objective, behaviorist doctrine to a new explanatory framework that accepts consciousness and the subjective is widely recognized and well documented (Baars, 1986; Davidson & Davidson, 1980; Dember, 1974; Fodor, 1981; Gardner, 1985; Hilgard, 1980; Kantor, 1979; Matson, 1971; Pylyshyn, 1973; Reese & Overton, 1972; Segal & Lachman, 1972; Skinner, 1985). This theoretic shift occurred with remarkable suddenness in the early 1970s (Pylyshyn, 1973), after behaviorism had reigned for more than half a century. Representing an about-face in the scientific conception and treatment of the relation of mind and brain, it has come to be referred to as the "consciousness," "cognitive," or "mentalist" revolution. It has also been called the "humanist" or "third" revolution (Matson, 1971), and it appears to constitute a true shift of paradigm in the sense described by Kuhn (1970).

The new mentalist thinking brings basic revisions of causal explanation that provide scientists and all of us with a new philosophy, a new outlook, a new way of understanding and explaining ourselves and the world. The full range of the contents and qualities of inner experience (that comprise the realm of the humanities) are not only given a new legitimacy in science but are also given primacy over the more basic physicochemical forces. The higher, more evolved, macro forces supersede the less evolved micro forces in control hierarchies. A new solution to the age-old mind-brain problem is involved, as well as a revised form of causation. The changed status in science of subjective values alters the relations between science and ethico-moral reasoning. These collective changes bring revised answers to the question, "What does modern science leave to believe in?" and affect traditional tensions between science and religion in a number of ways.

MUTUALLY EXCLUSIVE WORLDVIEWS

It seems fair to say that prior to the mentalist revolution, up through the late 1960s, mainstream science and religion actually had stood to one another as archenemies. All through the behaviorist-materialist era, science had been upholding a value-devoid, physically driven cosmos, ultimately lacking in those subjective humanistic attributes with which religion is most concerned. Things such as moral values, the human spirit, purpose, dignity, and freedom to choose, if they existed at all, were supposed to be only inconsequential epiphenomena or passive attributes of physical brain activity and best ignored in scientific explanation because, supposedly, they in no way changed the course of events in the real world, either in the brain or in the universe at large.

The foregoing characterization of pre-1970s science and religion as "archenemies" may appear a bit harsh in view of seeming exceptions such as Ralph Burhoe's Institute of Religion in an Age of Science (IRAS) and the associated *Zygon: Journal of Religion and Science* (Burhoe, 1970). It is presupposed, however, that I am discussing *mainstream* science and religion. It has long been a stated policy in both IRAS and *Zygon* that the attempt to join science and religion must be based on solid, mainstream science, not on fringe activities and minority opinions that might try to pass as science (Burhoe, 1967). For this reason, the IRAS project was constrained by policy to try to merge religion with the then-prevailing materialist, reductionist doctrines of mainstream science.

This was taken to mean, of course, that religion must be merged with radical behaviorism, sociobiology, the selfish gene concept, the quantum mechanics cosmos, and all the other reductive, mechanistic, atomistic views upheld in traditional scientific materialist thinking. Despite the good intentions and perseverance in this direction over several decades, this project never really succeeded from the standpoint of religion. It failed to remedy, in the words of W.T. Jones (1965), "the brute factuality . . . of cosmic meaninglessness . . . of life and death in an absurd, amoral universe" (p.20), a world indifferent to humanity and its purposes.

The actual relation of religion to traditional mainstream science seems to have been more realistically assessed by the Council of the National Academy of Sciences when they issued in 1981 the following resolution, quoted in the Academy's booklet on *Science and Creationism*: "Religion and science are separate and mutually exclusive realms of human thought, presentation of which in the same context leads to misunderstanding of both scientific theory and religious belief" (National Academy of Sciences, 1984, p.6). In other words, acceptance of the reductive physicalist beliefs traditionally upheld in science logically destroys the kinds of beliefs upheld in religion and vice versa. As already stressed, this mutually exclusive "archenemy" status is today a thing of the past, at least in behavioral science, as a result of the mentalist or cognitive revolution.

A THIRD CHOICE

Where formerly it had come down to a choice, in the last analysis, between two mutually contradictory accounts of the nature and origins of humankind and the universe, we now have a third choice in the new mentalist paradigm. Described initially as a midway compromise between classic reductive materialism and opposed forms of dualism, this new outlook on existence combines formerly antithetical features from both sides of the old spiritual-physical dichotomy into a single consistent worldview synthesis (Gardner, 1985; Popper, 1978; Slaatte, 1981; Sperry, 1965, 1983; Starr, 1984).

As a framework for belief, the new view of reality retains and integrates what seems most valid from each of the earlier views. It accepts mental and spiritual qualities as causal realities, but at the same time denies that they can exist separately in an unembodied state apart from the functioning brain. The new scheme manages to integrate the physical with the mental, the objective with the subjective, fact with value, free will with determinism, and positivistic thought with phenomenology (Slaatte, 1981; Sperry, 1985).

The consciousness revolution of the 1970s can be seen to represent a renunciation by a major scientific discipline of the reductionist "quantum mechanics philosophy" that had previously dominated scientific thinking. (This does not, of course, imply any renunciation of quantum theory per se.) At the same time, it represents also a further undermining of opposed dualistic thinking in philosophy and theology by explaining and accepting mind and the subjective entirely within a monistic framework (Natsoulas, 1987; Sperry, 1980). Instead of excluding mind and spirit, the new outlook puts subjective mental forces near the top of the brain's causal control hierarchy and gives them primacy in determining what a person is and does.

The traditional assumption in neuroscience, which was also long implicit in behaviorist philosophy, physics, biology, chemistry, and all the natural sciences, supposes everything to be determined from below upward, following the course of evolution (Armstrong, 1968; Feigl, 1967; Klee, 1984; Skinner, 1964, 1971). In this materialist "microdeterministic" view of nature, all mental and brain functions are determined by, and can be explained in terms of, brain physiology or neuronal activity. In turn, the neuronal activity can be explained in terms of biophysics and biochemistry-- with everything being determined and accounted for eventually in terms of subatomic physics and quantum mechanics--or some even more elemental "theory of everything."

The new mentalist-cognitive tenets replace this traditional reasoning with another. The control from below upward is retained but is claimed to not furnish the whole story. The full explanation requires that one also take into account new, previously nonexistent, emergent properties, including the mental, that interact causally at their own higher level and also exert causal control from above downward. The supervenient control exerted by the higher over lower level properties of a system, referred to also as "macro," "molar," or "emergent" determinism (Klee, 1984; Sperry, 1986, 1987), operates concurrently with the "micro" control from below upward. Mental states, as emergent properties of brain activity, thus exert downward control over their constituent neuronal events--at the same time that they are being determined by them. Microdeterminism is integrated with emergent determinism.

A simple analogy for the kind of higher (supervenient, downward) control envisaged compares it to that exercised by the programs of television from different channels over the flow of electrons in a TV receiver. Much as a TV program controls the electron flow, a train of thought in the brain, with its own cognitive dynamics and laws of progression, controls the brain's neuronal firing patterns. No interference with the underlying physics of neuronal discharge or electron emission is involved. Nothing in electron physics, however, can explain the sequencing of the TV program, that is, the plot development in a movie, the content of the news, or the comedian's delivery. Similarly, the laws of biophysics and biochemistry are not adequate to account for the cognitive sequencing of a train of thought. The interlevel, upward and downward controls work conjointly and continuously during the onward progression of events in time and are less sequential than spatial, coherent, and structural. The analogy breaks down if carried too far, of course, because the programs of the brain differ from those of television in that the brain can generate or create, largely from within itself, its own mental programs.

The principle of control from above downward, referred to as "downward causation" by Donald Campbell (1974), Karl Popper (Popper, 1978; Popper & Eccles, 1977), myself and others (Szentagothai, 1984) can be applied at all levels throughout nature. This outlook says that we and the universe are more than just swarms of "hurrying" atoms, electrons, and protons, that the higher holistic properties and qualities of the world to which the brain responds, including all the macrosocial phenomena of modern civilization, are just as real and causal for science as are the atoms and molecules on which they depend. The same principle of emergent control has more recently been invoked (Grene, 1987) to explain the units of causal selection in evolution, contradicting the extreme sociobiologic reductionisms that entered ethological thinking during the latter 1970s (Wilson, 1975).

The religion-science tensions of the past can be ascribed, not only to religion's reliance on dualistic supernatural explanation, but also in no small measure to the failure within science to recognize the causal reality and autonomy of the higher level forces. Successful merging of mainstream scientific and religious belief will logically require that science in general follow the lead of psychology and give up its traditional microdeterministic view of reality to accept the progressive emergence of higher, more evolved forms of causal control. Although this theoretic change might make little difference in physics, chemistry, molecular biology, and so on, it is crucial for the behavioral, evolutionary, social, and human sciences. In the rethinking of basic assumptions that have served to keep science and religion at odds, religion, on its side, would have to relinquish reliance on dualistic explanations. This it seems does not pose a major obstacle for modern theology (e.g., Burhoe, 1970; Byers, 1987; Kaufman, 1985; Starr, 1984).

FREE WILL, THE FACT-VALUE DICHOTOMY, AND A GLOBAL ETHIC

The turnabout on consciousness, involving a core principle of causal determinism of wide ontologic application, with changed perceptions of the self and physical reality, has potential for effecting pervasive global changes in human outlook. Some further conceptual consequences with special bearing on the religion-science controversy include (a) a resolution of the free will-determinism paradox that preserves moral choice and responsibility, (b) revisions in the traditional fact-value dichotomy that allow the derivation of ethical values from the factual knowledge of science, and (c) emergence of a science-based ideology for moral directive that, unlike currently prevailing schemes for ordering human priorities, holds promising prospects as the key to quality survival and a sustainable civilization (Brown, 1981; Daly, 1977; Kaufman, 1985; Schell, 1982; Sperry, 1983).

The free will-determinism paradox is resolved in mentalist theory by preserving both free will and determinism and integrating the two. "Micro" and "macro" forms of determinism are both retained and combined in such a way that, for any willed action, the sequence of antecedent causes in the brain includes subjective wants, purpose, choices, value judgments, and other subjective attributes of the cognitive self (Deci, 1980). Thus, from the standpoint of mentalist doctrine, as from that of common experience, one can will to do whatever one subjectively chooses, decides, or *wants* to do. The whole process is still controlled or determined, but primarily by emergent cognitive, subjective intentions of the conscious/unconscious mind (Grenander, 1983; Ripley, 1984).

Thus, freedom to will our actions as we wish is real, as are moral choice and responsibility. Yet none of these is uncaused. Uncaused behavior would be capricious, random, and out of our own control.

A changed science-values relation is another logical consequence of the new mentalism. Instead of maintaining the traditional unbridgeability of scientific fact and values, cognitive theory brings the two together in brain function. If conscious mental values not only arise from but also influence physical brain action, it then becomes possible to integrate subjective values with objective brain function and its physical consequences. Current concepts of cognitive processing make it possible to go from fact to value and from perception of what "is" to what "should" be (Sperry, 1985). The progression is not achieved directly but via cognitive intermediaries such as belief, understanding, perspectives, and the like.

For example, it is commonly accepted that scientific facts shape one's understanding and beliefs. These in turn determine what one values and color one's ideas about how things ought to be. Further, the cosmology of macrodeterminist science no longer destroys values and meaning through reduction of everything to elemental physics. The combined result has brought a major turnaround since the mid 1960s in the science-values relation (Edel, 1980; Graham, 1981), opening the way as well for corresponding developments in respect to an integration of scientific and religious belief.

In the revised, macrodeterminist outlook it becomes possible not only to build a descriptive science of values (Rottschafer, 1987) but also to get ethico-religious values from science in a prescriptive sense (Fletcher, 1987; Sperry, 1985). Historically, moral values have commonly been determined on the basis of fit with some accepted supreme plan for existence imputed to a divine intellect (Fletcher, 1987). Deriving values from science means a reconception of such master schemes of supernatural origin into one that is consistent with scientific evidence. This was deterred during the materialist-behaviorist era because science seemed to point to a cosmos lacking in values and higher meaning. Macromentalist theory, in contrast, provides a master plan based in emergent evolution, which, though not preconceived but gradually self-determined in its design, is nevertheless replete with intrinsic directives for determining values.

A primary source is found in the elaborate system of innate value preferences inherent in the human cognitive structure as a part of nature's genetic provisions for survival (Pugh, 1977); this system includes a basic social conscience, which is deemed central to morality (Fletcher, 1987). Values acquired later through experience are built on and tend normally to mesh with the inherent system and its associated drives, including a strong motivational thrust not only to survive in the status quo but also to strive for continued improvement. Values are both directly embodied and also implicit in this system and set guiding constraints for further derivation of other values.

More than this, when mentalist theory shows a revised scientific picture of both human and nonhuman nature and the forces in control, the result inevitably causes alterations at the more fundamental level of existent value and belief systems. A society's sense of the sacred, of what is most important in deciding priorities, good and evil, and how things "ought to be" rests ultimately on beliefs about our nature and origins and the kind of universe we live in. The mentalist paradigm establishes a new foundational framework for such beliefs. Rejecting dualisms on the one side and positivistic-reductionist views on the other, changes the ultimate criteria for determining ethical priorities.

A science-based moral code emerges in which the most valued things in life are neither relegated to another realm of existence nor reduced to quantum physics. The highest good, ultimate meaning, moral right and wrong, and so on are determined in terms of concordance with the master plan for existence set by evolving nature, including human nature with its sociocultural as well as genetic values (Kaufman, 1985). The backup ethical theory assumes as self-evident that survival of the cosmos and our planet's biosphere (without which there is nothing) constitutes a supreme good. The moral code to which the foregoing leads, expressed in simplest terms, interprets what is ethically good and morally right to be that which preserves and enhances the evolving quality of existence--and vice versa. When there is conflict about which existence deserves preference, the choice is made in terms of the "common good," ultimately in the perspective of the long-range evolving quality of the biosphere as a whole.

In the emergent interactionist view of causal determinism, it is not possible to physically separate the forces of creation from creation itself; the two become inextricably interfused. A Spinoza-Einstein-like concept of the cosmos is supported in which ultimate respect naturally centers, as in most religions, in the forces that made and control the universe, but these forces are conceived scientifically in emergent macrodeterminist terms (e.g., Kaufman, 1985; Sperry, 1983; Starr, 1984).

One comes out with a strong moral basis for environmentalism, population controls, conservation, and in general for protecting and enhancing the overall long-term evolving quality and diversity of this-world existence. The focus is on the whole ecosystem, loss of which, as by nuclear annihilation, would mean a much greater evolutionary set-back than loss of the human species alone. Implemented in legislation, the resultant value perspectives would predictably turn the tide of our worsening global predicament (Brown, 1981; Grenander, 1983; T.E. Jones, 1980; Schell, 1982; Speer, 1985).

Enhancement of the long-term evolving quality of existence seems a simple guideline policy for legislation in many respects, but it becomes in others a highly complex and involved criterion subject to different interpretations. As with any ethical code, the final criteria are determined only in broad principle, and much is left for argument in regard to specific issues.

IDEOLOGICAL BASE FOR WORLD JUSTICE

Among the extensive conceptual spin-offs of the mentalist paradigm, perhaps none is of more critical practical concern than the potential application of this paradigm in an ideology for world government. Although the pressing need for some kind of limited world security system has long been evident to help control thermonuclear and other impending global, environmental, and population-growth threats (e.g., Ferencz, 1985; Hudgens, 1986; Speer, 1985), major obstacles remain--not the least of which has been the lack of an acceptable ideologic foundation that could command worldwide respect despite local differences in culture, national loyalty, religious faith, political bias, and so on.

When it comes to ordering world priorities, formulating global policies, and the like, it helps to have some consensus on what is ultimately right and wrong, on what is the highest good, and on how things ought to be. It is most unlikely that different countries will agree to relinquish ancient ways and values in order to unite under any currently existing rival ideology. It is not inconceivable, on the other hand, that an effective majority might be willing to compromise, for purposes of international law, on a new, relatively neutral value-belief system founded in the truths and worldview of science.

Compared to other current belief systems, the outlook on existence supported in macromentalist philosophy tends to better satisfy some desired qualifications for building world accord (Toynbee & Ikeda, 1976). This philosophy is based on the neutrality, credibility, and universality of science and is relatively open and nonexclusive; thus, it can be expressed as a natural common denominator of human belief and can be translated to merge with other belief systems, including antireligious ideologies such as communism or secular humanism. It relies on principles that have worked successfully over eons in creating humankind and upholds as the highest frame of reference with which to settle international disputes, not the welfare of any chosen nation, peoples, faith, or culture, but rather the long-range survival and evolving quality of the biospheric as a whole--with humanity as the prime part of the system.

As an ultimate criterion for resolving differences between the rights of nations, religious groups, individuals, generations, and so on, this emergentist biospheric ethic would replace norms for justice based on intuitive humanitarian or narrowly humanistic guidelines or on otherworldly or "afterlife" dictates. It would replace also the official materialistic and "party" determinants of communist ideology, and utilitarian, "situational," hedonistic, or other ethical standards. Besides serving to protect the long-range quality of the biosphere, such a scientific global ethic and view of reality, evolving and improving as science advances, can be defended as our most valid reference frame for what is "true," "right," and most important. A world organization representing and protecting such principles and also bolstering the needed human hope for an unlimited future and meaning beyond the eventual demise of this planet--through a united space science program--might be perceived to deserve dedication and loyalty above even that to the nation.

In the same way that dialectical materialism is taken in communist countries to be the official philosophy of government (eventually for the entire world community in Soviet hopes), similarly the new macromentalist philosophy of behavioral and cognitive science (dialectal mentalism or cognitivism) can be considered a potential philosophy for world government. It would seemingly go far to reconcile the now deeply entrenched ideologic differences and distrust between the United States and Soviet Union. The conflicting superpower ideologies that pit capitalism against communism, atheism against theism, materialism against spiritual idealism, centralized controls against distributed free enterprise, religious freedom and separation of church and state against the opposite, and so on are widely perceived to be the single greatest obstacle to world accord (Hudgens, 1986; Speer, 1985). These differences cannot be resolved by technological developments.

Psychology's new mentalist doctrine extends into and challenges the theoretic foundations of these two opposed systems, offering some much-needed compromise. It agrees with the Soviet rejection of dualistic otherworldly guidelines in favor of empiric verifiable truths as a basis on which to mold social structure. At the same time, it concurs with Western rejection of dialectal materialism and of related Marxist views that society is determined primarily from below upward by material, economic, and basic subsistence forces. Although the essential importance of the lower level forces is recognized and accepted in the new outlook, priority is given to the higher, more evolved spiritual and idealistic dimensions in the cognitive structure. The implication is not to try to uplift or change human nature, but to use its highest, most evolved properties to control the less evolved ones through law and government for the common good.

Soviet social philosophy, in its reliance on earlier science during formative years, can be seen in the light of today's science to have overestimated the plasticity and homogeneity of human nature, as well as having underestimated the importance of some of the personal motivational structures. Both sides can thus claim to have been right on major issues, while both give way on others. Compromise in the new macrodeterminist cosmology of science would allow the two superpowers to begin to understand each other's differences within the same single reference frame instead of being totally at odds with incommensurable ideologies. Much the same applies to other countries and communities currently operating from mutually incompatible worldviews. Taken as an ideological base for world government, the new reality paradigm of behavioral and cognitive science could foreseeably foster and sustain the types of social change and value priorities needed if civilization is to survive and continue on a forward course.

REMAINING ISSUES

Conflict between scientific and religious belief gains added concern today in the context of worsening world conditions and an imperiled future. We are learning the hard way that real, lasting solutions to the major global ills of our times are not found in "crisis-management" techniques that treat the manifest symptoms directly and separately and rely on endless advances in applied science and technology. In the absence of world population controls, such advances result in vicious-spiral build-ups that need to be broken at the source through changes in human behavior and attitude, changes that can be effected most strategically at the level of the sustaining value and belief systems (Brown, 1981; T.E. Jones, 1980; Sperry, 1983).

The great power of these reigning belief systems, as determinants of behavior, decision making, and social policy can hardly be overrated. In today's crowded world, the beliefs of millions of followers of this or that religion--which influence the growth rate of world population, the ability of human communities to coexist, and the treatment of nature, irreplaceable resources, other species, and so--have tremendous consequences that become compounded in succeeding generations. Religious and ideologic beliefs, in particular, incorporate or imply a worldview or life-goal framework that then determines public judgment of how things ought to be in the world, the cultural sense of value, and ethical concepts of right and wrong and of social justice.

A crucial issue brought into new focus by the macromentalist outlook can be stated as follows: In ideologic or religious belief, is it any longer necessary or desirable to go beyond the limits of present knowledge and empirical verification? In other words, should humankind put its faith in the kind of truth within which scientific and religious belief are in accord, or should we continue to reach beyond this realm into others of less certainty? The answer, of course, is critical to many other issues.

Until the 1970s there seemed little choice; theology could hardly restrict itself to beliefs consistent with scientific doctrine, beliefs that, in the final analysis, became mutually exclusive and incompatible with the aims of religion. New reasons can be seen in today's changed outlook, however, for basing our belief systems, at least at the social level and *for purposes of legislation*, firmly within the realm of empirical verification. The principal argument relates to the power of belief systems in determining social policy and the future and says in effect that we can no longer afford the risk of mistakes in this critical area. Even a failure to correct past errors could easily mean our demise. If we do not succeed soon in adopting a theology that will protect the biosphere and if we do not find a common neutral belief system and global ethic on which most nations and most cultures and faiths can agree, then shortly there may not be any nations or theologies or sciences to worry about--or even any biosphere.

In today's scenario, the issue of survival (or better, quality survival) logically takes overwhelming precedence over all other moral imperatives (Kaufman, 1985; Schell, 1982). In this context, the new mentalist position of behavioral and cognitive science seems to hold promise, not only as a more valid paradigm for all science but also for all human belief.

*This article is based on an invited address to a conference on religion and science organized by the Committee on Human Values of the National Conference of Catholic Bishops, held in Plymouth, Michigan, September 1986. The assigned theme, "Is there a convergence in your discipline with religion?" was separately addressed by three other scientists representing physics, evolutionary theory, and biology. Advance instructions imposed no restrictions: "Feel free to do what you wish with the subject. . .the committee is interested in getting the important issues surrounding the religion/science tension on the table." I thank Erika Erdmann and three anonymous reviewers for their helpful comments. Support for the present work was provided from the C.Ed Nix and Doris J. Stein Funds and by the Ralph L. Smith Foundation.

REFERENCES

Armstrong, D.M. (1968). *A materialist theory of mind*. London: Routledg & Kegan Paul.

Baars, R.J. (1986). *The cognitive revolution in psychology*. New York: Guilford.

Bindra, D. (1970). The problem of subjective experience: Puzzlement on reading R.W. Sperry's "A modified concept of consciousness." *Psychological Review*, 77,581-584.

Brown, L.R. (1981). *Building a sustainable society*. New York: Norton.

Burhoe, R.W. (1967). Five steps in the evolution of man's knowledge of good and evil. *Zygon 2*, 77-96.

Burhoe, R.W. (1970). Potentials for religion from the sciences. *Zygon 5*, 110-129.

Byers, D.M. (Ed.). (1987). *Religion, science, and the search for wisdom*. Washington, DC: United States Catholic Conferences.

Campbell, D.T. (1974). Downward causation in hierarchically organized biological systems. In F.J. Ayala & T. Dobzhansky (Eds.), *Studies in the philosophy of biology* (pp.139-161). Berkeley: University of California Press.

Chomsky, N. (1959). Verbal behavior by B.F. Skinner. *Language 35*, 26-58.

Daly, H.E. (1977). *Steady-state economics*. San Francisco: Freeman.

Davidson, R.J., & Davidson, J.M. (1980). Introduction: The scientific study of human consciousness in psychobiological perspective. In J.M. Davidson (Ed.), *The psychobiology of consciousness* (pp.1-10). New York: Plenum Press.

Deci, E.L. (1980). *The psychology of self-determination.* Lexington, MA: D.C. Heath.

Dember, W.N. (1974). Motivation and the cognitive revolution. *American Psychologist, 29,* 161-168.

Edel, A. (1980). *Exploring fact and value* (Vol.2). New Brunswick, NJ: Transaction Books.

Feigl, H. (1967). *The "mental" and the "physical"* (with "postscript after ten years"). Minneapolis: University of Minnesota Press.

Ferencz, B.B. (1985). *A common sense guide to world peace.* New York: Oceana Publications.

Fletcher, J. (1987). Humanism and theism in biomedical ethics. *Perspectives in Biology and Medicine, 31,* 106-116.

Fodor, J.A. (1981). The mind-body problem. *Scientific American* 244(1), 114-123.

Gardner, H. (1985). *The mind's new science: A history of the cognitive revolution.* New York: Basic Books.

Graham, L.R. (1981). *Between science and values.* New York: Columbia University Press.

Grenander., M.E. (1983). The mind is its own place. *Methodology and Science, 16*(3), 181-192.

Grene, M. (1987). Hierarchies in biology. *American Scientist, 75,* 504-510.

Hilgard, E.R. (1980). Consciousness in contemporary psychology. *An Annual Review of Psychology, 31,* 1-26.

Hudgens, T.A. (1986). *Let's abolish war.* Denver: Bilr Corp.

Jones, T.E. (1980). *Options for the future.* New York: Praeger.

Jones, W.T. (1965). *The sciences and the humanities.* Berkeley: University of California Press.

Kantor, J.R. (1979). Psychology: Science or nonscience? *The Psychological Record, 29,* 155-163.

Kaufman, G.D. (1985). *Theology for a nuclear age.* Philadelphia, PA: Westminster Press.

Klee, R.L. (1984). Micro-determinism and concepts of emergence. *Philosophy of Science 51,* 44-63.

Kuhn, T. (1970). *The structure of scientific revolutions.* Chicago: University of Chicago Press.

Matson, F.W. (1971). Humanistic theory: The third revolution in psychology. *The Humanist, 31*(2), 7-11.

126

Miller, G.A., Galanter, E.H., & Pribram, K.H. (1960). *Plans and the structure of behavior*. New York: Holt, Rinehart & Winston.
National Academy of Sciences. (1984). *Science and creationism*. Washington, DC: National Academy Press.
Natsoulas, T. (1987). Roger Sperry's monist interactionism. *The Journal of Mind and Behavior, 8*, 1-12.
Neisser, U. (1967). *Cognitive psychology*. New York: Appleton-Century-Crofts.
Popper, K.R. (1972). Of clouds and clocks. In K. Popper (Ed.), *Objective knowledge* (pp.206-255). Oxford: Clarendon Press. (Second Arthur Holly Compton Memorial Lecture, presented April 1965).
Popper, K.R. (1978). Natural selection and the emergence of mind. *Dialectica, 32*, 339-355.
Popper, K.R., & Eccles, J.C. (1977). *The self and its brain*. New York: Springer International.
Pugh, G.E. (1977). *The biological origin of human values*. New York: Basic Books.
Pylyshyn, Z.W. (1973). What the mind's eye tells the mind's brain: A critique of mental imagery. *Psychological Bulletin, 80*, 1-24.
Reese, H.W., & Overton, W.F. (1972). On paradigm shifts. *American Psychologist, 27*, 1197-1199.
Ripley, C. (1984). Sperry's concept of consciousness. *Inquiry, 27*, 399-423.
Rottschaefer, W.A. (1987). Roger Sperry's science of values. *The Journal of Mind and Behavior, 8*, 23-35.
Schell, J. (1982). *The fate of the earth*. New York: Avon Books.
Segal, E.M., & Lachman, R. (1972). Complex behavior or higher mental process? Is there a paradigm shift? *American Psychologist, 27*, 46-55.
Skinner, B.F. (1964). Behaviorism at 50. In T. Wann (Ed.), *Behaviorism and phenomenology* (pp.79-108). Chicago: University of Chicago Press.
Skinner, B.F. (1971). *Beyond freedom and dignity*. New York: Knopf.
Skinner, B.F. (1985). Cognitive science and behaviourism. *British Journal of Psychology, 76*, 291-301.
Slaatte, H.A. (1981). The existential creativity of consciousness. *Contemporary Philosophy, 8*(8), 24.
Snow, C.P. (1959). *The two cultures and the scientific revolution*. New York: Cambridge University Press.
Speer, J.P. (1985). *World polity, conflict and war*. Fort Bragg, CA: Q.E.D. Press.
Sperry, R.W. (1965). Mind-brain and humanist values. In J.R. Platt (Ed.), *New views of the nature of man* (pp.71-92). Chicago: University of

Chicago Press. (Reprinted in *Bulletin of the Atomic Scientists*, 1966, 22[7], 2-6)

Sperry, R.W. (1969). A modified concept of consciousness. *Psychological Review*, 76, 532-536.

Sperry, R.W. (1970). An objective approach to subjective experience: Further explanation of a hypothesis. *Psychological Review, 77*, 585-590.

Sperry, R.W. (1980). Mind-brain interaction: Mentalism yes: dualism, no. *Neuroscience, 5*, 195-206. (Reprinted in R.W. Sperry, 1985, *Science and moral priority*. New York: Greenwood/Praeger)

Sperry, R.W. (1983). Changed concepts of brain and consciousness: Some value implications: 1982-83 Isthmus Foundation Lecture Series. *Perkins Journal, 36*(4), 21-32. (Reprinted in *Zygon*, 1985, 20, 41-57)

Sperry, R.W. (1985). The cognitive role of belief: Implication of the new mentalism with response to Howard Slaatte. *Contemporary Philosophy, 10*, 2-4.

Sperry, R.W. (1986). Discussion: Macro- versus micro-determinism. *Philosophy of Science, 53*, 265-270.

Sperry, R.W. (1987). Structure and significance of the consciousness revolution. *The Journal of Mind and Behavior, 8*, 37-66.

Starr, D. (1984). The crying need for a believable theology. *The Humanist, 44*, 13-16.

Szentagothai, J. (1984). Downward causation? *Annual Review of Neuroscience, 7*, 1-11.

Toynbee, A.J., & Ikeda, D. (1976). *Choose life* (A dialogue edited by R.L. Gage). London: Oxford University Press.

Wilson, E.O. (1975). *Sociobiology: The new synthesis*. Cambridge, MA: Harvard University Press.

Chapter Six

BRAIN SCIENCE AND THE HUMAN SPIRIT*

by

Colwyn Trevarthen

Abstract. In recent decades of its brief history, brain science has shed light on the source of psychological motives in brain tissues. We review the chemistry and anatomy of the neural core of human motivation. Its axon threads penetrate the cognitive fields of the hemispheres asymmetrically, subjecting the activity of cortical cells to constantly changing evaluations in self-organizing states of mind that seek communication with other minds. The core of the brain generates and responds to the rhythm and color of emotions, giving moral control to relationships between people and setting values to meanings in communication. The newborn human mind comes equipped with this organ and is ready to share transcendent states of emotion with an empathic partner. Within three years, the spontaneous fantasy-making play of a preschool child is mimicking adult roles and rituals. Thus mystical rites and mythic symbols of adult society come to express inborn feelings that form the time- and space-defying cooperation of human souls within the ancestral culture.

The great variety of sacred myths and rituals in different societies cannot conceal the influence of deep feelings and motives that all religions serve. Some desires seem to spring directly from the unchanging life processes of the human spirit, with power to question existence. Believers hold to values and feelings of good and evil that transform ordinary practical objects and tasks, making of them powerful symbols that affirm the zest for belief. The intrinsic passions of belief seek sympathetic response in the community of minds, and believers reject with fear or anger, even with hatred, those who disbelieve.[1]

How to explain the aesthetic, moral, and religious universals in human inspiration? For the empiricist all ideas penetrate from outside into a receptive mind fabric, born clear like a blank slate in each generation. But could such improbable coincidences of motive and consciousness come out of experiences built up over centuries in the memories of individual men and women? Could knowledge concentrate in that form by imitation and spread through the connected social histories of groups of people, then trade between all groups across continents and oceans? Or is it possible that they have their source in cosmic regularities of the environment that no group of humans can escape? If not imitated or remembered, are they received, as visionaries say, by a special kind of mind process in the form of advice from an all-knowing deity who resembles a supremely powerful parent or teacher?

Perhaps, after all, they grow in us. They might find their beginnings as actively conceived manifestations of genetic rules which we all possess, rules that govern the outward growth and interconnection of millions of nerve cells, making their active and communicating elements obey a psychogenetic strategy for place-seeking and pattern-forming. The chance experiences of individuals may become drawn into brain functions for fellowship in belief that were validated through natural selection in the evolutionary past of our species.

Victor Turner (1983a) believed that inherent forms of brain activity give rise to deep universals of culture. He proposed that anthropologists should take note of recent brain research in order to better understand the form of rituals and the content of myth. He courageously put his mind to the task of absorbing evidence from comparative and experimental brain science, neuropsychology and psychiatry, and built up a persuasive explanation why humans in very different situations are attracted to parallel images, legends, and ceremonials. He sought to define the inner satisfactions that customs bring to people by identifying anatomical and chemical categories of neuronal process that work together in each and every human being. He presumed these to be consequences of self-organizing and genetically constrained growth processes that link up and diversify the actions of nerve cells as they multiply and spread into the tracts and nuclei of the brain.

In responding to Turner's theory, it will not be sufficient to detail what we know of the complexity of information-receiving or movement-coordinating mechanisms in the brain. We will need, as Turner perceived, to interpret the deeply rooted, motivating, choosing, and evaluating systems that evolution has fashioned at the source of mental activity--the motive structures that mediate advantageous transactions between a unified knowing, imagining, and remembering self, its body, and the world.

Turner raises a question about how the inner working of the brain, with ancient evolutionary origins, might relate to spiritual vision and to the ritualistic forms that human individuals in their communities look to for support and confirmation, and by which they break free from the inconsistent impositions of reality. He promulgates a belief in motivator mechanisms of the brain that mix action and reflection, power and self-reward, anger and love, joy and despair, and faith and fear. He accepts the principle that patterns of social signaling have evolved to promote a community of beings that gain advantage in life by interacting cooperatively--linking themselves together mentally. Turner follows Eugene d'Aquili (1983) in extending the concept of an heritable structure of antithetical drives (such as ethologists attribute to animals and use to explain their "rituals" of courtship and mating, parental care, territorial fighting, etc.) to include the human cognitive modes of the hemispheres, viewed as being balanced in opposition--the energetic, pragmatic, and effective on the left side and the reflective, dreaming, and restoring on the right.[2] The brain division so described recalls Carl Jung's archetypal division of the mind and spirit into *animus* and *anima* (Turner 1983a, 238-39). Turner cites modern psychiatric, physiological, and pharmacological evidence as well as interpretations of the split brain and effects of unilateral cerebral lesions. This analysis he applies not so much to the ethnography and psychology of human techniques and artifacts as to more spiritual concerns and their celebration.

Turner's knowledge of African mythology inspired him to give a special role to "the Trickster" of play, an elusive force for jovial teasing and absurd rule-breaking, defiant of established routines and factual explanations. He saw playfulness as mixing up the ergic, reality-bound and the trophic, self-protecting, the animus and the anima, and the rational and the emotional in borderline "liminal" states of mind, pitting rival brain systems in a creative conflict that cracks the monopoly of concrete reality (Turner 1983a; 1983b).

I am fascinated by this insight because it is plain to me now, after a decade and a half watching spontaneous communicating between mother and infant, or toddler and toddler, that joking, teasing and imaginative, fantastical, rule-breaking play is the well-spring of energy for healthy mental growth in the individual child and the promoter of learning in affectionate relationships. Its absence in a young child is an infallible sign of motivational pathology and a forewarning of retarded mental development.[3]

Can we hope to bring all these exciting ideas of Turner's together in a theory of human cerebral nature and innate motivations for social cooperation and celebration as he recommends us to do? It is a grand challenge.

Doubts may well be felt that our scientific traditions are competent for this enquiry. Confronted with human consciousness and the complex antithetical purposes and values that it serves, our theories appear hidebound in rational objectivity or lost in a dualistic set of thinking that, by irrevocably separating the material from the spiritual, blocks the path to an understanding of motivations. As long as scientists believe that the only testable truth is in an uninterrupted physical reality outside the special psychological reality of minds, there is no way of conceiving either the inside springs of animal spirit or the fabric of human understanding that has evolved from them. Brain science is in the unique position of studying the only part of physical reality that has the design to contain or generate inner mental processes. Grasping this requires a shift in scientific attitudes, not just an extension of past physical models. Moreover, before we jump to the conclusion (perhaps encouraged by the rapidity of recent advances and the abundance of new findings that fill the journals and receive increasing attention in public media) that the task of making a brain science of spiritual, mental, or emotional matters will be no more awkward than any other physical analysis that science has attempted--merely a replacing of inaccurate superstitions with substantial and reliable data on brain matter and its chemistry, and with some more complex models of the causal machinery--it is well to remind ourselves just how little we know and how recently it is, and in what climate of thinking, that we have opened the Pandora's box of the brain to glimpse a little of what is inside. The history outlined below reveals a clear bias towards simplistic mechanical models that leave the creative power of motives obscure.

I believe, in spite of the obvious difficulties, that Turner's audacious challenge came at the right time to stimulate a new understanding. Brain science knows much more about the inner workings of the brain than it did just two decades ago. Now it can offer guidance concerning the origins of significant human motives. Psychology, too, is certainly more sophisticated today than over most of the past half century about the intrinsic, self-sustaining processes of mentation, including those that motivate and regulate both learning and social behavior. It is less reluctant to tackle the mysteries of cognitive, volitional, and emotional processes that taunt scientific efforts at reduction to the supposedly greater certainties of physics and chemistry. Scientific theories attempting to integrate cerebral facts at the level of psychological functioning are getting new confidence and credibility. They are beginning to find explanations for the human state of mind.

THE EVOLUTIONARY CONTINUUM OF BRAINS
AND OF BEHAVIORS

At the origin of the scientific view of ourselves is the Darwinian concept of evolution. A modern biologist expects human intelligence to resemble that of animals closest in the evolutionary scheme. In 1861 Thomas Huxley, lecturing to working men in London, took battle in support of *The Origin of Species*, recently published by his friend Charles Darwin (Darwin 1859). The lectures appeared in a best-seller entitled *Evidences as to Man's Place in Nature* (Huxley [1863] 1913). Huxley confronted those whose religious beliefs concerning creation forbad them to see humankind as related in form or function to any animal species. Eloquently, and with painstaking accuracy, he recited the evidence from comparative anatomy and embryology, paying particular attention to the latest information from dissection of preserved brains of monkeys, apes, and humans. He sifted evidence from reports of traveling naturalists and his own wide knowledge of human societies to show that behaviors of all tribes of human beings could be compared to behaviors of monkeys and apes.

But Huxley could have only gross knowledge of the brain and virtually no awareness of its inner histology or physiology. He concludes, "So far as cerebral structure goes, Man differs less from the Chimpanzee or the Orang than these do even from the Monkeys" (Huxley [1863] 1913, 69); but he goes on, "It must not be overlooked, however, that there is a very striking difference in the absolute mass and weight between the lowest human brain and that of the highest ape. . . . This is a very noteworthy circumstance, and doubtless will one day help to furnish an explanation of the great gulf which intervenes between the lowest man and the highest ape in intellectual power. . . . It is no doubt perfectly true, in a certain sense, that all difference of function is a result of difference of structure; or, in other words, of difference in the combination of the primary molecular forces of living substance" (Huxley [1863] 1913, 70). Moreover, Huxley thought that inconspicuous differences in brain mechanism combined with new peripheral organs, such as those of throat and mouth for speech, could produce great transformations in psychology and intellect.

Here we see the gifted prophet of natural history to be mistaken. Brain science now knows real and large-scale evolutionary transformations, not merely in "the combination of the primary molecular forces of living substance," but in the design and function of cell communities of the brain. In essence, however, it was not the anatomy but the psychological subtleties of the human mind that eluded Huxley, who was too preoccupied with a search for "structures." Without some psychological theory of the mental events that conceive the world and act upon it with choice we cannot begin to look for the brain mechanisms behind mental differences that separate humans from apes. Since Huxley's day, our thinking on brain and mind has been transformed.

A brief glance back over the history of brain science will suffice to warn us of the risks that lie in any attempt to bridge the gap between human communal mind and the human brain. Scientific materialism will explain deeper psychological events only partly and with great difficulty. But one has no right to make the traditional response of a dualist; we must not turn away and deny that these problems are tractable.

DISCOVERY OF THE BRAIN

Barely 300 years ago, an Oxford professor of medicine Thomas Willis argued that scientists should look for mind processes in solid brain matter.[4] Before that the cerebral processes of the mind and mental illness were utterly obscure; in effect, brain science was nonexistent. The ancient Greeks, Hippocrates of the fifth century B.C. greatest among them, had brilliant insights into brain activity and the effects of wounds or epilepsy, but these informed guesses were forgotten as centuries of savants since Galen, court physician to emperor Marcus Aurelius in second-century Rome, imagined the spirits of cold reason mingled with hot emotion in the ventricular cavities of the brain.   In the seventeenth century Rene Descartes' doctrine of reflexes, "mindless motor acts in man and animals" (Sherrington 1940, 161), could only provide an argument for placing mind, and also God, outside the machine of the body.

As Darwin was working on *The Descent of Man* (Darwin 1871), the best a mid-nineteenth century expert on the brain could do was ponder a mystery of bulbous masses and a tangle of white strands.[5] But great strides were made in the space of a few decades.   At the end of the century Sigmund Freud ([1895] 1954) was bold among neurologists to accept the intuition of the great Spanish "father of neuroanatomy" Santiage Ramon y Cajal that the brain was a tissue of separate nerve cells that communicated through discrete contacts, perhaps by chemicals (Freud [1895] 1954; Pribram 1969; Konner 1982,vii).   Beautiful global brain anatomies, full of intricate histological detail, were published at that time (see figure 6.1), but still the physiology of integrative neural action was virtually unknown.[6] Charting of the cortex of the brain in animals to locate different psychological functions began with the development of accurate experimental surgery and delicate electrical stimulation a little over 100 years ago.   Gustav Fritsch and Eduard Hitzig, Hermann Munk, David Ferrier, and Friedrich Goltz identified sensory perception territories for each of the modalities and defined a map of the motor organs of the body and limbs.[7]

When neurologists could localize lesions in humans, and when they had learned to analyze psychological reactions, they found that psychic integrations of differing kinds had a systematic relation to the locus of cortical damage.   These practices, too, were perfected in the latter decades of the last century.   Tragically, the human brain maps became clearer with the invention of high velocity rifles for war use and explosive shells that projected shrapnel with sufficient velocity to cut discrete pieces from the surface mantle of the brain.   Through all this advance in knowledge of the cortex there was uncertainty and bitter controversy over how local territories, with different relation to peripheral sensory or motor organs, could contribute to integrated consciousness and voluntary movement. Some thought mental operations could never be localized, that they were diffuse properties of a brain that could function only as a whole.

Concerning the special human form of mind, the greatest breakthrough was the discovery in the 1870s that language, for many scholars the defining feature of human intelligence, could be selectively impaired by either a lateral-frontal or a posterior-temporo-parietal lesion restricted to the left cerebral hemisphere (Broca 1865; Wernicke 1874; Freud 1953; Penfield & Roberts 1959; Blakemore 1977, 141-44; Trevarthen 1984a, 1159-60; see figure 6.3). The one-sided lesions that destroyed speech or comprehension of speech were in an anatomical *terra incognita* outside the primary sensory or motor areas. Their discovery inspired lively speculation on the anatomy of higher mental processes. It was soon observed that skillful coordinations of moving and perceiving, for such tasks as reading, making significant gestures, or formulating purposeful performance of a task, could be disrupted by a lesion that disconnected areas of the cerebral hemispheres and separated sensory and motor territories from integrative command centers placed on one side in the brain.

However, until Roger Sperry's work in the 1960s with the "split brain", the function of the greatest central connecting tract in the brain, the corpus callosum that bridges the cleft between the hemispheres and unifies the functions of left and right halves of the cortex, was a matter of speculation (Sperry 1967). This mass of nerve fibers is now estimated to contain 800 to 1,000 million fibers in one head, as many as the population of China. That inborn anatomical difference between the cerebral hemispheres of importance in human psychology could actually be seen in ordinary anatomical preparations was controversial until the mid 1970s.[8] Now we know they can be seen in the brains of fetuses half way through gestation.

A golden age of research on brain tissue began about 1870 when the method of staining single nerve cells black with silver deposits was discovered, and by the 1900s the fabric of the primary receptor territories, and many other cortical tissue types with less certain function, had been distinguished. Paul Flechsig demonstrated in 1901 that the primary sensory and motor cortices matured quickly after birth in a baby's brain but that

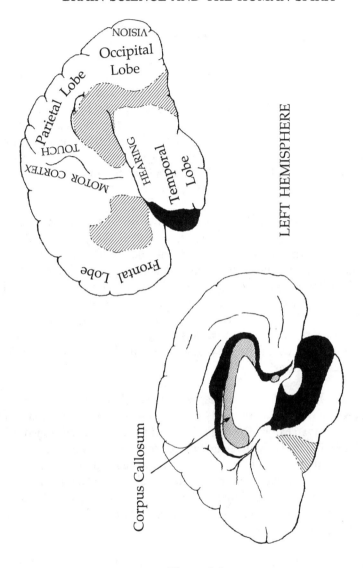

Figure 6.1

Cross-section of a human brain from Dejerine ([1895-1901] 1980) showing the corpus callosum, limbic structures (in black) and a portion of the late maturing "cultural" cortex (marked by a dashed line).

other territories took many years of childhood to complete differentiation.[9] The Australian Elliot Smith showed that the amount of neocortex, the territory in most immediate contact with receptors and motor organs and capable of refined sensory and motor discriminations in mastery of the external environment, increased from primitive to advanced mammals relative to older archicortex and paleocortex (Smith 1910). Evolution had built up the neocortex with increase of intelligent awareness and learning, older forebrain regions being committed to automatic, instinctive orienting reactions close to satisfaction of vital needs.

Charles Sherrington defined in 1906 how nerve fibers made contact with nerve cell bodies at junction points he called synapses, but the fine structure of the synapse was perceived only 60 to 70 years later.[10] At Oxford in the first decades of this century scientists in Sherrington's school worked out reflex integrations of the spinal cord by controlled stimulation of receptors in various intensities and combinations and by precise measurement of elicited response movements. They experimented with these basic sensory motor coordinations in animals which had their brains removed or disconnected from the cord--not the ideal procedure to elucidate higher mental functions!

Ivan Petrovich Pavlov in Russia, inheritor of the materialistic tradition for interpreting brain functions of Emil du Bois-Reymond, Hermann von Helmholtz, and Ivan Michailovich Sechenov, founded his conditioned reflex theory of learning on early investigations of sensory and motor maps in the cortex of animals exposed to rough tissue removals and simple behavioral tests (Pavlov [1927] 1960; Fearing [1930] 1970). Sherrington, who refers to Pavlov as a "reflexologist" and "Descartes greatest successor", admired his experiments but rejected his materialist explanation of the fabrication of the mind (Sherrington 1940).

The idea of chemical transmitters that carried excitation across the minute synaptic gaps between neurones and at nerve-muscle junctions was developed after 1914 by Henry Dale, Otto Loewi, and others. A physical model of how nerve impulses are started and how they travel down the nerve membrane, along with proof of the integrative blending of excitatory and inhibitory currents in postsynaptic cell bodies, came in the 1940s with the invention of microelectrodes, fine probes that could pick up electrical currents passing through the membranes of nerve cells.[11] Without these basic physiological facts it was impossible to even begin to conceive how nerve-cell circuits, seen clearly by anatomists since the 1870s, could process excitations and coordinate an animal's movements with perceptions of the outside world.

Up to this time nearly every scientist thought of the brain as a circuitry that had energy put into it from stimuli, even though they knew that the level of electrical activity in the brain fluctuated spontaneously in the sleep-wake cycle. Then, forty years ago, important psychological functions of the reticular core of the brain, regulating arousal of attention against sleep, were demonstrated by Horace Magoun and John French (Magoun 1958). This opened the way for new ideas on how the integrative activities of the cortex responsible for perceptual discrimination and learned guidance of movements could be sensitized or changed by the activity of brain-stem systems that also controlled vital body states.   The brain could be understood as capable of regulating its own mental states.

At present, new facts about cerebral functions come so fast--from brain scans, clinical neuropsychology, neuropharmacology, histochemistry of neurones, experimental embryology of the brain, brain grafts, and so on-- the picture we have in any year must, at best, be provisional.   And yet there are already findings that are enlightening for psychology and not unfriendly to traditional wisdom about the inspirations and maladies of the human spirit.

THE NEUROBIOLOGY OF MOTIVES

Adjustments within the core of the brain can select the physically insignificant for awareness from among a plethora of distinguishable elements in stimuli, can concentrate and aim the "searchlight" of attention and seek for goals, and can choose to forget the large and permanently retain the very slight and rare.   The complexity of these systems has become much clearer in the last decade (Scheibel 1984).

In the past century emotions have been identified by physiologists with sensory systems that monitor vital body functions, maintain tissue integrity, and ensure reproduction of the species.   Autonomic control systems that

balance visceral against somatic; restorative and sustaining against energy-
expending, effortful, and depleting; rest against action; pleasure against
pain; flight against fight have been taken as the basis for explanations of
emotion and emotional illness (McGeer, Eccles & McGeer 1978, 465-80;
Konner 1982, 137-42; Pribram 1984). Drives of hunger and sex, triggered
by events in gut and gonads, have been perceived as primary.

But transactions of the brain with physical nature outside the body are
controlled by independent nerve action in the brain core.[12] Spontaneous
changes in arousal, attention, or curiosity gate perceptions of the external
world and give pattern to motor action and learning. Consciousness,
though capable of reacting precisely to sensory stimulation, is under the
control of systems that balance exploration against knowing, seeking against
choosing, taking against rejecting, and remembering against forgetting.
Movement is made effective by these motivations for perception of useful
information.   Its voluntary control depends on active and selective
absorption of stimulus energy from the environment into images of events
in a space/time field for acting that has been generated spontaneously in the
brain.   These "programs" of the brain for its own information-seeking
purposes, that coordinate both perception of objects and movements, can be
identified with cognitive processing. But *there is one kind of motivation,
essential to the development of cultures, that transcends both the autonomic
and the cognitive.*

Mind states of a human being, whether to keep the body intact or to
further consciousness and intended action, *are made into information for
other minds.*   Human motives can be intimately shared through the
expressions of the face, the voice, or gesture. These actions bring, through
subtle regulation of mutual attention, a fusion of purposes between
individuals and a collective awareness of reality.[13] Here, at length, we
reach a level of brain work directly related to Turner's quest. We begin an
enquiry into the neurology of his *communitas.*[14]

Melvin Konner has described how, about 1890, before leaving objective
brain research behind him to explore the subjectivities of psychoanalysis,
Freud worked out a remarkable theory to explain how neural emotional
systems regulate neocortical transactions with reality (Freud 1953; Konner
1982, 130-33). As a young neurologist and neuroanatomist of great

promise, he confronted the new and exciting but simplistic view of language centers and one-way links between the word-hearing area of Carl Wernicke and the word-speaking area of Paul Broca, with a theory of processes for comprehending the meanings of words or for synthesizing ideas to be put into words. In his early papers, Freud was giving anatomical plausibility to notions that later, when he had given up attempting to formulate a neural model, became his metaphorical entities of id, ego, and superego. His informed speculations on the brain mechanisms of motivation at the dawn of psychoanalysis carry much sense to this day (Pribram 1969).

Paul MacLean followed the same tradition.[15] He took up the idea of James Papez that a circuit of structures in the inner rim of the hemispheres and penetrating basal ganglia, thalamus, and hypothalamus was the seat of emotions. He brought anatomy and physiology back to Freud's theory by direct examination with electrical stimulation of the centers in a monkey's brain that seem to command urges to sexual display, or the excitement of perceiving it. Taking a term invented by Broca, he names Papez's emotional system "limbic," that is, "on the fringe" of the cognitive neocortex.

MacLean noted that his squirrel monkey subjects displayed their genitals for the visual appreciation of social partners and also moved their faces to coordinate impulses to fight or mate. He perceived great significance in the ability of these animals to make social engagements by means of posturing, grimacing, and simple calls over a distance. He emphasized that the monkeys use an emotional code to regulate the compelling attractions and rivalries of sex. He expanded the concept beyond experiment to explain how humans, through expressions of love in partnership, find satisfaction for the drive to plan a safe and prosperous future for a family; and he guessed that the brain parts that carry monkeys into mating and generate social bonds must be homologous with those, much enlarged, that make it possible for humans to form lasting affectionate relationships. He proposed that enlargement of the motives of social and interpersonal life must involve projections from the limbic system into the prefrontal cortex, and such an anatomy was confirmed by Walle Nauta (1971). The regulation of emotional signals that can touch another mind is a mental necessity for humankind. The work of Freud, Papez, MacLean, Nauta, and many others since has helped identification of parts of the brain that form the essential crucible of the human spirit (McGeer, Eccles & McGeer 1978, 469-76; Pribram 1984).

MacLean's plan of a three component, "triune" brain is full of rich insights and is supported by careful research. Nevertheless, his idea that automatic reptilian and emotional early mammalian brains form separate, sometimes anarchic strata inside the human mind does not bear critical examination (Damasio & Van Hoesen 1983, 87). Every layer of the brain has been radically reworked by evolution, and new components have been added at the places where functional systems border one another, to make novel systems from their overlapping. All brain components are transformed in the making of human mentality which manifests itself in their interactions. At the same time, the fundamental relationships between instinctive motor patterns, autonomic emotional states, and cognitive processes that learn may be detected in a humble fish or a tiger salamander.[16] New human cerebral organization elaborates the whole plan that was established in ancestral species.

The inner generated spontaneity of motivation, making curiosity for experience and will for actions, plus the emotional linking together of motives between separate beings, are complementary to the building of cognitive, rational, and realistic faculties. Reason and emotion differ not as alternatives or mutually exclusive levels but as mutually dependent causes and explanations of mental life. This is being clarified by remarkable discoveries of different interlocking and balanced mechanisms within the reticular core of the brain. Here research on the tough ingenious rat, long a servant of behaviorists attempting to measure formation of conditioned reflexes, is in the forefront of the new scientific campaign to explore the many-colored motive networks in the periventricular core of the brain stem, and to understand their extensive penetration into the cognitive circuits of the cortex that receive sensory information or command motor action (Ungerstedt 1971; see figure 6.2). It is impossible to comprehend this kind of neural machinery without going into the recently discovered chemistry of the brain.

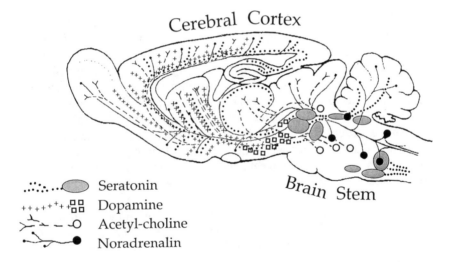

Figure 6.2

Section of a rat brain indicating approximate distribution of the brain-core transmitter systems important in motivation (based on McGeer, Eccles, and McGeer 1978; Ungerstedt 1971).

CHEMISTRY OF EMOTIONAL STATE AND HUMAN EMPATHY

Nerve cells interact by chemical substances that excite receptor gateways on the surface membranes of other nerve cells (McGeer, Eccles & McGeer 1978). Neurohormones or transmitters emitted from the nerve endings, or brought via blood capillaries from endocrine glands into the nervous system, have complex effects on nerve cell transmissions. Some chemicals instantaneously trigger the cell membrane to a discharge of impulses that travel in thousandths of a second from cell to cell down the network. Others have long-lasting, even permanent, effects on the chemistry and excitability inside the cell body. Some can regulate the chemistry of the receiver cell's cytoplasm to the extent of modifying gene transcription and protein synthesis and cell development.

In the motivational core of the brain there are intermingled cell clusters and a forest of cell communication lines that have a multiplicity of roles to play in balancing environment-sensitive perception against emotion, activity and effort against passive self-nurturance, fight against flight, and pleasure against pain. The whole dynamic multi-cellular federation integrates the antithetical states of a psychological subject and consolidates awareness of a "self"; it regulates the rate and intensity or force of motor output, focuses and aims a dozen different types of attention to sensory input, repairs diseased or disordered tissues, including the motivating tissues themselves, and reaches out to communicate with other organisms that mirror the excitements of the self and react with complementary messages or actions.

The chemical code of nerve cell communication in the brain stem has been discovered in the last fifty years (McGeer, Eccles & McGeer 1978). Adrenaline and acetylcholine in the peripheral autonomic nervous system, readying the body for intense effort and resisting pain, or settling it for sleep and recuperation, were detected about the turn of the century; however, transmitters in the brain itself were found in the 1930s, and the main quick-acting excitatory and inhibitory *ionotropic* agents of refined sensory and motor coordination were not discovered until the 1950s.

Slow *metabotropic* regulators of nerve cell activity and excitatory state act by releasing intracellular "second messenger" substances that give energy to chemical reactions of protoplasm, including protein synthesis.

They are secreted by a scattering of neurone groups in the brain stem that have been known for less than thirty years. While about one million in number, less than one-50,000th of the total population of neurones in a human cortex, regulator neurones have axons penetrating into all brain networks, perhaps five million endings arising from a single cell. They influence perception, learning, remembering, and motor programming by changing the state of cells in many deep nuclei of the brain and in the cerebral cortex. They are the telegraphic system of instinctive readiness in the nerve networks, capable of setting the balance of nerve energy in innate patterns and driving the rituals of social engagements, including those between the sexes or between parents and their offspring. These substances, acting in counterbalanced combinations to modulate all cerebral integrations, play a crucial role in altered states of consciousness and mental illness, in the day-to-day regulation of mood and personality, and in the moment-by-moment changes of emotion.

Historic experiments on the effects of electrical stimulations in the brain were carried out in the 1930s by Walter Hess. Hess described opposing systems. One produced arousal, increased muscle strength, active psychic alertness, and exploration; he called this *ergotropic* and identified it with stimulation of the posterior hypothalamus. The other induced behaviors promoting rest, recuperation, low body activity but high visceral processing, apathy, relaxation, and sleep; he named this system *trophotropic* and linked it to anterior hypothalamic stimulation. Later work by Hess, Heinrich Kluver and Paul Bucy, MacLean, and James Olds implicated an extensive system of brain stem and limbic cortex in this same regulation of motivations, appetites, and sexuality (Hess 1954; 1964; Olds 1962; Valenstein 1973). The evidence from cases of accidental injury to mesofrontal cortex, to the hippocampus, amygdala and limbic tissue, and to the hypothalamus and areas of the midline or ventral brain stem in humans is in agreement. Activation or suppression of these systems is associated with changes in vitality and alertness or sleepiness and confusion, and with pleasurable elation and warm floating feelings or irritability, anxiety, fear, and rage. They are involved in the symbolic effusions and "pressure of words" in schizophrenia, or in the withdrawn silence of the depressed or autistic individual. Sexual feelings and urges as well as visceral states are also altered by excitation or removal of these parts of the brain.[17]

In 1959 dopamine, abundant in the corpus striatum (key component of MacLean's reptilian brain), was implicated in Parkinsonism, a disorder of movement accompanied by a characteristic depression of motivation. At this time Bernard Brodie had the idea that noradrenaline is a central ergotropic agent while serotonin, first found in the early 1950s and concentrated in the hypothalamus and limbic system (MacLean's emotional brain of mammals), is the central trophotropic substance. Thus began a great era in discovery and synthesis of chemicals that could tranquilize, elevate mood, stimulate, and reduce psychotic symptoms, and of drugs that could create psychotic states of euphoria and hallucination. The most active substances, including reserpine, chlorpromazine, iproniazid, amphetamine, and lysergic acid, caused changes in the availability or action of serotonin, dopamine, noradrenaline, and adrenaline, or they mimicked the action of these substances. Hope for cures of mental illness drove researchers to untangle an immensely complex system, but unfortunately the antipsychotic drugs usually cause unpleasant Parkinson-like motor problems and agitation or depression.

In the 1960s and 1970s, ways were found to stain selectively natural transmitter chemicals in cell groups and fiber projection pathways, and at nerve cell endings where mental states and moods are regulated, making the transmitters easily visible under the microscope. The extensive penetration of these neurochemical systems into the classical sensory, motor, and associative tissues and the intricate convergence of their endings on integrator cells of cortex and brain stem were made vividly apparent. Then, in the mid 1970s, a new group of central transmitters was found regulating both the experience of pleasure and pain and the secretion of anterior pituitary hormones of growth and healing. Minute quantities of natural opiates could produce the effects of addictive opiate drugs like morphine: euphoria, sedation, relaxation of muscles, and relief from pain. The discovery of the enkephalins and related endorphines explained how traditional meditative or hypnotic techniques, or manipulations such as acupuncture, were effective in controlling the physical origin of pain; they caused the brain to produce its own analgesic (Marsden 1979). Secretory neurones of this type were found in the peripheral pain pathways and in the brain stem reticular formation and basal ganglia. They are probably involved in the whole range of appetitive drives for food, water, and sex, as well as in maternal behavior and transitory affective states of the limbic system.

The chemical systems of motivation are concentrated in the same brain structures as have been identified with emotions by clinical studies of temporal lobe epileptics, who experience depersonalized states and powerful emotional auras, and by electrical recording and stimulations with awake animals or in a few unhappy human patients who suffer uncontrollable aggression, fear or pain, or disturbing involuntary movements (Heilman & Satz 1983).

Brain science and clinical neuropsychology, linked to psychiatry and neurology, show up a bewildering variety of normal and broken-down states of personality that give evidence of the shape of the motivating fabric in human brains and how it is built up and maintained. Pharmacological drugs block or mimic the action of natural neurotransmitters, giving rise to abnormal impulses to move, whipping up storms of joy, anger or despair, perverting attention and blotting out remembering, and evoking psychotic fantasies with aimless outpourings of verbal and gestural symbols. Their evil as addictive drugs misused socially arises from their power to destroy the very basis of human affection, making expressions to others untrustworthy and driving creativity crazily inwards so it burns itself out in circular logic and narcissistic chains of association.

Epileptic discharges focused in limbic and association cortices, or in the deep nuclei with which these cortices communicate, likewise make false motives, inappropriate emotions, and illusory perceptions. Tumors in these places leave holes in consciousness or the patterns of voluntary purpose, or they change personality, sometimes leading to profound indifference, depression, or uncontrolled anger. Psychic defects caused by local injury in the limbic and deep parts of the brain display a bewildering spectrum, mixing cognitive and emotional effects (Heilman & Satz 1983).

MacLean has emphasized that the motivating mechanisms have been located by tracing epileptic discharges, applying electrical stimulation and surgery, and manipulating brain chemistry, leaving obscure how they can be excited by stimuli in normal life. One proven input to them is from hormones in the blood. Thyroid hormone in excess causes emotional instability, and apathy or depression if depleted. Sex hormones cause changes in aggressivity or gentleness as well as in erotic excitement. They are taken up by hypothalamus, septum, and amygdala, regions where Hess showed, in the 1930s, that instinctive sex behavior patterns could be triggered by electrical stimulation in hens and cats (Hess 1954; McGeer, Eccles & McGeer 1978, 468). But for consciousness a more significant input is the one through eyes and ears or through touch, taste, or smell which detect the organism's relationship with external conditions and events and assist in adjusting the state of the body to its circumstances. We can include the detectors of food and water, and the detectors of a safe, warm, and comfortable situation for rest and recuperation. These are of primary importance when an animal learns how to make the best of an environment that can be perceived by distance receptors.

While the motivating core of the human brain is supremely sensitive to signals from the environment, especially the human environment, it is also full of spontaneously generated nerve activity and it acts as source of excitatory and neurochemical signals for the rest of the brain. The anatomy of the brain core defines a coherent, multimodal space-time field of behavior. Orientations of attending in all modalities and movements of all body members are held together by associative systems of interneurones of the motivating system. Rhythmic measures of time and the tempo of movements, too, are created in pacemakers of the reticular network that can synchronize all parts of the body in cyclical expressive effusions that need bear no immediate relation to the timing of events in the outside world.

The unified configurations and rhythms of expressive behavior constitute a common code for interpersonal attunement. By this code we share motivation, through imitating the forms of actions and the rhythms of movement of our partners. The messages of motivation are carried from a patterned and integrated emitter in one brain to tuned and matching receivers in other brains. In a sense, the cadences and shapes of movement that are caused by different fluctuating states of interneuronal chemistry in one brain stem can be the cause of matching or complementary patterns of chemistry in another brain stem.

The power of learned associations and of symbolic formulae to act as languages for communicating human feelings and experiences must be derived from these empathic mechanisms that attune emotions between individuals directly. Both experiences of reality and symbols are given values derived from emotional referencing between human beings who match their evaluations. That is why meanings of objects and symbols have universal dimensions in psychic space and time, such as rate and rhythm of movement, brightness or darkness, color values, warmth or cold, and loving and trusting or fearfulness--all qualities differently labeled in the chemistry and anatomy of the emotional brain core. It is barely a quarter of a century since the outlines of this inner evaluative council of the brain became known. Clearly we have much to learn about its vital workings.

MOTIVATION FOR LEARNING

One persistent mechanistic view of brain physiology and of reductionist psychology that turns to physiology for explanations is that the neocortex is a retentive fabric without prejudice, a network that starts its postnatal maturation with no functional design, in which associations of experience are made in response to patterns of chance in encounters with the outside world.   This cortex stores or encodes the history of stimuli traced *a posteriori*.   An adult human mind so built is thought of as essentially pragmatic or rational and logically deterministic, ruled by a truth-telling propositional language that transmits cognitive structures into the brains of children. They learn practical tasks by practice and how to deal with facts and the logic of combinations of facts by absorbing reason in language. Rules of inference acquired in school lead to progressively more powerful propositions about truth in both practical and social worlds.

This analysis flatters text-proud and physicalistic European philosophies that place motives and values in a dependent relation to practical and realistic necessities, and to reason. It is favored by empiricist doctrines of education such as that advocated by John Locke,[18] and it is congenial to the contemporary physicalism of the computer-minded. But, in the eye of an evolutionary or developmental biologist the child's brain is less passive and less empty of values than conceived by these philosophies. It is a strategy-planning controller of a vital and self-regulating being. It is the organ that represents in its genetically transmitted self-fabricating design a set of adaptive purposes for behavior that physical and logical programs so far created by systems engineers can imitate only in caricature. Activity patterns and responsive settings generated within the brain before birth are independent of outside facts at that stage of development, and after the brain is born into perception of an outside world it gains desired forms of acting by reference to categories of perceiving and moving and to states of motivation and emotion created earlier, in evolution and *in utero*. As the humanistic educators Comenius and Friedrich Froebel taught, children learn largely by development of their natural impulses to share knowledge.[19]

In the last five years it has become clearly apparent that brains never solidify into the static nerve cell networks they seem to be in anatomical pictures of physiological tests of reflex integration. They retain a lifelong embryogenic dynamism and develop perpetually (Trevarthen 1980a). In a spontaneously active cerebral federation the activities, growth, and indeed the survival of every nerve cell depend upon the balance of excitation it receives from other nerve cells. Growing neurones cooperate and compete in vast assemblies. Moving and changing populations interact to generate flowerings of structure where fusions and destructions of elements occur, and competing activities stabilize in elaborate equilibria. Damage is repaired, sometimes with novel rewirings. From time to time parts of the developing brain undergo catastrophic fall or upheaval with death of vast numbers of cells. Throughout the life cycle within an overall organization that resists deformation, neurones are uniting in new functional teams--not just drilled by patterns in stimuli but also under the regulation of rewarding and punishing patterns of motivation that the brain generates in itself.[20]

TISSUES THAT LEARN CULTURE

A striking anatomical feature in maps for human brain functions is a large, slow-maturing zone of cortex where limbic inward-directed and neocortical outward-directed tissues meet and intensively interact (see figure 6.3).

This zone appears to have evolved in humans to carry out the cooperative learning activities that make culture possible (Trevarthen 1983a; 1984a). It is the area of greatest difference between ape and human brain, and lesions in it cause the most bizarre cognitive disorders; the aphasias, which lead to failures in the use of language to communicate and to think; the apraxias, which affect the planning of intricate, and arbitrary, serial motor skills; neglect syndromes, which leave a patient unable to generate

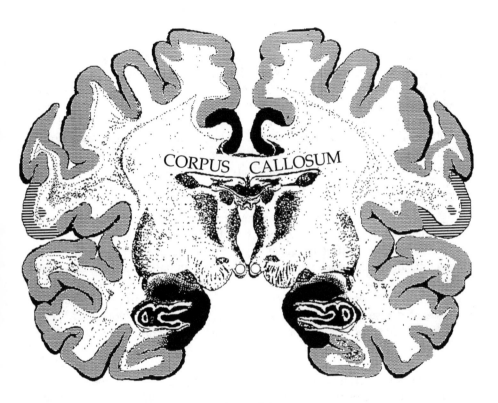

Figure 6.3

Diagrams of the human cortex showing limbic tissue in black and "tissues of culture," Brodmann's territories numbers 37, 39, 40, 44-46, cross-hatched (original).

and use an awareness of one side of his or her body, of the space around, or of objects in it; and the specific agnosias, where a class of objects important in normal intelligent life is not comprehended and is poorly perceived. Prosopagnosia, for example, is an extraordinary loss of the ability to recognize people by their appearance; of course it is socially incapacitating.

The lesions that cause these defects either disconnect tissues by breaking nerve tracts that allow motives to integrate with perceptions or actions, or they demolish an integrative center where motives are elaborated. In every case they change the functions of primary sensory and/or motor projections known for more than 100 years and also of the still poorly understood reticular and limbic projections of the brain core. This component of the human cortex seems to be both source and pinnacle of remembering, where experiences are represented in forms that have the most concentrated meaning for the subject.

I see these tissues as receiving the best of information from both inner-directed and outer-directed cerebral worlds. On the one hand they are most finely tuned to the affective states engendered by self-awareness and to that peculiar innate awareness of people that causes imitation and sympathy. On the other hand they receive the most synthetic, most abstract forms of association between experiences, as well as the most sifted and densely correlated resultant memories, and their rationalized overworkings. They also include areas, such as the supplementary motor cortex, that can initiate actions.

Furthermore, this part of the cortex integrates a link between the unconscious motor plan of the cerebellum, which predicts kinetics of body action and delicately tunes them to feedback from sensors of force in body members and round their joints, and the space and object perceiving images of the projection zones of the cerebral cortex. The latter images give propulsive and prehensile movements their precise and appropriate targets in the outside world.

In short, the learning processes in this ultra-neo, hyperlimbic cortex tissue at the junction of the main cerebral lobes are the ones that give meanings form. They generate actions and experiences that have been validated by shared emotions and common experience in an instinctively, and sometimes stormily, cooperative community of human minds.

It is to the motivation and emotion side of this critical mind apparatus, not to the rational inferential side, that we must turn to get clarification of religious, artistic, theatrical, or playful experiences. The senses of holiness, of morality, of beauty, and of humor project the attitudes that people have towards experience. They arise because people need to and want to communicate evaluations of experience and because they must test their motives for comprehension and cooperation to the limit.

The grasp of reality is precarious in the sacred, the ethical, the aesthetic, or the playful or tragic dramatic events; but it is also most powerful in significance, which explains why parables of tradition compel attention and why they are so instructive. They show ways that all manner of new experiences may be interpreted in terms of universal feelings compatible with an ancient human lore.

MODES OF CONSCIOUSNESS AND LEARNING IN SPLIT BRAINS

Pioneering split-brain experiments of Ronald Myers and Roger Sperry in the 1950s proved that the great interhemispheric bridge, the corpus callosum, could transmit details of learned consciousness from one cerebral hemisphere to the other (Sperry 1961). Their tests showed that each half of a cat's brain separated from its partner could direct behavior of all the cat's body.

I used learning experiments with split-brain monkeys to demonstrate that perceiving and remembering are not just an automatic consequence of the cortex being aimed at and receiving any stimulus that might be suitable to direct the actions that the animal is set to perform (Trevarthen 1965). The two anatomically equal halves of the divided monkey brain could be getting identical stimuli, but only one side, the one engaged in directing a hand to push a lever for a peanut, would learn. The other half brain, which was not involved in responding, seemed unconscious and retained nothing. The obvious conclusion was that a cerebral cortex has to be readied inwardly for awareness and learning to occur. Perceiving required wanting to act or an active interest in the consequences of action as well as an input of relevant sensory experience.

In the 1960s a few epileptic patients whose sickness was not responding well to drugs were relieved of seizures by commissurotomy. Disconnection of the hemispheres prevented spread of electrical discharges. The now famous psychological tests performed in Sperry's laboratory at Caltech (Sperry 1967) revealed that in these human beings a readiness to know and learn with one hemisphere at a time was part of a strategy to act with a particular kind of problem-solving program. Their left and right minds were different. While the cerebral hemispheres of a monkey are almost equal alternative systems of consciousness and learning, human hemispheres were revealed to be specialized for complementary domains of awareness. They perceive different meanings in identical stimuli and each solves best its own kind of mental problem. This conclusion accords well with a century of observations of people with injury in one or the other side of the brain and with many recent experiments in which normal people have been tested with stimuli routed to one hemisphere at a time (Bradshaw & Nettleton 1983; Trevarthen 1984a). Most people, we now believe, have different concepts of experience, different aptitudes for learning, and different creative strategies for using experience to guide thoughts and actions in their two cerebral hemispheres.[21]

By analysis of the dynamics of perceiving in commissurotomy patients, Jerre Levy and I were able to show that adjustments in the whole brain, including brain-stem circuits that operate below consciousness, could turn on or off all or part of high-level processes in the cerebral cortex of one hemisphere (Levy and Trevarthen 1976). Both awareness and ability to move could be adjusted by this channeling of internal facilitation or activation into one or the other half of the divided forebrain. We called this "meta-control" of consciousness. It qualifies the permanent differences in functional capacity of the separated hemispheres. Indeed, the common pattern of differences between the two human cerebral hemispheres may turn out to be related to alternative ways in which the motivating and orienting mechanisms of the brain stem can be set to deal with the outside world.

The right hemisphere appears to have a more diffuse and more coherent representation of all the body and its parts, and of the space that radiates out from the body as the field into which attentions and actions are projected. The left hemisphere has a more crisply differentiated representation, more focused on just the right hand and just the right side of body-centered space as this is represented in visual, auditory, and tactile spheres. In consequence of this asymmetry, injury to the right posterior cortex often leads to an unawareness or neglect of the left of the body or the left of space, but such indifference to one side of reality is not produced by a left-hemisphere lesion of the same size. The right hemisphere, because it has more complete representation of space round the body, appears to be better equipped for the primary organizing of attention to stimuli. In addition, this hemisphere is better at recognizing faces and bodies and at making drawings or arranging elements to make patterns or schematic diagrams. Geometric puzzles are used with brain injured patients as tests for failure of predominantly right-sided abilities.

Of course the most dramatic difference between the human hemispheres, vividly demonstrated in the early experiments of Sperry and Michael Gazzaniga (1967), is that when each is on its own, lacking connections to its partner, only the left one can speak. Since the days of Broca and Wernicke over a century ago, it has been thought that all language functions are much more strongly represented in the left hemisphere. But exploration of language function in commissurotomy patients soon revealed that the surface effects are misleading.

In fact the right hemisphere contributes much to the understanding and conceiving of language, even when it has been disconnected from the speaking partner (Hughlings Jackson 1932, 129-45; Trevarthen 1984a). Its poor perception of fine features of speech, its failure in rhyming when it has to imagine the sounds of speech, and its inability to emit any articulatory movements of speech except very rare fragments may all be consequences of a congenital restriction of a unique part of the speech apparatus to the left hemisphere, a part that performs a final state of programming to insert the smallest units of speech expression into slots of meaning that the right hemisphere can conceive on its own. The right hemisphere, listening to language, can pick up much of the sense, especially that part of it that translates readily into a scenario of being and acting. It relates words to a pragmatic and emotive world that can be perfectly well seen, heard, felt, and understood without coding into words--a world like that of a young child, remembered directly and not explained by a propositional argument (Ross 1984).

Besides transmitting semantic information about facts and features of an objective world, the structure of language must encode rules for engagement of awareness, feeling, and purpose between conscious subjects. Sentences explain how subjects are acting on objects or on other subjects. The syntax and case inflections define changing motivations and purposeful tendencies. Language must, therefore, involve a cerebral regulation of how the inner situation of one person can reach out and cooperate with what is going on in the feelings of another person.[22] The propositional and informative functions of language ride upon an assertive interpersonal engagement that tries, by appeal to a common expressive code, to make the other mind take something in. These contrast with the self-regulatory, remembering, and thinking functions of language in a private world where messages of speech mingle freely with images and thoughts in wordless form.

Perhaps the partitioning of language functions we observe in human brains is a product of an ancient tendency for the left brain to be outgoing and assertive and the right to be more receptive, accommodating, and self-sustaining. Support for this idea comes from asymmetries favoring the right hemisphere in nonlinguistic areas of mental activity mentioned above, including the private management of action of the body by an integrated self who perceives both the configuration and motions of its body and the relation of the body in time to the geography of surroundings. This difference is reflected in the very mysterious, universal and prehistoric tendency for one hand to be the most public, most expressive and most symbolic one. In a majority of people everywhere it is the right hand, but for some people it is just as definitely the left.[23]

If we direct attention to the emotional and temperamental side of human behavior, an intriguing partitioning of the personality seems to emerge in differences between the hemispheres (Heilman & Satz 1983; Trevarthen 1984a, 1174). Along with their attentional neglect and reduced body scheme, patients with right-sided strokes or other right-brain pathology seem temperamentally brittle in response to experience, extraverted, insensitive to others' emotions, literal in their impressions of phenomena rather than metaphorical, and deficient or inappropriate in sense of humor. People with left-hemisphere lesions tend to be not only impaired in language but also withdrawn and yet retaining social sensitivity and a metaphorical or poetic imagination that may be revealed in their mistakes with language or in interpretations they make of pictures. The symptoms seem to relate to the subjects' way of assimilating situations to themselves, physically or emotionally, and to constitute a form of primary adaptation to those situations.

Thus, the left hemisphere seems to be revealed as having a more active commitment to execute acts on the physical or human world while the right is more private and receptive. The left seems to seek initiative and to express itself in declarative mode. There is evidence from epileptics suggesting that in emotional pathology the left hemisphere tends towards manic, aggressive states while the right is more depressive and submissive (Flor-Henry 1983). These are of course important poles in the emotional balancing of viewpoints between persons who are attempting to share consciousness and transfer information about it or act cooperatively within it. Infusion of feeling into experience makes it communicable and gives meaning to metaphorical and narrative representation. Fantasy always draws richly on metaphor as well as a sense of unfolding drama. The right hemisphere of most of us may have more complete mastery of an essential motivation for this generation of a story in experience.

There is widespread interest now in these indications of differences in the personalities and emotions of the two hemispheres of the human brain. Some believe that the articulate and rational left hemisphere has, in our culture, had unfair hegemony over an intuitive right hemisphere. They appear to be rebelling against our deep-seated Western belief that reason must master emotion and hold it in check, a belief that owes its strength to the rational philosophy that has dominated our Western culture since the seventeenth century. Knowing facts and arguing from them with appeal to truth, objective reality, and necessity, independent of personal feelings, must involve different brain mechanisms from the having and sharing of emotions or the influencing of others by arousing in them imaginary and moving connotations and intuitive evaluations.

But communication needs both these kinds of mental strategy. They must work together, as seeking and evaluating do in control of adaptive behaviors of very simple animals. It is difficult to imagine that a human mind could work at all if reason and emotion were separated surgically. There is evidence that commissurotomy patients exhibit an impoverishment of emotion and lowered vigilance in attention, but each of the separated hemispheres can achieve elaborate consciousness and can react with social sensitivity.[24]

We have learned much from the discovery of the contrasting mentalities of our left and right hemispheres, but this is only one way of viewing complementary mental states.

First, it fails to recognize that there are other anatomical axes along which one may seek contrasts in motivational process. For example, frontal and posterior parts of both hemispheres differ in their relationship to perception, to generation of motor impulses, to emotions, and to cerebral trophotropic regulations of the body's physiological functioning. There is a mapping across the cortex in each hemisphere, and through its subcortical nuclei, of the same components of mental activity as are used to characterize left and right parts of the brain.

Second, given that clear-cut hemispheric differences in mental style and in motivations exist, they certainly normally interact in synchrony and with the closest coordination. Various states of mind may arise not from the separate action of the two hemispheres, but from their joint action. Consider an example: Is the energy of play and ritual the result of left and right hemispheres in dialogue, of basal ganglia and limbic structures interacting with neocortex, or of frontal parts of the cortex engaging with parietal and temporal parts?[25]

Split-brain studies showed how cortical states of consciousness are regulated by the motivation for response. They showed that refined perception and learning were confined to the cortex, and they revealed the power of underlying directives of attention and evaluation from the brain stem. They also gave a new view of complementary cognitive strategies in human consciousness. These too seem now to originate in deeper asymmetries of motives for acting on the world and for communicating.

Consistent differences between the cognitive functions of the hemispheres seem to bear a relationship to different motivations for engagement of a person with the outside world or with other persons. Further evidence for this kind of inherent structure in human motives for cooperative awareness comes from recent research on the communicative behavior of infants.

THE HUMAN SPIRIT IN CHILDREN

About 1970 psychologists began to study films and television recording of mothers and infants playing happily and intimately without interference. They saw behaviors of wonderful complexity. Within hours of birth a baby can join in a delicately regulated exchange of feeling with a responsive and loving mother, showing a remarkable precocity in appreciation of the pulse and musicality of human expression. By two months, subtle conversation-like exchanges occur (Trevarthen 1974; 1983b). The new discoveries stimulated experiments which prove that newborn infants are tuned to many signals from the mother's body, that they can identify her from her odor, her voice, and the rhythms of her movements, and that they can imitate her face movements (Field & Fox 1985). Even the most skeptical, and there has been an intellectual resistance to this evidence, have to admit that a human being is born with a capacity to empathize with another who is sought as a trusted and loving caretaker.

I have been studying the development of this human empathy, attempting to discover how the infant regulates the attentions of the mother in play. For me the most important discovery is that the infant, aware of persons before attending to objects that can be manipulated, has a growing interest in learning about the world by sharing experiences and tasks and by tracking what others know and understand through observation of their actions. I see the child working toward a symbolic, cultural understanding well before he or she utters first words in the mother tongue (Trevarthen 1979; 1980b).

The patterns in the behavior of infants give evidence of inborn cerebral organizations that set mental life in motion. They show up universal laws of emotion by which interactions between persons are regulated (Trevarthen 1984a; 1985a). From birth, there is a deep antithesis between the joyful affection that promotes coming together of persons and their joining to share motives harmoniously, and the anger or fear that exploits or withdraws from another and destroys sharing. After three months, play between infant and a trusted caretaker joins affection to that measured aggression called teasing in a dynamic and lively dance across the boundary between dependence and independence of consciousness and will. In a happy relationship it reinforces bonds of trust and confidence (Trevarthen 1983a; 1984a).

Infants display from the beginning a spontaneous integrity of action and expression that corresponds with the *anemos* of the ancient Greeks, an invisible wind that moves, and the *anima* of Latin that became the Judeo-Christian "soul." This stirring spirit (akin to the breadth of life, *pneuma*), with insistent beat and subtle rhythmic variations, resists analysis in machine terms. All parts of the baby's body move together to express shades of feeling. The expressive flowing of an infant's emotion is highly responsive. It encourages a mother, deeply moved by the birth of her infant, to feel she is appreciated by another being who is intimately like herself. A new system of two persons--a self-sustaining relationship--is made of their behaving together (Stern 1985; Braten, 1988).

The practical curiosity about the world that an infant builds up in the first six months is not simply the expression of self-regulated independence of perception and acting. In it interpersonal motives remain strong, so the exploring infant is inherently cooperative and communicative. Play with objects opens the relationship with the mother towards the world they can learn about together (Hubley & Trevarthen 1979). While the infant is striving to understand objects, with intent following of gaze and reaching out with the hands, he or she is intimately sensitive to what others do. The baby soon becomes expert at seeking information about how acts of a trusted partner, recognized as part of a relationship and different from strangers, may extend a project in hand.

The will to manipulate and explore is expressed as a message to people, as being shy or showing off, that is, trying to escape attentions of others or trying to cause them to accept the interest or purpose behind any action or novel experience (Trevarthen 1983b; 1985b). Soon familiar playthings and tricks of expression absorb an evaluation not only from the way they reward the feelings of the child directly but, even more powerfully, through the expressions of approval, pleasure, or dislike that others give forth when the child attends to these things or acts that way.

A mother who loves her child is ready to be a pupil to this growing curiosity about the shared world. Her behavior gives pattern and development to infant motives for expression, and this is the basis for an affectionate teaching relationship. Through it the mother becomes a traveling supporting consciousness for the infant's mental differentiation, driven forward by her instinctive impulse to be guided by the infant's signals of curiosity and pleasure. The friendship between mother and infant, though asymmetric in complexity and purpose, is held together by the same emotions as in all other human friendships. It uses the same affective code to establish mutual awareness, the same concordance of motives and regulated variation in dependence and independence of wills (Trevarthen 1984b; Stern 1985).

Developments in the stage called *infant*, a word derived from the Latin meaning "without speech," though related to the child's eventually gaining command of speech, are independent of words. Also, later developments are not a simple consequence of thinking in words; they rely upon the interpersonal and emotional patterns practiced and developed in communication in the first months, at least a year before the first true word. Even a two-month-old can actively contribute utterances and gestures to precise intercoordination of a communication game (Trevarthen 1983b). By six months he or she will show playful, humorous interest in the clashes of purpose that arise in play with the mother. Both enjoy teasing, which is a regulated use of resistive or aggressive moves that test the skill and affection of the other (Trevarthen 1984b; Trevarthen 1990). It is a way of challenging that laughs at the efforts of the other to respond.

There is an impulse from early weeks for the infant to express the germ of an idea in gesture and utterance, and this expressiveness has power to become the unique human gift of language (Trevarthen & Marwick 1986). Towards the end of the first year simple word-like sounds and hand signs are imitated by the baby and displayed to gain recognition for others. Called "protolanguage" by Michael Halliday (1975), these signs immediately serve as a common currency in the family to represent shared ideas and to label intentions or designate important experiences or people.

This ushers in an ebullient production of fantasies in play that rework all experiences to make them into sociodramatic entities, pieces of a picture or story being created with others, a miniature symbolic world to be lived in with them (Trevarthen and Logotheti 1987; Trevarthen 1987, 1990).

At one year most infants use gestures and vocalizations to engage the interests and attentions of familiar persons, and they understand instructions and want to comply (Trevarthen & Marwick 1986). They watch, gesture, and listen to utterances, fixing gaze on the partner's face to get as much information as possible about the message. In other words, they begin to show that they want cooperative action, hunting for signs that help them to perform tasks in collaboration. Pretending to be someone else, pretending to carry out actions that another will understand, or for the benefit of another, pretending to use banal or meaningless things as tools, consumables, or emblems that are full of meaning and meaningful action-- such acts of mental creation appear in the spontaneous repertoire of an eighteen-month-old who has few words (Trevarthen 1985b; Trevarthen and Logotheti 1987).

The requisite imagining and motivation for this "symbolic" kind of communication arises asymmetrically in the child's brain before language is mastered. It is coupled to the strange unconscious preference to use one hand, usually the right, for such communication (see note 23). It does not need words but is clearly of fundamental importance to the understanding and use of words in language, and it can take in spoken messages from adults who are trying to assist. Details of the ways toddlers play with people, especially how three-year-olds develop play with peers in friendship, make it clear that the adaptive function of fantasy is to construct a world of metaphor that is sharable and collectively usable.[26]

The play of animals that so amuses us, like play of humans, contributes to the development of social awareness. The cognitive representations involved in it have to be separable from those that govern what each subject is doing for himself, so they can be presented with clear emotional force for assimilation by another. Just imagine kittens at play: Do they not strut and posture and dodge within the awareness of another being, real or imagined? John Fentress finds that wolf cubs play at the thrust and dodge of a fight even when on their own, but the instinctive moves only make sense in a real combat with a fighting partner (Havkin & Fentress 1985).

The actions of play are communications. This is understood in Gregory Bateson's theory of metacommunication (Bateson 1972). Bateson focuses on the paradox of play where every act is different from what it seems to be doing, drawing attention to what it could be. Play biting, hiding, or dodging is not "serious" with a simple purpose for the player alone: it is always combined with an expression of feeling that signals "this is play." In humans metacommunication becomes the generator of meanings and the foundation of rituals that give collective social events significance.[27]

It might be thought outrageous to suggest that we can designate elements of brain activity for such emotional and playful subtleties of spirit in the infant and toddler and for such sensitivities to the spirit of others, especially the mother and friends, but there are signs of how parts of the brain are implicated in the early growth of the human mind (Trevarthen 1983a; 1985a). We have a few pointers to the cerebral growth changes underlying early postnatal developments in motivation for human contact.

First, the affective signaling in the primary intersubjective contact of the first two months has much that is homologous with emotional signaling of animals. The cerebral mechanisms of brain stem, midbrain reticular formation, basal ganglia, and limbic system that govern vocal expressions of monkeys certainly will have homologues in humans, and the same applies to movements of facial expression. Detlev Ploog, a pupil of MacLean, suggests that early coos and cries of infants are involuntary and unlearned, closely similar to the calls that he has studied in squirrel monkeys to determine their neuroanatomical basis (Ploog 1979). However, coos of two-month-olds already have morphological characteristics that show they are rudiments of human speech. This does not mean they are produced by the cortical speech areas because even in adults speech still involves processes in subcortical (limbic and thalamic) centers. It seems that the subcortical components, already formed for speech, mature ahead of the neocortical ones.

A wave of cell differentiation and maturation of intercellular contacts spreads across the posterior cerebral cortex of a baby from the occipital pole through the integrative parietal cortices shortly after birth. This correlates with rapid improvements in visual perception in the first six months and with the development of efficient manipulation. Developments in frontal parts of the brain a few months later have been correlated with development in the infant's ability to predict the place of interesting objects in spite of periodic rearrangements and disappearances as the objects are moved about, behind, or inside other objects by an adult (Goldman-Rakic 1984). They may be vital in imitation and observational learning.

One special feature of human communication, present in rudimentary form in monkeys and capable of "cultural" molding in the apes, is the use of hands to give messages. Ordinary people move their hands to express feelings and ideas in parallel with speech. Most of us use the right hand as the dominant expressor of ideas and the left as a supporting partner that helps lay out the context for what is to be expressed. In deaf people the hands can become transmitters of a full sign language, as rapid as speech and carrying all the subtleties of emotion and reference. Hand gestures of young infants also show asymmetry, expressive responses to maternal speech being most often made by the right hand (Trevarthen 1985b). This second remarkable precocity in human expression, coupled to cooing vocalizations that lead to speech, may also be due to inherent asymmetry in brain parts beneath the neocortex in limbic cortex, basal ganglia, and thalamus (see note 23).

Intersubjective mirroring essential to the establishment and progress of normal intellectual development may involve the medio-frontal limbic system and medial cortex in front of the corpus callosum. Damage to these regions in monkeys causes a loss of social skill and an apparent fall in the kinds of motivation that are essential to maintaining a lively and confident position in a group. The poor animals become isolated and withdrawn (Myers 1972).

In human beings the same kind of loss of spirit for communication and cooperation is seen when a stroke or infection leads to a lesion in this territory of the brain. Rare cases have been reported where a damage in the meso-limbic cortex or supplementary motor area causes a social apathy and muteness, although the patient is not paralyzed, retains high intelligence, and can still understand what other people refer to when they speak (Damasio & Van Hoesen 1983). There is evidence that defects in the meso-limbic frontal parts of the brain underlie the tragic conditions where infants and toddlers are autistic and fail to develop communication with the human world except in poor and fragile forms.[28]

Autistic toddlers, who avoid direct contact with their caretakers and cannot share the pleasure of play, show mysterious numinous states of joy. They gaze up to the sky opening their hands to a private experience and emit a saint-like smile. Autistic children, typically inclined to intense concentration of their minds or the exploration of sensations and playing seriously with visual, tactual, or auditory effects of their own making, can have remarkable gifts. Cases are known that draw with astonishing artistic maturity, that write sensitive poetry with wonderful imagery, and that make brilliant calculations or beautiful musical sounds. Clearly they retain a sense of beauty and a pleasure in mystical experience that can have symbolic value to others. When observed closely they are seen to be supremely sensitive to others while avoiding eye contact or touching and exhibiting no joy in sharing.

I believe these sad children, whose development needs the closest, most sympathetic and perceptive support, reveal to us an antithesis in the human spirit of which we are all secretly aware. They seem to have a lesson to teach us abut the austere and lonely origin of religious or artistic inspiration. There is no doubt about the awe such inspiration can command.

CONCLUSIONS

"The Spiritualist and the associationist must both be 'cerebralists,' to the extent at least of admitting that certain peculiarities in the way of working of their own favorite principles are explicable only by the fact that the brain laws are codeterminant of the result" (James [1890] 1950, 1:4).

Since the Harvard psychologist William James wrote those words a mere 100 years ago, some coherent knowledge has been won of the cerebral mechanisms of mind. James reviewed body-imaging maps that respond to sensory input in separate modalities or that excite movements of body segments. In these windows of perception and outlets of will humans and intelligent animals are easily compared. In addition, neurologists have located tissues at the confluence of the main lobes of the left hemisphere in the human brain that are vital for coordinating speech or for comprehending language. Now we know that language areas are one part of a newly evolved cortical zone that contains the power to grow the myriad memories and skills required for participation in the collective enterprise of culture.

The "tissues of culture" all tend to asymmetry; in a majority of persons certain ones are stronger in the left brain while others are better served in the right hemisphere. Greater mysteries remain within the deeper motive systems that have decisive control over both the development and the functioning of the reality-oriented and cognitive brain--from the embryo, when neurones are beginning to distribute themselves in brain nuclei and the cortical mantle of the hemispheres, to the failing but experienced and wise networks of the aged adult.

In the last fifteen years a system of fibers has been found penetrating from clusters of neurones in the brain core into every region of the neocortex and into surrounding sensory and motor fields of the brain stem. This core brain is much more differentiated than had been imagined; it creates kaleidoscopic changes in the balances between evaluative and motivating impulses that impinge on every element of the integrative networks of the mind. We find, too, that the cerebral hemispheres with their different cognitive styles and preferences have characteristic emotional and temperamental differences. Perhaps these are due to an asymmetry in the neurochemical activators that direct growth of anatomical patterns in brain systems long before birth and long before their psychological engagement with reality.

The motivating brain is responsible for the patterns of emotion, for the activating or depressing changes of attention or fatigue, in perception, learning, remembering, and acting. It contributes a subjective unity of evaluation to memories and becomes part of the mechanism of their recall. It switches the patterning of movement or readiness to react of the whole organism between energetic, information-seeking vigor of action against the environment and inner-directed withdrawing to sustain or recuperate in a reflective state of rest. When stress, disease, or drugs that mimic or block the natural transmitters interfere with the balance of action between emotional components, they can create abnormal excitement and awareness, illusory experiences, moods of elation or depression, transcendent dream states, joy or terror or rage, and grotesque distortions of communicative expression, many of which may have an erotic aspect.

But these emotional parts of the brain are not just involved in pathological states or instinctive drives. They give vitality to normal living. They must concern not only the psychiatrist or neuropsychologist but every student of the deep processes of the human spirit and their development, and they must be implicated in any scientific examination of religious experience. Their patterned activity is behind the rhythm and drama of music, dance and theater, the aesthetic evaluation of art, and the love or hate that binds human beings in fellowship or that segregates followers of different teachers or political leaders into suspicious, vengeful camps. These parts make up the peace and ecstasy of fulfillment in communication, or the anxiety and pain of suffering in loneliness.

The place of emotion in the growth of human consciousness, grace of moving, and interest for learning is clear from the earliest play between infant and mother and from the games of fantasy that are shared in early childhood friendships. The creative energy of these engagements shows us an innocent human reaching out to learn from others the symbols and roles of an ancient but endlessly renewable way of living and cooperating. In childhood, liking and learning are inseparable. As we perceive the emotions of childhood more clearly, we know better what questions to ask concerning the brain mechanisms that generate the essential feeling and consciousness of being human.

There may be no alternative for the scientist but to study by the best means available the unique mental physics of the brain itself in order to comprehend the human spirit and how the feelings of a child reach out to experience to give it form and value. In a broader psychological perspective we must recognize that every symbol, role, and ritual is a product of tradition. In a mature mind the passions of moral, artistic, theatrical, and practical sharing are crystallized in intricate habits of perception, expression, practice, and thought. The underlying motives are there, much stronger than in infancy and still capable of asserting their primordial equilibria and contrasts in the same uncompromising forms with universal human appeal. But they are also specified and disciplined in relation to an historic fabric of belief and conventional action. They are made relevant to elements of a particular reality conquered by ancestors and currently exploited in traditional ways.

Different societies use different statements of belief or knowledge that require different cognitive aptitudes and that carry connotations in different material, ethical, and artistic contexts. Consciousness is attracted to the innumerable learned referents that interest shares. Symbols are not exempted from this traditional specifying, even though their power and utility spring from the unconditional principles of motivation by which humans seek comfort, contentment, happiness, inspiration, or excitement and flee their opposites, communicating these feelings to each other. Icons blend the power of directly perceived tempo, symmetry, color, and force of representation with traditional styles and codes of expression that are in no way present in the mind at birth. Archetypes are both innately motivated and conventional; the "inner experience" of religion works within the "protection and guidance of dogma and ritual" (Jung 1938). Their truth comes from this union of inner values and outward facts historically experienced and made explicitly traditional, timeless affordances of nature felt emotionally and made part of culture through learning within "communitas."[29]

If we attempt to break the unity of feeling-with-experience in human consciousness, the analysis ends in confusion. Sociobiology seeks explanations of taboos and prejudices concerning social and interpersonal contracts by reference to the economics of biological inheritance only. When Edward O. Wilson (1980) would find the causes of these feelings and beliefs in scientific materialism and nerve cell biology, he unwittingly gives but lip service to the role of emotions in the life of a community that transmits traditional wisdom as well as its genes. He reduces human motivation to the resemblance of a survival kit of instincts appropriate to a social insect. Gene-culture coevolution theory enlightens us to the problem of human mental evolution but does not solve it. We might agree that "an understanding of the roots of human nature now seems essential to ethical philosophy" (Wilson 1980, 431). First we must understand the nature of emotions and their service to life of real persons. We need more than concepts of "sensory screening, interneurone coding, memory and other cognitive processes" plus "responsiveness to the behavior of others" (Wilson 1980, 428) to understand how culture is learned.

Veteran brain scientist John Eccles (1979) puts the soul, the "self-conscious mind," quite outside the neuronal machinery. We can accept with Eccles the integrator principle that evaluates and motivates mental life into a unified self, but with Sperry (1985) we look inside the total organization of the brain, not somewhere else, for the evidence on how self-consciousness and its values arise. We look particularly into a component of the brain that is richly and specifically concerned with maintaining "communitas," with gaining self-consciousness through sympathy with the souls of fellow humans.

To understand the caldron of the spirit that brain science brings to light *we need a philosophy of mind that unifies Spinozan belief in a self-maintaining vitality of will with a Buberian recognition that truth lies in a personal relationship, one to another. The human spirit defines itself in qualities of fellowship discovered in play and achieves fulfillment in companionship made strong with ritual.* Indeed, Victor Turner has directed us to the right track.

*An earlier version of this paper was presented at the Thirty-first Annual Conference ("Recent Discoveries in Neurobiology--Do They Matter for Religion, the Social Sciences, and the Humanities?") of the Institute on Religion in an Age of Science, Star Island, New Hampshire, 28 July-August 1984. Professor Trevarthen has further revised the material subsequent to its publication in *Zygon* and specifically for this volume.

NOTES

1. Robin Fox (1980) discusses theories of anthropologist Claude Levi-Strauss and sociologist Emile Durkheim concerning universals in human psychology. He points out the difficulties that arise for these authors from dichotomizing intellect from emotion and social from natural. Fox later sketched an illuminating history of sociopolitical philosophy and controversies about the "innate" in human intelligence (Fox 1985). Randall Collins (1984), a sociologist, discussing "the role of emotions in social structure," contends that "interaction rituals" regulate

emotions which serve as the driving force for functions of society. Robert Levy (1984), an anthropologist, views emotions in a comparative perspective, claiming a new anthropological orientation that perceives emotions as universal organizers of communication and knowledge. Such ideas give credibility to the "collective unconscious" of Carl Jung (1938). Mary Midgley (1984, 38-39), discussing the "endless trouble" anthropologists go to to explain moral paradoxes between cultures, notes that, "the assumption of shared moral compass-bearings is what makes it possible for us to praise and learn from other cultures, and also to accept criticisms which outsiders pass on our own culture." Furthermore, in assessing Freud's view of culture, "unless we suppose our species to have run an evolutionary course quite contrary to that of other social species, we ought to conclude--that culture is the fruit of exceptionally well-developed social instincts, not that it is a kind of weed-killer put down to control those few we possess" (Midgley 1984, 159).

2. The antithetical temperamental functions that d'Aquili (1983) would separate between the hemispheres have been recognized since T. Ribot (1917) described temperamental types. His distinctions were taken up by William James (1907) who contrasted "tender-minded" and "tough-minded" individuals. These correspond, in turn, with the "introvert" and "extravert" of Jung (1917). E. Kretschmer (1925) described "cyclothymic" and "schizothymic" types as "two great chemical hormone groups." Motivational differences between the cerebral hemispheres are discussed below.

3. Depressed infants do not play (Rosenblatt 1977). Autistic children lack the rapport with others that is essential to participation in joking play, and this affects their learning (Kanner 1943; Richer 1978).

4. Original sources may be found in Richard Jung's history of concepts of sensory systems (Jung 1984). A popular account of theories of mind in the brain is presented by Colin Blakemore (1977). Charles Sherrington gave the Gifford lectures on natural theology in Edinburgh in 1937-38. His book, *Man on His Nature* (Sherrington 1940) is a classical appraisal by a physiologist of the mind/brain problem. His pupil Sir John Eccles gave the Gifford lectures in 1977-78 and produced an updated dualistic interpretation from the viewpoint of a leading brain scientist in *The Human Mystery* (Eccles 1979).

5. Darwin published *The Descent of Man* eleven years before his death. He delayed presenting his view of human evolution partly out of respect for the

religious beliefs of his family. His thinking on the matter began over thirty years earlier (see Gruber & Barrett 1974).

6. Exquisite examples of anatomical drawings of the human brain, showing fine details of tissue structure, were published by Dejerine ([1895-1901] 1980).

7. For a contemporary review of the experiments of Fritz and Hitzig, Munk, Ferrier, Goltz, and others, see William James ([1890] 1950, 1:12-80).

8. Interest in anatomical differences between the hemispheres was revived by Norman Geschwind and W. Levitsky (1968). See also Trevarthen (1984a, 1139-44) and Rosen and Galaburda (1985).

9. Flechsig made a pioneering demonstration of how areas of the human cerebral cortex develop at different rates (Flechsig 1901).

10. For a recent account of how the fine structure of synapses was found, see McGeer, Eccles, and McGeer (1978, 7-10).

11. McGeer, Eccles, and McGeer (1978, 141-46, and following chapters) describe transmitters and their discovery.

12. Sherrington (1940, 172) refers to the central place that Baruch Spinoza gave to will, which he described as "a manner of thinking and understanding" that is essential to the mind. Modern ideas on spontaneous cerebral activity behind movement are lucidly presented, with classical articles in original form, by C.R. Gallistel (1980). Michael Arbib (1984) interprets the thinking of the great Russian physiologist of movement Nicholas Bernstein and his argument that self-directed activity is the distinguishing mark of living things.

13. Darwin (1872) pioneered modern research on emotional expressions. The communicative function of emotions has been neglected in psychology (Trevarthen 1984b).

14. In his concept of "communitas" Turner (1974) captured the innate fellowship of feeling that is capable of setting itself in opposition to the conventions of society (societas). As Roy Willis (1985) explains in his obituary for Turner, anthropology has assimilated the concept without full recognition of its importance.

15. The theories of J.W. Papez (1937) and MacLean (1949; 1958) are discussed by A.R. Damasio and C.W. Van Hoesen (1983) who present a modern neuropsychological account of emotional systems.

16. Charles Herrick (1948) in a classic study of the brain of the tiger salamander perceived the evolutionary relationship of the neocortex to core integrator circuits of the brain stem adjacent to the hypothalamus (ventrolateral peduncular neuropil).

17. Stimulation of brain core structures to help direct brain surgery in human patients can produce strong emotional states (Damasio & Van Hoesen 1983, 101-4; Mark & Ervin 1970).

18. John Locke (1632-1704) had perfect trust in truth and reason; he thought the child lacks these at first and acquires them by formation of habits. He compared the young child to "white paper or wax" (Quick 1910).

19. Jan Amos Komensky, known best as Comenius (1592-1670), in contrast to Locke thought of the child as a "reasonable creature" from birth. He emphasized the natural process of learning from adults, as did Friedrich Froebel (1782-1852) who shared Comenius's belief in the importance of early years in a child's mental development (Quick 1910).

20. Wolf Singer (1984) showed that development of the visual cortex in a kitten requires both patterned visual stimulation and activity from the brain core mediated by the neurotransmitters acetylcholine and noradrenaline. The role of limbic structures (amygdala and hippocampus) in recognition memory has been demonstrated by recent research with monkeys (Mishkin 1982). Robert Zajonc (1980; 1984) has performed psychological experiments showing that emotion has a primary organization and that it can regulate cognition.

21. Lesions at different locations in the human brain produce distinct cognitive and emotional effects, and the two cerebral hemispheres differ in both the nature and severity of effects with a lesion of a given size and location (Blakemore 1977; Corballis 1983; Trevarthen 1984).

22. Speech act theory emphasizes the intentional and interpersonal functions of language against the traditional theory that language is propositional and fact stating (Searle 1969).

23. In the original version of this paper published in *Zygon*, three of Leonardo da Vinci's drawings were reproduced to illustrate how asymmeric influences from the brain determine which hand will make movements, intuitive or learned, to communicate feelings and ideas. Leonardo was left-handed, as one can see from the shading in his drawings, but he drew the postures and movements of right-handed models as he saw them and he obeyed the sacred rules for the gestures of religious subjects. In "The Madonna and Child with a Bowl of Fruit" (RF 486, Cabinet des Dessins, Musee du Louvre) he portrayed a one-year-old baby boy playfully feeding fruit to his young mother in a way that is instantly and delightfully recognizable. A baby who is to become a right-handed adult would normally behave just like this, preferring the right hand to make an interpersonal offering. In "An Apostle with Right Hand Raised" (Albertina Museum, Vienna) and "A Study for Youthful John The Baptist" (Windsor Library, London) we see the obligatory use of the right hand for sacred messages, a traditional wisdom, convention giving the living motivation a specific meaning and moral force. Right-handedness for gestures of communication, and for many skilled culturally-important abilities, is inherent in about ninety percent of people (see Hertz, 1909; Corballis, 1983; Trevarthen, 1985b).

24. James Henry (1982) contrasts the power-control-agent with the social status-communion-attachment axes in human personality and social conduct. Competitive tension leads to a denial of feelings and absence of compassion. He cites evidence from Hoppe and Bogen (1977) that commissurotomy patients are alexithymic, that is, they lack mythopoetic skills or the ability to link affectively loaded images into a meaningful story.

25. Victor Turner (1983b) following the lead of Barbara Lex (1979) and d'Aquili and Laughlin (1979) considers whether play may pit the hemispheric temperaments against one another. It is noteworthy that children show playful motivation before six months of age, when cortical structures of the hemispheres are still to undergo elaborate development (Trevarthen 1980a; 1983a). Hemispheric motivational asymmetries probably originate deep in subcortical regions.

26. Fantasy play blossoms in toddlers, though why it does is a mystery (Winner & Gardner 1979). The world of imagination with all its subjective color and emotional complexity appeals strongly to young children who love a fantastical and thrilling story (Bettelheim 1977).

27. Play of children and adult ritual have much in common; both involve participants in temporary sociodramatic roles *vis a vis* others (Turner 1974; Handelman 1977). Play weaves a baffling mixture of equilibrium and disequilibrium; it is an active psychological process in its own right, not derivative of imagination, exploration, construction, or practice (Sutton-Smith & Kelly-Byrne 1984). As play contributes to relationships of child to child or child to adult, so ritual assists the maintenance of "communitas" in a society structured by traditions.

28. Childhood autism was first described with unsurpassed clarity by Kanner (1943). Its consequences for social and cognitive growth are considered by Richer (1978). Damasio and Maurer (1978) propose a neurological explanation.

29. Ernest Renan, the biographer of Jesus, vividly describes how the inspiration of Christianity arose from the religious beliefs current at his time and place and was then transformed by his spirit. "To show that religion founded by Jesus was the natural consequence of that which had gone before, does not diminish its excellence; but only proves that it had a reason for its existence that it was legitimate, that is to say, conformable to the instinct and wants of the heart in a given age" (Renan [1863] 1927, 390). "Jesus is the highest of these pillars which show to man whence he comes and whither he ought to tend. In him was condensed all that is good and elevated in our nature" (Renan [1863] 1927, 392).

REFERENCES

Arbib, Michael A. 1984. "From Synergies and Embryos to Motor Schemas."
    In *Human Motor Actions: Bernstein Reassessed*, ed. H.T.A. Whiting, 545-
    62. Amsterdam: North Holland.
Bateson, Gregory. 1972. *Steps to an Ecology of Mind*. New York:
    Ballantine. (See paper entitled "A theory of play and fantasy.")
Bettelheim, Bruno. 1977. *The Uses of Enchantment*. New York: Vintage
    Books.
Blakemore, Colin. 1977. *Mechanics of the Mind*. Cambridge: Cambridge
    Univ. Press.
Bradshaw, John L. and N.C. Nettleton. 1983. *Human Cerebral Asymmetry*.
    Englewood Cliffs, N.J.: Prentice-Hall.
Braten, Stein. 1988. "Dialogic Mind: The Infant and Adult in
    Protoconversation." In *Nature, Cognition and System*, ed. M. Cavallo, 187-
    205. Dordrecht: Kluwer Academic Publications.
Broca, Paul. 1865. "Sur la Faculte de Language Articule." *Bulletin de la
    Societe de Anthropologie*, Paris 6:337-93.
Collins, Randall. 1984. "The Role of Emotion in Social Structure." In
    Approaches to Emotion, ed. Klaus P. Scherer and Paul Ekman, 385-96.
    Hillsdale, N.J.: Erlbaum.
Corballis, Michael. 1983. *Human Laterality*. New York: Academic Press.
Damasio, A.R. and R.G. Maurer. 1978. "A Neurological Model for
    Childhood Autism." *Archives of Neurology* 35:777-86.
Damasio, A.R. and G.W. Van Hoesen. 1983. "Emotional Distrubances
    Associated with Focal Lesions of the Limbic Frontal Lobe." In
    Neuropsychology of Human Emotion, ed. Kenneth M. Heilman and Paul
    Satz, 85-110. London: Guilford Press.
d'Aquili, Eugene G. 1983. "The Myth-Ritual Complex: A Biogenetic
    Structural Analysis." *Zygon: Journal of Religion and Science* 18
    (September):247-69.
d'Aquili, Eugene G. and Charles D. Laughlin, Jr. 1979. "The Neurobiology
    of Myth and Ritual." In *The Spectrum of Ritual: A Biogenetic and
    Structural Analysis*, ed. Eugene G. d'Aquili et al., 152-82. New York:
    Columbia Univ. Press.
Darwin, Charles. 1859. *The Origin of Species*. London: Murray.
_____. 1871. *The Descent of Man, and Selection in Relation to Sex*.
    London: Murray.
_____. 1872. *The Expression of Emotion in Man and Animals*. London:

Methuen.

Dejerine, Jules. [1895-1901] 1980. *Anatomie des Centres Nerveux*. 2 vols. Paris: Masson.

Eccles, John C. 1979. *The Human Mystery*. Berlin: Springer International.

Fearing, F. [1930] 1970. *Reflex Action*. Cambridge, Mass.: MIT Press.

Field, Tiffany M. and N.A. Fox. 1985. *Social Perception in Infants*. Norwood, N.J.: Ablex.

Flechsig, Paul. 1901. "Developmental (Myelogenetic) Localisation of the Cerebral Cortex in the Human Subject." *Lancet* 2:1027-29.

Flor-Henry, Pierre. 1983. In *Neuropsychology of Human Emotion*. ed. Kenneth M. Heilman and Paul Satz, 193-217. New York: Guilford Press.

Fox, Robin. 1980. *The Red Lamp of Incest*. New York: Dutton.

———. 1985. "*Sumus Ergo Cogitamus*: Cognitive Science and the Western Intellectual Tradition." In *Neonate Cognition*, ed. Jacques Mehler and Robin Fox, 29-36. Hillsdale, N.J.: Erlbaum.

Freud, Sigmund. 1953. On *Aphasia: A Critical Study*. Trans. E. Stengel. New York: International Universities Press.

———. [1895] 1954. "Project for a Scientific Psychology." In *The Origins of Psychoanalysis: Letters to Wilhelm Fliess, Drafts and Notes*, 347-445. New York: Basic Books.

Gallistel, C.R. 1980. *The Organization of Action: A New Synthesis*. Hillsdale, N.J.: Erlbaum.

Geschwind, Norman and W. Levitsky. 1968. "Human Brain: Left-Right Asymmetries in Temporal Speech Region." *Science* 161:186-87.

Goldman-Rakic, Patricia S. 1984. "The Frontal Lobes: Uncharted Provinces of the Brain." *Trends in Neurosciences* 7:425-29.

Gruber, Howard E. and Paul H. Barrett. 1974. *Darwin on Man*. London: Wildwood House.

Halliday, Michael A.K. 1975. *Learning How to Mean: Explorations in the Development of Language*. London: Edward Arnold.

Handelman, Don. 1977. "Play and Ritual: Complementary Frames of Metacommunication." In *It's a Funny Thing, Humour*, ed. Anthony J. Chapman and Hugh C. Foot, 185-92. Oxford: Pergamon.

Havkin, G.Z. and John C. Fentress. 1985. "The Form of Combative Strategy in Interactions among Wolf Pups (*Canis lupus*)." *Zeitschrift fur Tierpsychologie/Journal of Comparative Ethology* 68:177-200.

Heilman, Kenneth M. and Paul Satz, eds. 1983. *Neuropsychology of Human Emotion*. London: Guilford Press.

Henry James P. 1982. "The Relation of Social to Biological Processes in Disease." *Social Science and Medicine* 16:369-80.

Herrick, Charles J. 1948. *The Brain of the Tiger Salamander*. Chicago:

Univ. of Chicago Press.

Hertz, Robert. 1909. "La Pre-eminence de la Main Droite: Etude sur la Polarite Religieuse." *Revue Philosophique* 68:553-80.

Hess, W.R. 1954. *Diencephalon: Autonomic and Extrapyramidal Functions.* New York: Grune & Stratton.

Hoppe, I.D. and Joseph E. Bogen. 1977. "Alexithymia in Twelve Commissurotomized Patients." *Psychotherapy and Psychosomatics* 28:148-55.

Hubley, Penelope and Colwyn Trevarthen. 1979. "Sharing a Task in Infancy." In *Social Interaction During Infancy*, ed. Ina Uzgiris, 57-80. New Directions for Child Development, No. 4. San Francisco: Jossey-Bass.

Hughlings Jackson, John. 1932. *Selected Writings of John Highlings Jackson*, ed. J. Taylor. London: Hodder & Stoughton.

Huxley, Thomas H. [1863] 1913. *Man's Place in Nature.* London: Watts. Originally published as *Evidences as to Man's Place in Nature*, 1863.

James, William. [1890] 1950. *The Principles of Psychology.* 2 vols. New York: Henry Holt.

_____. 1907. *Pragmatism.* London: Longmans.

Jung, Carl G. 1917. *Collected Papers on Analytical Psychology*, 2nd ed. London: Balliere, Tindall & Cox.

_____. 1938. *Psychology and Religion.* New Haven, Conn.: Yale Univ. Press.

Jung, Richard. 1984. "Sensory Research in Historical Perspective: Some Philosophical Foundations of Perception." In *Handbook of Physiology Section I, The Nervous System*, Vol. III *Sensory Processes*, Part I, volume ed. Ian Darian-Smith, 1-74. Bethesda Md.: American Physiological Society.

Kanner, L. 1943. "Autistic Disturbances of Affective Contact." *Nervous Child* 2:217-50.

Konner, Melvin. 1982. *The Tangled Wing.* New York: Harper & Row.

Kretschmer, E. 1925. *Physique and Character.* London: Kegan Paul.

Levy, Jerre and Colwyn Trevarthen. 1976. "Metacontrol of Hemispheric Function in Human Split-Brain Patients." *Journal of Experimental Psychology: Human Perception and Performance* 2:299-312.

Levy, Robert I. 1984. "The Emotions in Comparative Perspective." In *Approaches to Emotion*, ed. Klaus R. Scherer and Paul Ekman, 397-412. Hilsdale, N.J.: Erlbaum.

Lex, Barbara. 1979. "Neurobiology of Ritual Trance." In *The Spectrum of Ritual: A Biogenetic Structural Analysis*, ed. Eugene G. d'Aquili et al., 117-51. New York: Columbia Univ. Press.

MacLean, Paul D. 1949. "Psychosomatic Disease and the 'Visceral Brain,' Recent Developments Bearing on Papez Theory of Emotion."

Psychosomatic Medicine 11:338-53.

_____. 1958. "Contrasting Functions of Limbic and Neocortical Systems of the Brain and their Relevance to Psycho-social Aspects of Medicine." *American Journal of Medicine* 25:611-26.

Magoun, H.W. 1958. *The Waking Brain*, Springfield, Ill.: Charles C. Thomas.

Mark, V.H. and F. R. Ervin. 1970. *Violence and the Brain.* New York: Harper & Row.

Marsden, C.D. 1979. "The Emotion of Pain and its Chemistry." In *Brain and Mind*, Ciba Foundation Symposium 69, new series, ed. Gordon Wolstenholme and Maeve O'Connor, 305-13. Amsterdam: Excerpta Medica.

McGeer, P.L., J.C. Eccles, and E.G. McGeer. 1978. *Molecular Neurobiology of the Mammalian Brain.* New York: Plenum.

Midgley, Mary. 1984. *Wickedness.* London: Routledge & Kegan Paul.

Mishkin, Mortimer. 1982. "A Memory System in the Monkey." *Philosophical Transactions of the Royal Society*, London, Series B, 85-95.

Myers, Ronald E. 1972. "Role of Prefrontal and Anterior Temporal Cortex in Social Behaviour and Affect in Monkeys." *Acta Neurobiologica Experimentalis* 32:567-79.

Nauta, Walle. 1971. "The Problem of the Frontal Lobe: A Reinterpretation." *Journal of Psychiatric Research* 8:167-87.

Olds, James. 1962. "Hypothalamic Substrates of Reward." *Physiological Reviews* 42:554-604.

Papez, J.W. 1937. "A Proposed Mechanism of Emotion." *Archives of Neurology and Psychiatry* 38:725-44.

Palov, Ivan P. [1927] 1960. *Conditioned Reflexes.* New York: Dover.

Penfield, Wilder and L. Roberts. 1959. *Speech and Brain Mechanisms.* Princeton, N.J.: Princeton Univ. Press.

Ploog, Detlev. 1979. "Phonation, Emotion, Cognition, With Reference to the Brain Mechanisms Involved." In *Brain and Mind*, Ciba Foundation Symposium 69, new series, ed. Gordon Wolstenholme and Maeve O'Connor, 79-98. Amsterdam: Excerpta Medica.

Pribram, Karl H. 1969. "The Foundation of Psychoanalytic Theory: Freud's Neuropsychological Model." In *Brain and Behavior, vol. 4: Adaptation*, ed. Karl H. Pribram, 395-432. Harmondsworth and Baltimore: Penguin.

_____. 1984. "Emotion: A Neurobehavioural Analysis." In *Approaches to Emotion*, ed. Klaus R. Scherer and Paul Ekman, 13-38. Hillsdale, N.J.: Erlbaum.

Quick, R.H. 1910. *Essays on Educational Reformers.* London: Longmans & Green.

Ribot, Th. 1917. *Psychologie des Sentiments*, 10th ed. Paris: Felix Alcan.
Richer, John M. 1978. "The Partial Noncommunication of Culture to Autistic Children." In *Austism: A Reappraisal of Concepts and Treatment*, ed. M. Rutter and E. Schopler, 47-61. New York: Plenum.
Rosen, G.D. and A.M. Galaburda. 1985. "The Development of Language: A Question of Asymmetry and Deviation." In *Neonate Cognition*, ed. Jacques Mehler and Robin Fox, 307-25. Hillsdale, N.J.: Erlbaum.
Rosenblatt, Deborah. 1977. "Developmental Trends in Infant Play." In *Biology of Play*, ed. Barbara Tizard and D. Harvey, 33-44. London: Heinemann.
Ross, Elliott D. 1984. "Right Hemisphere's Role in Language, Affective Behavior and Emotion." *Trends in Neuroscience* 7:342-46.
Scheibel, Arnold B. 1984. "The Brain Stem, Reticular Core and Sensory Function." In *Handbook of Physiology, Section I, The Nervous System, Vol. III. Sensory Processes*, Part I, volume ed. Ian Darian-Smith, 213-56. Bethesda, Md.: American Physiological Society.
Searle, John R. 1969. *Speech Acts: An Essay in the Philosophy of Language*. London: Cambridge Univ. Press.
Sherrington, Charles S. 1906. *Integrative Action of the Nervous System*. New Haven, Conn.: Yale Univ. Press.
_____. 1940. *Man on His Nature*. Cambridge: Cambridge Univ. Press.
Singer, Wolf. 1984. "Learning to See: Mechanisms in Experience-Dependent Development." In *The Biology of Learning*, ed. Peter Marler and H.S. Terrace, 461-77. Berlin: Springer.
Smith, Elliot. 1910. "Some Problems Relating to the Evolution of the Brain." *Lancet* 1:221-27.
Sperry, Roger W. 1961. "Cerebral Organization and Behavior." *Science* 133:1749-57.
_____. 1967. "Mental Unity Following Surgical Disconnection of the Cerebral Hemispheres." *The Harvey Lectures* 62:293-323.
_____. 1985. "Changed Concepts of Brain and Consciousness: Some Value Implications." *Zygon: Journal of Religion and Science* 20 (March):41-57.
Sperry, Roger W. and Michael S. Gazzaniga. 1967. "Language Following Surgical Disconnection of the Commissures." In *Brain Mechanisms Underlying Speech and Language*, ed. F.L. Darley, 108-21. New York: Grune & Stratton.
Stern, Daniel. 1985. *The Interpersonal World of the Infant: A View from Psychoanalysis and Developmental Psychology*. New York: Basic Books.
Sutton-Smith, Brian and Diana Kelly-Byrne. 1984. "The Phenomenon of Biopolarity in Play Theories." In *Child's Play: Developmental and Applied*, ed. D. Yawkey and Anthony D. Pelligrini, 29-47. Hillsdale,

N.J.: Erlbaum.

Trevarthen, Colwyn. 1965. "Functional Interactions Between the Cerebral Hemispheres of the Split-Brain Monkey." In *Functions of the Corpus Callosum*, ed. E.G. Ettlinger, Ciba Foundation Study Group, No. 20, 24-40. London: Churchill.

_____. 1974. "Conversations with a Two-month-old." *New Scientist* 2 (May):230-35.

_____. 1979. "Instincts for Human Understanding and Cultural Cooperation: Their Development in Infancy." In *Human Ethology*, ed. Mario von Cranach, K. Foppa, W. Lepenies, and D. Ploog, 530-71. Cambridge: Cambridge Univ. Press.

_____. 1980a. "Neurological Development and the Growth of Psychological Functions." In *Developmental Psychology and Society*, ed. J. Sants, 46-95. London: Macmillan.

_____. 1980b. "The Foundations of Intersubjectivity: Development of Interpersonal and Cooperative Understanding in Infants." In *The Social Foundations of Language and Thought: Essays in Honor of J.S. Bruner*, ed. D.Olson, 316-42. New York: W.W. Norton.

_____. 1983a. "Cerebral Mechanisms for Language: Prenatal and Postnatal Development." In *Neuropsychology of Language, Reading and Spelling*, ed. U.Kirk, 45-80. New York: Academic

_____. 1983b. "Interpersonal Abilities of Infants as Generators for Transmission of Language and Culture." In *The Behaviour of Human Infants*, ed. A. Oliverio and M. Zapella, 145-76. London and New York: Plenum.

_____. 1984a. "Hemispheric Specialization." In *Handbook of Physiology*, ed. I.Darian-Smith, 1129-90. Washington: American Physiological Society.

_____. 1984b. "Emotions in Infancy: Regulators of Contacts and Relationships with Persons." In *Approaches to Emotion*, ed. K. Scherer and P. Ekman, 129-57. Hillsdale, N.J.: Erlbaum.

_____. 1985a. "Facial Expressions of Emotion in Mother-Infant Interaction." *Human Neurobiology* 4:21-32.

_____. 1985b. "Form, Significance and Psychological Potential of Hand Gestures of Infants." In *The Biological Foundation of Gestures: Motor and Semiotic Aspects*, ed. J-L. Nespoulous, P. Perron, and A. Roch Lecours, 149-202. Cambridge, Mass.: MIT Press.

_____. 1987. "Sharing Makes Sense: Intersubjectivity and the Making of an Infant's Meaning." In *Language Topics: Essays in Honour of Michael Halliday*, eds. Ross Steele and Terry Threadgold, Vol.1, 177-99. Amsterdam and Philadelphia: John Benjamins.

_____. 1990. "Signs Before Speech." In *The Semiotic Web, 1989*, eds. Thomas A. Sebeok and Jean Umiker Sebeok. Berlin/New York/

Amsterdam: Mouton de Gruyter.

Trevarthen, Colwyn and Katerina Logotheti. 1987. "First Symbols and the Nature of Human Knowledge." In *Symbolisme et Connaissance/ Symbolism and Knowledge*, eds. Jacques Montangero, Anastasis Tryphon and Sylvain Dionnet. Cahier No. 8, Jean Piaget Archives Fondation, 65-92. Geneva: Jean Piaget Archives Fondation.

Trevarthen, Colwyn and Helen Marwick. 1986. "Signs of Motivation for Speech in Infants, and the Nature of a Mother's Support for Development of Language." In *Precursors of Early Speech*, ed. Bjorn Linblom and Rolf Zetterstrom. Basingstoke, England: Macmillan.

Turner, Victor. 1974. *Dramas, Fields and Metaphors*. Ithaca, N.Y.: Cornell Univ. Press.

_____. 1983a. "Body, Brain and Culture." *Zygon: Journal of Religion and Science* 18 (September):221-45.

_____. 1983b. "Play and Drama: The Horns of a Dilemma." In *The World of Play*, ed. Frank E. Manning, 217-24. West Point, N.Y.: Leisure Press.

Ungerstedt, U. 1971. "Stereotaxic Mapping of the Monoamine Pathways in the Rat Brain." *Acta Physiologica Scandinavica* Supplement No. 367:1-48.

Valenstein, Elliot S. 1973. *Brain Stimulation and Motivation*. Chicago: Scott, Foresman.

Wernicke, Carl. 1874. *Der Aphasische Synpotemenkomplex*. Poland: M. Cohn & Weigart.

Wills, Roy. 1985. Victor Witter Turner." *Africa* 1:73-75.

Wilson, Edward O. 1980. "The Relation of Science to Theology." *Zygon: Journal of Religion and Science* 15 (December):425-34.

Winner, Ellen and Howard Gardner, eds. 1979. *Fact, Fiction and Fantasy*. New Directions for Child Development, No. 6. San Francisco: Jossey-Bass.

Zajonic, Robert B. 1980. "Feeling and Thinking: Preferences Need no Inferences." *American Psychologist* 35:151-75.

_____. 1984. "On Primacy of Affect." In *Approaches to Emotion*, ed. Klaus R. Sherer and Paul Ekman, 259-70. Hilsdale, N.J.: Erlbaum.

Chapter Seven

THE HUMAN BRAIN AND HUMAN DESTINY:
A PATTERN FOR OLD BRAIN EMPATHY
WITH THE EMERGENCE OF MIND*

by

James B. Ashbrook

ABSTRACT. The human brain combines empathy and imagination
via the old brain which sets our destiny in the evolutionary scheme of things.
This new understanding of cognition is an emergent phenomenon--basically
an expressive ordering of reality as part of "a single natural system." The
holographic and subsymbolic paradigms suggest that we live in a contextual
universe, one which we create and yet one in which we are required to adapt.
The inadequacy of the new brain--especially the left hemisphere's rational
view of destiny--is replaced by a view of a new relatedness in reality in
which human destiny comes from and depends upon the mutual interchange
between the new brain (cultural knowledge) and the old brain (genetic
wisdom) for the survival of what is significant to the whole systemic context
in which we live.

People tend to separate destiny from origin, omega from alpha. It is as
though who we are (genetically and historically) bears little relationship to
where we are going and who we will be when we get there. Destiny takes
on the sole meaning of future development unhindered by continuity with
nature or adaptation in the present.

Such a narrow, tunnel view of human destiny is comparable to the
reverence given to our ideas of the new brain--the neocortex. This
evolutionary development has been taken as our crowning glory, that which
separates us from all other mammals and the rest of creation. That
separation allows us to transcend the complexities of the human brain when
the definition of being--life's fullness--resides primarily in the new brain,
more particularly the left hemisphere, thus distancing us from the whole
created order. This view of destiny cuts us off from the physical universe
which gives us life.

I call this view the "new brain" illusion, more particularly the illusion of the left hemisphere. The illusion is dispelled in recognizing that the rationality of the left half of the new brain is an outmoded and distorted understanding of the human mind. The new brain is an extension and elaboration of the old brain--the reptilian and mammalian brains which set our place in the evolutionary scheme of the universe.

An understanding of human destiny requires that we reject the new brain-left hemisphere superiority and rediscover old brain-new brain--or full mind--interdependence. A multidimensional approach to human destiny takes into account the complexities of the human brain--its biological roots *and* its cognitive reaches. While not reduced to the brain, our destiny involves--yes, and requires--the whole brain. In light of this new understanding of the whole brain, we ask the question of what might be the relationship between our brain and our destiny? How does the way the brain is shed light on what humanity is about?

A superfical view of what is happening in the brain sciences could be characterized as a move downward from psyche as mind to soma as body, from mind to brain, from spirit to matter. The dramatic attention to the chemical make-up of the brain as "the hardware of consciousness" (Hooper & Teresi [1986] 1987) supports that impression. In efforts to cope with various forms of mental dysfunction, scientists have turned increasingly to psychopharmacological processes (Snyder 1974). For instance, chemical imbalance contributes to severe depression and so is treated medically. Instead of exploring how a person feels or thinks, effort is directed to the brain's biochemistry. Quite simply, the focus marks a shift from "oppressive beliefs" and "troubled minds" to "broken bodies" (Andreasen 1985; Ashbrook 1990). Genetic, biochemical, and neurological factors contribute to disturbed behavior (Tanguary 1985).

A closer look, however, reveals a more complex picture (Ashbrook 1990). Biological intervention alone is not enough. We need think only of the disillusionment surrounding the deinstitutionalization of mentally ill people by putting them back into the community. Families, support networks, societal conditions, interpretive frames of meaning affect our lives as much as chemistry. These enhance or restrict what is done medically.

A multidimensional approach to human life and human destiny thereby takes into account the complexities of body-mind interaction. Those interactions include biological brains, cultural beliefs, social conditions, interpersonal patterns, and individual minds. The idea that the mind is not separate from the body is bringing about changes in the way we understand ourselves. The revised view understands that the mind is very much part of the old brain even as the old brain is very much part of the mind.

THE CHANGE IN HOW WE VIEW OURSELVES

In efforts to understand how values and beliefs are mapped onto the brain, part of psychology has been moving upward from soma as physical to psyche as cognitive. Traditional distinctions such as mind-body or matter-spirit no longer fit the empirical data. Researcher Howard Gardner interprets this phenomenon as the cognitive revolution. For him and others, it has become "the mind's new science" (Gardner 1985).

Until the last two decades we have been limited in understanding the connection between soma and psyche, human nature and human destiny. Now we are on the threshold of a reconstruing, catching up with what the poetic and religious traditions have always known. We are neither our own origin nor our own destiny. In the imagery of the writer of The Revelation of John, the Lord God is both our alpha--our beginning--and our omega--our fulfillment (Rev. 1:8; 21:6; 22:13).

In reflecting on his experience of himself, Augustine voiced the dilemma of our trying to understand our destiny in terms of consciousness: "I do not myself grasp all that I am. Thus the mind is too narrow to contain itself. But where can that part be which it does not contain?" (Augustine 1955, Bk. X, viii,210).

The cognitive revolution is returning "mind" to an embodied place in our understanding of ourselves and how we function. Popular books are heralding the unity of body and mind (see Benson 1984; Borysenko 1987). No longer can we view ourselves--nor even other mammals--as passive objects, mechanical organisms, to be manipulated chemically with no attention to the experiential reality which is expressed in and through the physical. We are discovering the crucial role the limbic system plays in that unity. There is a bodily base in all that we feel, imagine, and about which we reason (Rossi 1986; see also Johnson 1987). This includes our sense of destiny.

The cognitive revolution gives "human" meaning to the mind's biological origin, integrating nature and nurture, instinct and experience. As brain, the concept of mind gives "human" meaning to the evolutionary matrix out of which both itself and culture have emerged. Similarly, as brain, the concept of mind gives "human" meaning to the universe in which it finds itself. The human brain literally embodies the "human" meaning of divine purpose. Let me explain.

The brain constructs a reasonable view of reality by imaging or representing in a mental schema how things go together. To have a brain and to give a reasonable explanation of the world are one and the same. To have a brain is to be a co-creator of what matters most in human life. There is no way the mind cannot *not* interpret what it observes and imagines (Gazzaniga 1988).

Except in conditions which suspend or negate its natural functioning, the brain does not work by itself. We are part of, and we shape, universes of influence--social, cultural, cosmic. In truth, we live in a contextual universe, a universe of meaning which we create as much as a universe of meaning which we find.

Cognitive psychologist Urich Neisser describes that relationship between cognition and reality with a cleverly concise statement: "No choice is ever free of the information on which it is based. Nevertheless, that information is selected by the chooser. . . . On the other hand, no choice is ever determined by the environment directly. Still, that environment supplies the information the chooser will use" (Neisser 1976, 182). In other words, in relation to the environment mind must be understood as semi-autonomous.

Mind is "semi" (autonomous) in the sense that the neocortex--the new brain of the two hemispheres--is always processing information both from the old cortex and from what it observes in the environment. Therefore mind is not creating something out of nothing. Cognition manifests a perceptual realism (Lakoff 1987).

Mind is (semi) "autonomous" in that its associations, connections, gestalts precede and go beyond sensory input. It selects and combines input in novel ways. The cerebral cortex transforms the regularities of the old reptilian and the mammalian brains into emergent mental representations. The results are what the triune brain of three minds takes to be real and right, or true (MacLean 1970). Cognition reveals an experiential construction (Lakoff 1987).

These cognitive creations express our emotional convictions of the way the world is put together. The reptilian and mammalian brains do not displace the new brain nor does the new brain displace the older brains. In effect, the concept of mind expresses the human meaning of the physical brain (Ashbrook 1984).

THE EMERGENT MIND AS THE EXPRESSIVE BRAIN

By understanding the older and newer brains as one mind we can approach the cognitive dimension of life as an emergent phenomenon of a basically expressive ordering. Mind comes out of nature and does not function apart from nature. Mind shapes [the way we construe] the physical world even as the physical world shapes mind. Mind creates our destiny even as our destiny comes in and through our mind.

The cognitive--or mental, to use the more conventional word--bridges what we take to be physical and what we regard as human. Matter and meaning are both aspects of biochemical activity. Molecular biology and brain studies point to "the inseparability or oneness of the reality designated by the two domains called 'life' and 'matter' and the two domains called 'mind' and 'matter'" (Burhoe 1981, 126). Their features and reaches are shaped by the fields of influence--contexts--in which they are located and with which they interact. The brain, as human matter, both reflects the historical reality of the world and shapes that reality on the basis of its own input, including its reptilian and mammalian input. We integrate our cultural contexts and our genetic inheritances into the living realities which we are (Trevarthen 1986).

At the loose interface between physical data and vivid personal experience--that nonphysical yet imaginable space which science interpreter Gordon Rattray Taylor (1979) defines as mind--we find clues to the human meaning of being in a physical universe (Sperry 1982). Those clues consist of "such fancy trimmings as a sense of identity, a sense of humor or a sense of deity" (Taylor 1979, 17-19). These trimmings reflect core features of our brain: our identity as persons; our capacity for perspective through humor; and the nature of the contextual universe in which we locate ourselves, or what in religious language we call God. We are part of "a single natural system" (Burhoe 1981, 82, 74-75), an "emergent interactionism" or "mentalist monism" as Roger Sperry (1982) puts it.

Unexpectedly, the cognitive revolution is contributing to the pivotal notion of mind (Gardner 1985). Instead of referring to mind per se, the mind's new science focuses on the centrality of mental representations. We conceive an objective world by uniting three elements into one mental representation: what our senses tell us; the truth or weight of our perceptions tested or checked out against what we remember through use of memory; and an integrating synthesis by means of morality--or sense of order or rightness--in our universe (Johnson 1987; Lakoff 1987). A set of constructs--variously labeled schemas, images, rules, frames, transformations, and other mental structures and operations--is being used to explain cognitive phenomena. These phenomena range from what we see, to understanding stories, to what I call "belief" which is the configuration of assumptions we make about the really real, in short, about our human destiny.

I view this breakthrough in making sense of human life as a wider view of cognition than the older dualistic view of mind as separate from body. This more natural cognition can incorporate physical explanations at the level of the neuronal brain, socio-psychological explanations at the level of the socio-cultural mind (Gardner 1985, 383; TenHouten 1985), and spiritual explanations at the level of the soul (Ashbrook 1989).

Left-brain cognition follows the rules of formal logic. Its information comes from what it observes. It uses language in a way which creates a second-order vocabulary. That is, its vocabulary is less about actual events and objects and more about whether statements are consistent or inconsistent (Gardner 1985, 385). We make sense of life--and create consistency--through the way we interpret life. It is the left brain's analytic processing that makes reality appear objectively stable. Whether reality is stable or not our perception of it conforms to immediate perceived needs or desires. That allows no place for argument or disagreement. Thus our world view is potentially misleading. When isolated from input from the rest of the brain, the left hemisphere taken by itself is simply the limited mind of myopic rationality. It takes what it thinks--and says--as the last word about reality.

In contrast, right-brain cognition works according to a situational logic. Its information arises from an imaginative construction of patterns or wholes. These mosaics of what is meaningful come about as a result of processing which can be described as simultaneous. Though it never works completely independently of left brain input, especially in the frontal area, the right brain functions in a way that falls "into patterns with huge numbers of interconnections and a minimum of formal symbolic processing" (DeAngelis 1987; Rumelhart et al. [1986] 1987; see Pribram 1986).

The ability of the right hemisphere seems to be based on "the *pars-pro-toto* principle, that is, the immediate recognition of a totality on the basis of one essential detail" (Watzlawick 1978, 69-73). Everything is there--all at once, by a leap of imagination. We see *archetypes*, according to neurophysiologist Paul D. MacLean, partial representations which we take for the whole (Hooper and Teresi [1986] 1987, 47).

Pars-pro-toto is a way of seeing things obliquely--not looking at an object or event straight on or with a direct, studied look but rather from a glancing, off-centered view. This may be similar to "seeing through a glass darkly" (1 Cor. 13:12). And it may be exactly the way that part of the brain has to operate later on in order to make symbolic connections possible through images which are seen, though they are not seen in an objective or physical sense.

THE HOLOGRAPHIC PARADIGM

Research scientists such as Karl Pribram identify this phenomenon of the oblique imaging of the whole as the *holographic paradigm* (Wilber 1985; Pribram 1985; Pribram 1986, 514). We do not "see" objects directly, rather we "construct" objects as when we listen to music from two stereo speakers so balanced that the sound seems to come from a point midway between them (Wilder 1985, 9).

Holography is a form of optical storage in which each individual section (part) of a photographic plate contains the image of the whole picture in condensed form. If you take a holographic picture of a person, for instance, and cut a section out of the person's head, and then enlarge that section to the original size of the picture, you do not get a big head but rather the whole person (Wilber 1985, 2).

Belief patterns, I suggest, are basically holographic. When theologians talk about unity-in-diversity, therefore, they are saying that the whole is in the part; and when they speak of diversity-in-unity, they are indicating that the part contains the whole. Any and every part of the hologram reconstructs the whole image.

From research and reflection on the precise mathematical holographic transformations of waves of information (which are distributed over the entire photographic film) into whole images, Pribram speculates about the classic dichotomy between the physical and the mental (Pribram 1986; 1985). On the basis of the holographic paradigm he rejects the mentalist who gives the primary weight of evidence to experience and phenomenology as well as the materialist who gives the primary weight of evidence to "the contents of the experience" and the physical. For him, "structure" constitutes both mind and brain in that each proceeds in a different direction in conceptualizing and realizing systems of information (Pribram 1986, 512).

The brain, according to Pribram, does not organize input gained from the physical world (through the senses) and from this construct "mental properties." Instead--and this is the astonishing speculation--"Mental properties are the pervasive organizing principles of the universe, which includes the brain" (Pribram 1985, 29-30).

From this perspective, the brain-mind reflects the basic structure of the universe. It is *the relationships* which exist among the many observations that are cognitive and thereby mental phenomena. This leads Pribram to suggest that "perhaps the very fundamental properties of the universe are therefore mental and not material" (Pribram 1985, 29). Order itself constitutes the really real and not the components which make up order. In theological language this has been called "Logos," the "Word."

The question then becomes whether mind and cognition are "emergents or expressions of some basic ordering principle" (Pribram 1985, 33-34). If mind is "emergent" from nature, then mind evolves from brain and brain evolves from matter and matter means the separate and many particles of dust. If mind is an "expression" of nature, then mind reveals a basic undivided, whole universe of imaged relationships. Then the separate "entities" which we observe in ordinary time and space are images which we "read out" from each part which has access to the whole even as the whole is present in each part.

A photographic lens focuses, objectifies, and sharpens boundaries between the parts of any scene. It functions in a left brain step-by-step manner. In contrast, holographic operations are distributed, implicit, unbounded, and holistic. These operate in a right brain all-at-once process which draws directly upon the subsymbolic, parallel, distributed activity of the limbic system. Our senses "make sense" of reality "by tuning in (and out) selective portions of this [holographic] domain" (Pribram 1986, 517-18).

Thus, the brain is an analyzer and transformer of energy and relationships. Reality consists of the imaged configurations of energy systems rather than raw objective stimuli. Only the ordinary world of experience is made up of physical matter. Real reality is "neither material nor mental, but neutral . . . [an] informational structure" which organizes energy (Pribram 1986, 512).

As Howard Gardner characterizes this wider form of cognition, we do not approach the "more complex and belief-tainted processes such as classification of ontological domains or judgments concerning rival courses of action . . . in a manner that can be characterized as logical or rational or that entail step-by-step symbolic processing" (Gardner 1985, 385). What we believe to be true, what we take to be right, what we decide is the best way to proceed in a specific situation all require a patterning of reality which involves something other than a logical progression. Instead, we use biases, images, hunches, vague patterns--yes, and beliefs as well. Our destiny arises from our imaging and imagining, and our imagining is, finally, confirmed by optimal evolutionary adaptation.

For me, faith is the experiential anchoring of what matters most in life. It appears in the old brain, below the conscious level of the two hemispheres. That bodily sense of reality then gets voiced in terms of what we believe.

As the Letter to the Hebrews puts it, "faith is the assurance of things hoped for, the conviction of things not seen" (Heb. 11:1 RSV). "Assurance" and "conviction" about what matters are right brain responses to limbic activity in the service of survival of the self and continuity of the species. Belief thereby is a transformation of biological experience into conceptual explanation. Beliefs are left brain explanations of visceral experience. They give conceptual focus to our sense of destiny. They derive from limbic environmental empathy and direct us back to that context.

The formal categories of the left brain tend to take on permanence. It is as though these categories of "what's there"--objects, experiences, and events, or even ourselves, the world, and God--actually exist as objective "entities" so that when we think about them our mind is "mirroring" the "entity" in the external world. But in viewing our categories as existing independent of ourselves we fail to take account of the fact that these perceptions are always "messy, intuitive, [and] subject to subjective representations" (Gardner 1985, 380-86).

These intuitive representations reflect right brain and limbic decision-making as to what is perceived to be there and whether that is desirable or undesirable, to be approached or avoided, to be sought or fought. Here in the messiness of life we find the issue of our destiny. That issue includes "the role of the surrounding context, the affective aspects of experience, and the effects of cultural and historical factors" on how we act (Gardner 1985, 387). Everything we think or feel occurs in a context of meaning. We construct that meaning based on bodily experience and the imaginative use of reason (Johnson 1987; Lakoff 1987). And as Thomas Aquinas expressed the belief, God as our source is always our good (Burrell 1973, 169-70).

THE SUBSYMBOLIC PARADIGM

Some scientists are now calling this whole brain process the *subsymbolic paradigm*. That means "the most powerful level of description of cognitive systems is hypothesized to be lower than the level that is naturally described by symbol manipulation" (Rumelhart et al. [1986] 1987, vol. 1:195). We ordinarily think of that symbol manipulation as language. For all the power of the symbolic-sequential capability of our left hemisphere (what we ordinarily know as the rational mind), it is the subsymbolic activity of our total cortex--primal, emotional, and rational--which accounts more adequately for what we know and how we know it. The left brain, whose "mental processes can be modeled as programs running on a digital computer" (Palmer 1987), simply does not function without the subsymbolic activity of the rest of the brain. These subsymbolic processes may be best modeled as "the flux of global patterns of activation over the entire network" (Palmer 1987). In fact no part of the old brain functions without the symbolic activity of the left and right hemispheres of the new brain.

In other words, the left brain, with its vigilance and explanations, approaches reality in terms of a symbolic paradigm. The symbolic paradigm is restricted to the new brain and more especially to its rational mind, though it is important to remember that it is the relational mind of the right brain which creates the whole symbolic paradigm. I suggest that this process of abstracting realistic features from immediately perceived experience contributes to the dualistic distinction between an objective physical world and a subjective phenomenal realm.

In contrast to such a dualistic view, brain research is directing us toward an approach to reality more in terms of a subsymbolic paradigm. The approach gives greater weight to natural processes in meaning-making. These processes are technically known as category construction and definitional classification (Lakoff 1987; Johnson 1987). The questions of classification are these: What features constitute "an object?" and How is that object distinguished from all other objects?

Only by studying how alike things are can we arrive at their differences or see those differences when they do exist. Concepts of perfection, adaptation, and invention can occur as a result of this perception of likeness. The perception might lead to an idea of beauty, of joy and order which transcends our presence and opens the mind and soul to a holy place or idea of God. For we always come back at this point to a realization that the order was there before we were and we ourselves did not make it.

With Aquinas we can say that God is the name by which we identify "the origin and the goal of this inbuilt orientation" (Burrell 1979, 31) of order: we are "directed to God as to an end that surpasses the grasp of [our] reason. . . . But the end must first be known by [us] who are to direct [our] thoughts and actions to the end" (Aquinas 1945, vol. 1.6) of perfected ordering.

These natural processes operate at every level of brain organization, and by so doing they are identified as massively parallel and widely distributed in both what is represented and how it is controlled. They combine memory and novel associations of memories. This mind-ful brain makes us different from the machine-like (rational) left hemisphere and the mammalian-like (emotionally motivated) right hemisphere. We construct a world--the realism of the symbolic paradigm--in terms of our subsymbolic experience. Our destiny includes and requires biological-genetic activity.

No matter how sophisticated we make machines we are still better at "perceiving objects in natural scenes" than any machine. We are quicker at noting relationships. We more easily understand commands and retrieve "contextually appropriate information from memory" (Rumelhardt et al. [1986] 1987, vol. 1:3). We make plans and carry them out more effectively than even the most sophisticated computer.

In essence, we are "smarter than today's computers." The reason lies in the fact that our brain is better suited to deal with tasks which require "the simultaneous consideration of many pieces of information or constraints," since every constraint may be vague, ambiguous, and inadequately specified. Furthermore, "most everyday situations cannot rigidly be assigned to just a single" frame of reference or schemata of meaning (Rumelhardt et al. [1986] 1987, vol. 1:9). This kind of common-sense complexity requires a grasp of the context in which we act, and it is precisely the context which is of our own making. Further, the context we make reflects our destiny as we imagine it to be.

In relation to animals, we are better at sequential symbolic processing. Traditionally we have called this "rationality" our capacity to imagine, to think, to plan, to implement, to evaluate in conscious ways. The capacity points to the higher-ordering processing in which we engage--the macrostructures of meaning. There is no way our cultural heritage, with its technology and its artistry, can be explained simply on the basis of genetics alone (Burhoe 1981; 1987). Unlike other animals we can pass on to future generations accumulated information about the past. That is why so much of our experience consists of what we learn instead of what is instinctual. We have more cortex uncommitted to motor or sensory function at birth than any other mammal (Penfield 1975, 20).

According to the mythical interpretations of our origin in the Book of Genesis, we are breathing dust (Gen. 2:7). We embody all that is and is to be, created, as the phrase has it, "in the image and likeness" of that Reality which is and will be what it will be (Gen. 1:27; Exod. 3:14). Undoubtedly, this capacity to order "Order"--to have dominion over everything (Gen. 1:28b) by "naming" it (Gen. 2:19-20) and thereby objectifying it--reflects the higher-order processing of the neocortex, a recognition of the larger contextual universe in which the human brain exists.

In effect, every logical piece of information is embedded in a distributed, parallel, simultaneous, contextual network of meaning. I take this subsymbolic, microstructure of meaning to refer to the neuronal activity of the brain. What gains our attention because it is new, different, and/or disturbing is seen, then grasped, as it resembles what we have seen before.

We catalogue objects according to their apparent similarity in terms of how they appear, the associations we make about them, and the feelings we identify with them in memory.

Parallel to that microstructure of meaning in the older brain, I regard that activity of meaning-making as inevitably part of the symbolic, macrostructures of meaning in the new brain. These conscious processes are the "observed regularities" in our world (Rumelhardt et al. [1986] 1987, vol. 2:548). In their most global form these observed regularities are belief patterns--what might be viewed as the imaged realities of holography and our projection of our perceived destiny.

I suggest that these belief patterns are a result of our observed order of things in our universe--the overwhelming sense we sometimes arrive at that all our knowledge, all our being only leads back to this order which if we find, we find ourselves a part of it. We often call that part of ourselves that reaches it our connection with God. It becomes our purpose and our existence defined.

Even though language is our most regularized structure of meaning, language is turning out to be metaphorical, not objective (Lakoff and Johnson 1980; Gerhart and Russell 1984). Concepts define everyday realities by structuring what we perceive, how we get around, and how we relate to each other. This is the order that the likeness of things establishes. But concepts arise out of metaphors, which means that concepts reflect our experience more than a mirrored reality of absolute truth. "*The essence of metaphor is understanding and experiencing one kind of thing in terms of another*" (Lakoff and Johnson 1980, 5; italics in original). Only a subsymbolic, parallel, distributed process can generate these kinds of unpredictable associations.

Differences of opinion, for example, can be viewed as "a dance," though they usually are conceived as "an argument"--and arguments are structured as "war." We need only think of phrases we use in describing much of our conversation with each other: "Your claims are *indefensible.*" "He *attacked* every weak point in my argument." "His criticisms were right *on target*." "He *shot down* all of my arguments" (Lakoff and Johnson 1980, 4: emphasis in original).

The metaphorical basis of how we think and talk makes language an imaginative creation based on visceral experience and visual perception. Words are not permanent, substantial, independent entities. Symbolic regularities exist in our conscious mind more than in the distributed processes of dynamic interaction. Words and ideas are finite, subjective, abstract configurations of reasonable sensibilities. We develop a coherent system of metaphors which we then use as the basis of the abstract concept.

Figurative and denotative language patterns--the poetic and the mechanical, the religious and the scientific, the metaphorical and the analogical, respectively--are not fundamentally different types of meaning arising from fundamentally different processes in the brain. Instead, I submit that what is suggestive and what is exact, what is psyche and what is soma, what is purposeful and what is physical, what is mind and what is brain are "coarse categories describing the nature of the meanings synthesized" by *parallel distributed processing networks* (Rumelhardt et al. [1986] 1987, vol. 2:550). Instead of local representations of the symbolic process being primary in cognition, a distributed dynamic network with feedback loops is more basic.

When the mind is working optimally, it is constructing phenomena across time and space. There are no hard and fast boundaries. As a folk saying puts it: we lose ourselves in thought. This is how and why the cognitive revolution is carrying us into a wider realm of mental representation than Enlightenment Reason suspected existed.

THE INADEQUACY OF THE INTERPRETIVE LEFT HEMISPHERE

From the 1500s on, the Western world has been dominated by the scientific revolution and its counterpart in the intellectual tradition which found coherence between science and the humanities (Bronowski and Mazlish 1960). Enlightenment Reason combined the lawfulness of mathematical certainty and the objectivity of empirical observation with the logic of formal rationality (Barbour 1966). In very specific ways we are the inheritors of the dualism of Rene Descartes (1596-1650) and the mechanism of Isaac Newton (1642-1727).

Ironically, Descartes' method of seeing the universe as a mathematical and logical structure came specifically from a mystical experience. It occurred during the night of November 10, 1619, when he was 23 years old (Bronowski and Mazlish 1960, 216-29). By doubting everything, he forged the empirical method of observation and the logical method of formal reasoning. In this way he arrived at a view of the universe which was "both realistic and orderly" (Bronowski and Mazlish 1960, 229). Because he distrusted the imagination, he drew a sharp cleavage between the inward experience of mind and the outward examination of matter. Even so, he remained a devout Catholic all his life and treasured the memory of his dream discovery.

In a similarly ironic way, Newton's method of combining mathematics and experimentation came neither from observation nor deduction alone. Rather, his discovery of the law of gravity and his metaphor that nature is a law-abiding machine required "creative imagination" and his belief in God (Barbour 1966, 34-55). He, and the other English scientists of the second half of the seventeenth century, directed their investigations "to the glory of God and the benefit of the human race" (Barbour 1966, 37). Whether God was the Divine Clockmaker who wound up the world like a clock, the Cosmic Plumber who mended leaks in the system, the Ultimate Conservative who maintained the status quo, or the Cosmic Architect who built the universe, religion was more a matter of "intellectual demonstration" than of "living experience" (Barbour 1966, 40).

That rational, objective certainty--which I identify as the symbolic paradigm of the interpretive left hemisphere--sprang from and depended upon relational patterned imagination: what I identify with the subsymbolic paradigm of parallel distributed processing and the holographic paradigm. To the early modernists science was "a religious task," and so it can be today. Without using explicit "religious" language, we can say that *human destiny requires integrating nonconscious subsymbolic experience and conscious symbolic realism, genetic givens and cultural inheritance.*

Cautious scientists insist we are "a long way from connecting our more abstract networks with particular brain structures" (Rumelhardt et al. [1986] 1987, vol.2:552). Even so, it is evident that our brain's reasoning capacity is an interpretation of our right brain's meaning-making sensibility. Despite the vigilance of the left hemisphere, our right brain's responsiveness to the felt-meaning of the environment continues to be primary. Whole brain processing is more fundamental than half brain activity (Levy 1985).

Ordinary consciousness carries on with all the exact representationalism which assumes that the maps we make in our heads correspond to the territory we actually are and the territory in which we find ourselves. But maps are never the territory (Korzybski 1933; Hooper and Teresi [1986] 1987, 103-4). Increasingly we are recognizing that no amount of human mastery can dispel the cosmic mystery which we incarnate. Our three-pound universe reveals an integrated and integrating reality, a higher-order processing of lower-level randomness (see Gen. 1-3).

In light of the mystery of our three-pound universe one might ask: If following the nature we are made in, namely the image of God, and if God is the order and ordering logic of the universe, and if such an order and ordering reflects stringent, analytical processing, then why should not humanity, as made in God's image, duplicate such an order and ordering analytical process?

So I suggest in understanding mind that we move from the cognitive focus on mental representation to understanding mind as a way to summarize all that includes the human meaning of the brain: bodily perception, imagination, culture, values, beliefs, destiny. What we learn about cognition, based on what the brain knows and how that is represented mentally, leads us to what matters ultimately; namely, what we take God to be, the alpha and omega of our destiny. Here we deal with the survival of what is significant and the significance of what survives (Burhoe 1981, 158).

WHOLE MIND AND NEW DESTINY

The concept of mind, expressing as it does the human destiny of the human brain, directs our attention downward into the organized regularities of the reptilian-mammalian levels and equally encourages us to turn outward toward the emergent aspects of human purposes (Ashbrook 1986). The royal road toward understanding how culture is mapped onto brains, as

Gardner puts it, is the representational level (Gardner 1985, 390-91). The whole mind makes belief more credible and destiny more immediate.

To speak of "the whole mind" is to refer to the "whole" brain--old cortex and new cortex together, inseparable, interdependent. Consciousness consists of both the pattern-making construction of the right hemisphere and the observing-objectifying activity of the left hemisphere. Yet consciousness derives from the environmentally empathic, adaptational activity of the nonconsious, subsymbolic older brains. Consequently, the concept *mind* includes both nonconscious information as well as conscious representation.

The roots of the mythic Tree of Life (Gen. 2:9a) go down into the genes--our reptilian and mammalian heritage--and its branches--the neocortex or the mythic Tree of Knowledge (Gen. 2:9b)--stretch out into the ecosystems in which we participate. Through all of this processing God works, providing us with our purposes, our values, our convictions, our commitments. Just as mind discloses the human significance of brain, so mind points to what I understand to be the intentionality of God.

The prophet Jeremiah expressed this inner link between God's purposes and humanity's understanding when he had Yahweh God say: "Deep within I will plant my Law, writing it on the heart" (Jer. 31:33 JB). In biblical psychology, the heart is the unifying and central focus and equivalent of the personality, the seat of our psychic life including emotions, intellect, volition, the moral life, and the point of contact with God (Sellers 1962). In technical terms, theology and ontology are dependent upon epistemology, and epistemology depends upon the functioning of the brain (Ashbrook 1989). The nature of God, the nature of human nature, the nature of the universe, the nature of human destiny are matters which depend upon how we know and how we process what we know.

I believe the distinction between disclosed and discovered truth, or between revelation and reason, is misleading. Such dichotomies reflect the Cartesian split between mind and body and the earlier Hellenic duality of body and soul. It is precisely such splits that the newer brain sciences and this newer form of theology are overcoming. The revised view of cognition makes sense; the old view of cognition does not.

A RENEWED RELATEDNESS IN REALITY

In relation to the larger scheme of things we wonder: How can we be who we are in the midst of the mystery that is ourselves? In relation to more immediate situations we ask: How can we survive and find satisfaction in an environment which is both threatening and inviting?

For me, these issues of our nature and destiny are linked inseparably with the data of evolutionary development, brain-mind activity, cross-cultural comparisons, and religious expressions, most particularly biblical and theological images, events, and interpretations. Despite the supposed conflict between the selfish genes of our biological nature and the pro-social motivation of our human capacity for symbolization, evidence points increasingly toward our destiny as one in which we are to be "in harmony with the universe" (d'Aquili 1983, 266-67).

In truth, I question whether we are citizens of two worlds--a world of biology and a world of culture (Theissen [1984] 1985, 145), because I believe it is more accurate to say that we as organisms are expressions of--participants in and citizens of--one reality, a reality in which we must "choose" to be at home and for which we are responsible. Our brain--the whole mind--reveals "parallel but interrelated processes, one biological and the other cultural . . . [with] separate mechanisms for the production," selection, and transmission of variations over time (Csikszenthmihalyi 1987). As theologian Philip Hefner characterizes the issue of genes and culture, humanity "is always struggling to integrate its biological equipment into the cultural configuration which the human has become" (Hefner 1986, 3).

Take the everyday experience of sweating as an illustration of the struggle to integrate genetic input and cultural context. We sweat differently in different situations. The profuse sweating which accompanies strenuous exercise has a beneficial effect on the body and the mind (Achterberg 1985, 139). It reduces the stress of the sympathetic nervous system and activates the relaxation of the parasympathetic system. Blood flow to the skin is increased (Achterberg 1985, 33-35). Yet the profuse sweating which comes in situations of extreme anxiety, focused fear, and even mild threat activates the survival reactions of the limbic system. The resulting tension sets off an alarm which puts the system on alert, aroused, vigilant, running full speed (Selye 1976).

The point is straight forward: we change to fit into what we experience to be happening in our world. And those changes result from the activation of the old brain and the imagination of the new brain: genes and culture, subsymbolic and symbolic processing. Our destiny comes from the whole mind, cortical and subcortical, new brain emergence and old brain empathy.

Consider, as an example, the very real changes women are going through in being both mother and a person with a "career." This is not a new situation for women because such has been the experience of many women in the past. Rather, the problem is more general now. We do not talk about "work" which women did in the past when they "worked" outside the home. Instead, we refer to that pattern as "career," especially for those with education. To be paid for doing something carries the message for a woman and others that she is "worth" something. She is "doing something" significant.

These new cultural expectations and demands radiate all kinds of effects: family structure, redefining of "traditional" male and female roles in the social, economic, and political sectors. In the process we as a society are undergoing new and different ideas of nurturing and caring for our young. Beyond these changes we can think of the more fundamental changes in family structure that are coming about because women in greater numbers are single heads of generally very poor families. The pattern is being called "the feminization of poverty."

Parallel but interrelated processes--biological and cultural--are everywhere evident. Consider the social pattern of the single-parent woman. How might her "mind" gather her life together if she is on welfare and supporting one, two, three, or more children? Vigilance is likely to be more in the service of the children--the continuity of the species--than in the survival of the self, a limbic activity with the arousal of the amygdala utilized by the septum for protection and nurturing. In less adaptive circumstances vigilance serves to maintain a woman's own survival, with the needs of her children quite secondary; a limbic activity with septal activation subsumed by the sympathetic arousal of the amygdala. At the most adaptive level, care of her children requires care for herself as well--a level of moral development in which a balance of care and rights, intimacy and identity, interdependence and integrity constitute maturity (Gilligan [1982] 1983, 151-74); an integration of all limbic activity for optimal environmental adaptation.

Contemporary experiences of patriarchal oppression and ecological precariousness suggest a reversal of the concern for genetic-cultural integration. Perhaps the issue is less one of integrating our "biological equipment into the cultural configuration," as Hefner (1986) and others have stressed, and more one of integrating our cultural patterns into our biological and ecological universe. When viewed this way, transcendence of the human situation requires that we move from the new brain's prominence and domination back into the old brain's primacy and purpose, namely, the best evolutionary adaptation under the circumstance. *Our destiny lies in the recovery of our relatedness to the whole of creation, not in our getting beyond that origin.* Only as the symbolic paradigm arises from *and returns* to the subsymbolic, parallel, distributed paradigm of what is going on in our contextual universe, only thus do we become the human creatures that we are.

The various data bases of brain and belief, of the physical and the human, of matter and spirit, are intelligible by virtue of both the empirical and the experiential approaches to what is true in human experience. These bases are not reducible to each other, yet they are related. They are not the same, yet they are interdependent. They are not autonomous, yet they are distinguishable. Whether they are emergent or expressive (see Pribram 1985) is not easily determined.

Paul D. MacLean speculates about our place in the cosmos: "Human beings . . . are the only creatures known to shed tears with crying. Is it possible that the misting of the eyes so commonly experienced upon observing an altruistic act is in any way owing to a reciprocal innervation of mechanisms for parental rescue and for crying represented in the cingulate gyrus [of the limbic system]?" He goes on to point out that "human beings and their antecedents are the only creatures known to have used fire." Then MacLean advances his own conviction about human destiny in the form of a question: "In the course of millions of years did there arise some connection between smoke and tears and activities surrounding fire, including ceremonies involved in disposing of departed loved ones?" (MacLean 1985b).

Tears and transcendence link us to an evolutionary adaptation which reveals both our origin and our destiny. We are not simply here, like the alligators or the fruit flies. Rather, we are here on earth, in this universe, in a way that calls forth our caring for one another--in death as well as in life.

This empathic caring marks the most striking change in evolutionary adaptation. Brain and family evolved together (MacLean 1982). Empathic caring came with the long period of dependency necessary for children to get them to functioning "adulthood." With these demands unceasing and the rewards often unseen, early huminoids must have gone through radical old brain-new brain transformation to insure survival of the species along with differentiation of the self. Parent-offspring smiles and soothing sounds reinforced attachment behavior necessary for physical survival and emotional security on the one hand and activated exploratory activity in response to novelty on the other (Paterson and Moran 1988). The consequence was seeing the child as part of oneself within the family, and with the appearance of religion (Burhoe 1981) seeing the other--nonkin stranger and enemy alike--as neighbor to be loved as one loves oneself (Lev. 19:18; Matt. 5:43; 19:19; 22:39; Mark 12:31; Luke 10:27; Rom. 13:9; Gal. 5:14; James 2:8). Process thought points to this caring when it claims that "sympathy, 'feeling of feeling,' is an ultimate principle, applicable to deity and every other singular activity" (Hartshorne 1975, 92).

Research psychologist George Wolf picked up that emphasis upon altruistic empathy in an article on "The Place of the Brain in an Ocean of Feelings" (Wolf 1984). He described visiting a laboratory "in which the activities of individual neurons were being monitored by transducing [transforming and translating] the neural impulses to pulses of sound." In the midst of the "popping" sounds of the neural impulses, he heard what he described as "a soft moan." The researcher told him that "it was the sound of a dying cell--a high frequency discharge as the cell's life ebbed away." Wolf claimed that his "empathic interpretation" of that event could be taken as "an empirical-hypothesis," yet he himself believed that "the moan was an expression of a feeling that all sentient creatures share--it was a feeling of perishing" (Wolf 1984, 119).

Perhaps in the end we represent moral order in the mind because when observed over time we see nothing but order in nature: parts relating to other parts, each to another to make a whole. This idea of order is so stupendous we develop symbols to describe it, symbols which continue for us--as it must have for our ancestors in the furtherst reaches of time when they first formed words--to express and articulate the inexplicable.

A cell's soft moan as its life ebbs away, a mammal's cry in recognition of separation from nurturing care, human tears in the presence of death, religious testimony to a gracious God, theological expressions of transcendent purposes, values and beliefs--each of these bridges the simply physical and the surely spiritual.   MacLean says in the language of evolutionary psychiatry what I am groping to say in the language of theology: "Perhaps we can trace to this situation [of the separation call] the evolutionary roots of unity of the family, unity of the clan, unity of the larger societies, as well as the human philosophic yearning for an abstract kind of unity" (MacLean 1985a, 415).

But that abstract unity is turning out to be a concrete unity--a oneness with the whole created order through every level of organization, from dust to breath to belief to dust--brain is being and being is brain.   Or in the poetic words of Emily Dickinson: "The brain is just the weight of God" (in MacLean 1988). It bears the glory of divine destiny. As we understand ourselves and our place in our world, we are understanding the relatedness of everything that is.   The thrust of the ecology movement represents but another change in a world which is changing our understanding of who we are in the universe in which we find ourselves.

In our penultimate knowing, we see through the obscuring lens of our perceptual-cognitive biases, the cognitive maps or mental representations of culture, if you will.   In the imagery of the apostle Paul, we see through a glass darkly (1 Cor. 13:12).   Even so, we are discovering that matter and meaning, the physical and the psychic, the sensory and the spiritual are more alike than different.   Whatever the mutative selectivity that has combined dust and breath, we cherish it. We are object-seeking creatures and meaning-making animals.

The old brain (with its genetic knowledge) and the new brain (with its cultural knowledge) make meaning-making understandable in new ways. Even as symbolic meaning is demystified, we are coming to a deep sense of mystery in the materiality of the human brain and the mentality of the physical universe--our destiny as human beings. We live in a universe in which variety is constantly being created and the world is ever renewed (Ps. 104). New things are always being disclosed, created out of the hidden unformedness in which we dwell (Is. 48). The hidden wisdom which permeates our universe (the older cortex) is being revealed through the image and likeness of the creative Spirit in us (the whole cortex). And that Spirit explores everything, even the depths of our own creative imaginative Spirit (1 Cor. 2:10).

*In a different form, these ideas were presented in a paper to the Science and Theology Section of the American Academy of Religion in Boston, December 1987. The author expresses appreciation to Ralph Wendell Burhoe for extended discussion of the issues, to Karl Peters for editorial suggestions and Barbara Stinchcombe, who assisted with style.

REFERENCES

Achterberg, Jeanne. 1985. *Imagery in Healing: Shamanism and Modern Medicine*. Boston: New Science Library/Shambhala.

Andreasen, Roberta. 1985. *The Broken Brain: The Biological Revolution in Psychiatry*. New York: Basic Books.

Aquinas, Thomas. 1945. *Basic Writings of Saint Thomas Aquinas* vols. I & II edited and annotated, with an Introduction by Anton C. Pegis. New York: Random House.

Ashbrook, James B. 1984. "Neurotheology: The Working Brain and the Work of Theology." *Zygon: Journal of Religion and Science* 19 (September):331-50.

_____. 1986. "Brain, Mind and God." *The Christian Century* (March 19):295-98.

_____. 1989. "The Whole Brain as the Basis for the Analogical Expression of God." *Zygon: Journal of Religion and Science* 24 (March):65-81.

_____. 1990. "Between Broken Brains and Oppressive Beliefs: Troubled Mind." In *Religious and Ethical Factors in Psychiatric Practice*, ed. Don S. Browning, Thomas Jobe, and Ian S. Evison, 226-44. New York: Nelson Hall.

Augustine. 1955. *Confessions and Enchiridion*, ed. and trans. Albert C. Outler. Philadelphia: Westminster.

Barbour, Ian G. 1966. *Issues in Science and Religion*. Englewood Cliffs, NJ: Prentice-Hall.

Benson, Herbert. 1984. *Beyond the Relaxation Response: How to Harness the Healing Power of your Personal Beliefs*. With William Proctor. New York: Times Books.

Borysenko, Joan. 1987. *Minding the Body, Mending the Mind*. With Larry Rothstein. Forward by Herbert Benson. Reading, MA: Addison-Wesley.

Bronowski, Jacob and Bruce Mazlish. 1960. *The Western Intellectual Tradition: From Leonardo to Hegel*. New York: Harper & Brothers.

Burhoe, Ralph Wendell. 1981. *Toward A Scientific Theology*. Belfast: Christian Journals Limited.

_____. 1987. Personal conversation and notes critiquing James B. Ashbrook "From Being to Brain: Natural Theology in an Empirical Mode." Paper presented to the Science and Theology Section of the American Academy of Religion, Boston.

Burrell, David. 1973. *Analogy and Philosophical Language*. New Haven: Yale Univ. Press.

_____. 1979. *Aquinas: God & Action*. London: Routledge & Kegan Paul.

Csikszenthmihalyi, Mihaly. 1987. "On the Relationship Between Cultural Evolution and Human Welfare." Paper for the American Academy of Science meeting, Chicago.

d'Aquili, Eugene G. 1983. "The Myth-Ritual Complex: A Biogenetic Structural Analysis." *Zygon: Journal of Religion and Science* 18 (September):247-69.

DeAngelis, Tori. 1987. "Computer Theorist (David Rumelhart) Nabs MacArthur Prize." *APA Monitor* August 28:28.

Gardner, Howard. 1985. *The Mind's New Science: A History of the Cognitive Revolution*. New York: Basic Books.

Gazzaniga, Michael. 1988. *Mind Matters: How the Mind and Brain Interact to Create our Conscious Lives*. Forward by Robert Bazell. Boston: Houghton Mifflin Bradford Books.

Gerhart, Mary and Allan Russell. 1984. *Metaphorical Process: The Creation of Scientific and Religious Understanding*. Foreword by Paul Ricoeur. Fort Worth: Texas Christian Univ. Press.

Gilligan, Carol. [1982] 1983. *In a Different Voice: Psychological Theory and Women's Development*. Cambridge, MA: Harvard Univ. Press.

Hartshorne, Charles. 1975. "Physics and Psychics: The Place of Mind in Nature." In *Mind in Nature*, ed. John B. Cobb, Jr. and David Ray Griffin, 89-97. Washington, D.C.: University Press of America.

Hefner, Philip. 1986. "Evolutionary Interpretation of The Christian Faith." Mimeographed paper for the Seminar on Science and Religion. Chicago: Lutheran School of Theology.

Hooper, Judith and Dick Teresi. [1986] 1987. *The 3-Pound Universe: The Brain*. Foreword by Isaac Asimov. New York: Laurel, Dell.

Johnson, Mark. 1987. *The Body in the Mind: The Bodily Basis of Meaning, Imagination, and Reason*. Chicago: The Univ. of Chicago Press.

Korzybski, A. 1933. *Science and Sanity*. 4th ed. Lakeville, CT: The International Non-Aristotelian Library.

Lakoff, George. 1987. *Women, Fire, and Dangerous Things: What Categories Reveal about the Mind*. Chicago: The Univ. of Chicago Press.

_____ and Mark Johnson. 1980. *Metaphors We Live By*. Chicago: The Univ. of Chicago Press.

Levy, Jerre. 1985. "Interhemispheric Collaboration: Single-Mindedness in the Asymmetrical Brain." In *Hemisphere Function and Collaboration in the Child*, ed. Catherine T. Best, 11-29. Orlando, FL: Academic Press.

MacLean, Paul D. 1970. "The Triune Brain, Emotion, and Scientific Bias." In *The Neurosciences: Second Study Program*, editor-in-chief F.O. Schmitt, 336-49. New York: The Rockefeller Univ. Press.

_____. 1982. "The Co-Evolution of the Brain and Family." In *Anthroquest: The L.S.B. Leakey Foundation News* 24 (1):14-15.

_____. 1985a. "Brain Evolution Relating to Family, Play and the Separation Call." *Archives of General Psychiatry* 42 (April):405-17.

_____. 1985b. "Evolutionary Psychiatry and the Triune Brain." *Psychological Medicine* 15:219-21.

_____. 1988. Emily Dickinson poem quoted in personal correspondence, December 20.

Neisser, Urich. 1976. *Cognition and Reality*. San Francisco: W.H. Freeman.

Palmer, Stephen E. 1987. "PDP: A New Paradigm for Cognitive Theory." Review of David E. Rummelhart et al. *Contemporary Psychology* 32 (11):925-28.

Paterson, Randolph J. and Greg Moran. 1988. "Attachment Theory, Personality Development, and Psychotherapy." *Clinical Psychology Review* 8:611-36.

Penfield, Wilder. 1975. *The Mystery of the Mind: A Critical Study of Consciousness and the Human Brain*. Princeton, NJ: Princeton Univ. Press.

Pribram, Karl. 1985. "What the Fuss is all About." In *The Holographic Paradigm*, ed. Ken Wilber, 27-34. Boston: New Science Library/Shambhala.

_____. 1986. "The Cognitive Revolution and Mind/Brain Issues." *American Psychologist* 41 (May):507-20.

Rossi, Ernest Lawrence. 1986. *The Psychobiology of Mind-Body Healing: New Concepts of Therapeutic Hypnosis*. New York: W.W.Norton.

Rumelhart, David E., James L. McClelland, and the PDP Research Group. [1986]1987. *Explorations in the Microstructure of Cognition: Computational Models of Cognition and Perception*. 1: *Foundations*; 2: *Psychological and Biological Models*. Cambridge, MA: MIT Press.

Sellers, O.R. 1962. "Heart." In *The Interpreter's Dictionary of the Bible: E-I*, ed. George A. Buttrick, 549-50. New York: Abingdon.

Selye, H. 1976. *The Stress of Life*. New York: McGraw-Hill.

Snyder, Solomon H. 1974. *Madness and the Brain*. New York: McGraw-Hill.

Sperry, Roger. 1982. *Science and Moral Priority: Merging Mind, Brain, and Human Values*. New York: Columbia Univ. Press.

Tanguay, Peter E. 1985. "Implications of Hemispheric Specialization for Psychiatry." In *The Dual Brain: Hemispheric Specialization in Humans*, ed. D.Frank Benson and Eran Zaidel, 375-84. New York: The Guilford Press.

Taylor, Gordon Rattray. 1979. *The Natural History of the Mind*. New York: E.P.Dutton.

TenHouten, Warren D. 1985. "Cerebral-Lateralization Theory and the Sociology of Knowledge." In *The Dual Brain: Hemispheric Specialization in Humans*, ed. D. Frank Benson and Eran Zaidel, 341-58. New York: The Guilford Press.

Theissen, Gerd. [1984] 1985. *Biblical Faith: An Evolutionary Approach*. Philadelphia: Fortress Press.

Trevarthen, Colwyn. 1986. "Brain Sciences and the Human Spirit." *Zygon: Journal of Religion and Science* 21 (June):161-200.

Watzlawick, Paul. 1978. *The Language of Change: Elements of Therapeutic Communication*. New York: Basic Books.

Wilber, Ken, ed. 1985. *The Holographic Paradigm and Other Paradoxes: Exploring the Leading Edges of Science*. Boston: New Science Library/Shambhala.

Wolf, George. 1984. "The Place of the Brain in an Ocean of Feelings." In *Existence and Actuality: Conversations with Charles Hartshorne*, ed. John B. Cobb, Jr. and Franklin I. Gamwell, 167-84. Chicago: The Univ. of Chicago Press.

CONTRIBUTORS

James B. Ashbrook, Professor of Religion and Personality, Garrett-Evangelical Theological Seminary and advisory member of The Graduate Faculty, Northwestern University, Evanston, IL.

Eugene G. d'Aquili, Professor of Clinical Psychiatry, University of Pennsylvania, Philadelphia, PA.

Paul D. MacLean, Senior Research Scientist, National Institute of Mental Health, Bethesda, MD.

Roger W. Sperry, Trustee Professor Emeritus of Psychobiology, California Institute of Technology, Pasadena, CA.

Colwyn Trevarthen, Professor of Child Psychology and Psychobiology, University of Edinburgh, Scotland.

Victor Turner, William R. Kenan, Jr., Professor of Anthropology, University of Virginia, Charlottesville, VA. Deceased.

·